500 POPULAR

ANNUALS & PERENNIALS

FOR NEW ZEALAND GARDENERS

D0179075

VIKING

VIKING
Penguin Books (NZ) Ltd, Cnr Rosedale and Airborne Roads, Albany,
Auckland 1310, New Zealand
Penguin Books Ltd, 27 Wrights Lane, London W8 5TZ, England
Penguin USA, 375 Hudson Street, New York, NY 10014,
United States
Penguin Books Australia Ltd, 487 Maroondah Highway, Ringwood,
Australia 3134
Penguin Books Canada Ltd, 10 Alcorn Avenue, Toronto,
Ontario, Canada M4V 3B2

Penguin Books Ltd, Registered Offices: Harmondsworth,
Middlesex, England

ISBN 0670 88247X

Film Separation PICA Color Separation Overseas Pte Ltd
Printed in Hong Kong by Sing Cheong Printing Co Ltd

CONTENTS

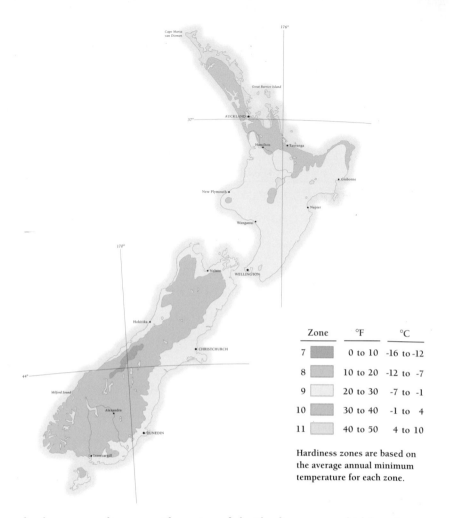

Zone	°F	°C
7	0 to 10	-16 to -12
8	10 to 20	-12 to -7
9	20 to 30	-7 to -1
10	30 to 40	-1 to 4
11	40 to 50	4 to 10

Hardiness zones are based on the average annual minimum temperature for each zone.

This map has been prepared to agree with a system of plant hardiness zones which have been accepted as an international standard and range from 1 to 12. It shows the lowest minimum winter temperatures which can be expected on the average in different regions of New Zealand. Note that ZONES 1 to 6, which involve much lower temperatures, and ZONE 12, which involves very high temperatures, don't occur in New Zealand.

In the A–Z section of this book a zone number (for example, ZONE 8) is given at the end of each species entry. That number, which corresponds to a zone shown here, indicates the coldest areas in which the particular plant is likely to survive through an average winter. Note that these are not necessarily the areas in which it will grow best. Because the zone number refers to *minimum* temperatures, a plant given ZONE 7, for example, will obviously grow perfectly well in ZONE 8 but not in ZONE 6. In the lower zones, plants such as annuals and perennials can be started from seed in a covered area, then planted out when the likelihood of the last frost is over. Plants grown in a zone considerably higher than the zone with the minimum winter temperature in which they will survive might grow well but they are likely to behave differently. Note also that some readers may find the numbers a little conservative; we felt it best to err on the side of caution. The map does not attempt to indicate a plant's water requirements or drought hardiness; where significant, this information is given in the text.

Introduction

Annuals and perennials give a garden more than the occasional splash of bright color. In many cases they 'make' a garden—giving it its essential character, its atmosphere and sense of place. Few gardens seem complete without the presence of these plants and their flourish of flowers mark the seasons as surely as the weather.

Often what begins with a few tentative purchases and trial runs leads to a

The stately *Agapanthus* prefers full sun.

lifetime of happy, harmless plant collecting. Friendships are cemented and remembered with personal gifts of such plants. In some families plants become 'family' plants when they move from place to place and between the generations with 'their' family. For some, just the scent or sight of a particular plant will bring back treasured affections and experiences of the past. Whether the gardener has the space and time for a stunning pair of matched herbaceous borders or is limited to a couple of tubs on a verandah, the presence of annuals and perennials can give great pleasure and add a personal touch to the commonplace.

Both annuals and perennials have the unwarranted reputation of being time-consuming, space-consuming, money-consuming and water-consuming. But the key issue is, of course, how the available resources are used. The possession of unlimited resources will not necessarily make for the creation of

You can put your own stamp on a garden by selecting the colors you like, such as the strong colors of *Tagetes erecta*, *Tagetes patula* and *Salvia viridis*.

a lovely garden filled with annuals and perennials. It can help, but a little plant knowledge, a little know-how, a few good friends and some good books are far more effective.

Planting combinations

By combining perennials with annuals in a more informal manner, the garden loses that 'all or nothing' effect which is so evident when a bed of annuals has 'finished' and is again planted out with tiny seedlings. By placing clumps of perennials beside drifts of annuals the eye is drawn from one accent to another, say from a group of low-growing annuals in front to the taller perennial flower spikes behind. Annuals are marvellous for providing a festive welcome to an entrance or a splash of color to a shrub border when the garden is to be used for a special event.

For a continuous effect, group them with perennials, staggering the flowering times of the plants so that when a small pocket of annuals is nearly past its prime a perennial just behind is about to flower. This complementary display can take a few seasons to achieve, as many perennials need two years to bloom, but don't give up, as experimenting in this way is one of the most rewarding aspects of gardening.

Apart from color combinations within a garden, try to tie in the house color to that of a garden display so they complement one another: a red or red-orange toned house looks good surrounded by bright oranges, yellows, rusty reds and creams, while a white or pastel painted house blends well with soft blue, mauve, pink and white flowers plus masses of silver foliage.

Just as important as linking the house to the garden, is the overall siting of the garden beds. Most annuals demand full

Even after flowering, the attractive seed heads of this poppy complement the scarlet flowers of the *Penstemon*.

sun to flower well so be sure to choose an aspect where the plants will receive as much light, particularly morning sun, as possible. Give them generously wide beds ensuring the colorful display will not be overwhelmed by shrub foliage or robbed of nutrients by the roots of nearby permanent plants.

🌿 Outstanding Perennials with 🌿 a Long Flowering Season	
Argyranthemum species	*Hemerocallis* 'Stella D'Oro'
Brachycombe multifida	*Knautia macedonica*
Catananche caerulea	*Oenothera speciosa*
Centranthus rubra	*Nepeta faassenii*
Convolvulus sabatius	*Scaevola* 'Mauve Clusters'
Diascia species	*Phlomis fruticans*
Felicia amelloides	*Silene diocia*

Instant color effects

One of the most welcome developments in recent years has been the increase in

With their long spikes of large, brilliant, strongly colored flowers, lupins are a joy in any garden.

the number of annuals and perennials available in 'instant color' pots. Once red geraniums were the only available way to provide a splash of color in early spring; now, right through the seasons a pot or tray of mature flowering annuals can be purchased to add instant color to a garden dead spot or patio. And don't overlook hanging baskets filled with annuals to highlight a garden color scheme. If potting up seedlings to make a basket full of your own instant color, take care to choose plants that will fall gracefully over the edge of the basket. If you are using large pots or tubs, both uprights and sprawling plant types can produce a very decorative display.

Annuals, by their very nature, aim to set as many seeds as possible within a very short life span. Gardeners can extend the flowering period by cutting the blooms for indoor use or nipping off faded flowers before they seed and so decide it's all over for another year. If you follow this procedure, remember it is good practice to provide regular nourishment to the plants in the form of a quick-acting fertilizer designed to promote flowers rather than foliage growth.

Plant names
Species
What we call a species is the form in which a plant was found in the wild. The membership of a particular genus is denoted by the first word in a plant's name while the subsequent word usually refers to some aspect of the plant's appearance, native habitat or to the person who discovered or introduced the plant to gardeners. These two botanical names are, by custom, written in italics.

Cultivars
Following these two names there is often a name contained in quotation marks and written in normal print. This is the

name of what is called a cultivar—or selection—and denotes a particular form of the species. The cultivar's name is often of great significance to gardeners as these plants have particular and recognisable characteristics. They may display larger flowers than the common wild form, or the flowers and leaves may be in different shades and have different markings. The scent may be more pronounced, the plant larger, smaller, fatter, thinner, be more upright, more spreading, have a neater appearance or a longer flowering season. In other words, these named cultivars are worth knowing about. Plant breeders regularly introduce new named strains and cultivars.

Hybrids

Hybrids are plants which are bred by crossing one species with another and their presence is indicated by the use of the symbol '×' or the words 'Hybrid', 'hybridus' or 'hybrida'. Hybrids are bred to increase the vigor and splendor of plants and to alter their appearance. Most hybrids do not grow true from seeds.

Common names

Today, with gene therapy rapidly becoming a part of normal plant breeding, the gardener can expect many interesting developments in plant appearance and behavior.

Common names are like nicknames. Some are so well known as to make those who use botanical names in ordinary conversation appear pretentious! Others are now obscure to the point of being more or less obsolete. However, as many plants bear the same or very similar common names, they are of limited use. Botanical names may appear a little daunting when first

encountered but they are essential tools in the processes of identifying and buying plants.

Definitions
Perennials

A perennial is a plant with a life cycle longer than two growing seasons. During each year of a perennial's life a plant will flower and set seed in the season which is appropriate to a particular climate and situation. Perennials which survive the tough times by becoming dormant and spending the season below ground are referred to as 'deciduous perennials'. Those which are on view throughout the year are referred to as 'evergreen perennials'.

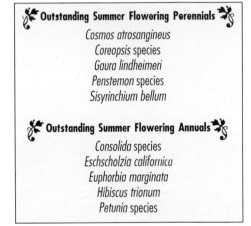

Outstanding Summer Flowering Perennials

Cosmos atrosangineus
Coreopsis species
Gaura lindheimeri
Penstemon species
Sisyrinchium bellum

Outstanding Summer Flowering Annuals

Consolida species
Eschscholzia californica
Euphorbia marginata
Hibiscus trionum
Petunia species

Annuals

Plants which live for a single season and die after flowering are called annuals. In cold climates this definition is clear cut as these plants, once they have flowered, die with the first frosts of winter. In climates where no hard frosts occur, these distinctions become a little blurred as some so-called annuals are, in point of fact, frost tender short-lived perennials which have been selected and bred in the cold climates of the northern hemisphere for use as flowering annuals. (For example, *Nicotiana sylvestris* is a true open-pollinated annual which appears in spring, flowers, sets seed and dies as winter approaches. Whereas the *N. alata* derivatives found on seedling benches appear to have the potential for a longer life. They can also be propagated through division.)

However, it is worth remembering that some of these so-called annuals were bred to provide one quick display and while they may prove capable of survival for several years they may also fail to perform with any flamboyance in their second and subsequent seasons.

Outstanding Spring Flowering Annuals

Hesperis matrionalis
Limnanthes douglasii
Lunaria annua
Myosotis alpestris
Nigella damascena

Biennials

A biennial is a plant with a life cycle that spans two growing seasons; establishing a rootstock in the first then flowering, setting seed and dying in the second. Many biennials evolved in cold regions and often react to mild climates by flowering in their first year.

Buying and choice

When choosing plants the first thing to do is to find out which plants grow well in your locality, to acquire those with appeal, and to learn how to get the best from them.

Then, when ready to experiment,

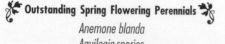

Outstanding Spring Flowering Perennials

Anemone blanda
Aquilegia species
Aurina saxatilis
Onixotis triqueta
Pulsatilla vulgaris

A display of annuals and perennials like these *Nicotiana*, *Begonia*, *Verbena* and *Ageratum* can take a lot from the soil. You must nourish the soil if you want to repeat the display season after season.

explore other plants which enjoy similar climates and conditions and add a few to your collection. Knowing the native locations of desirable plants will do much to help the beginner to match plants to climates and conditions. Suburban nurseries often acquire their plants from a variety of sources, with the result that not all their flowery offerings will thrive in the garden next door unless nurtured by an expert. It really does pay to do your homework.

As confidence, experience and enthusiasm builds, the gardener will learn to mimic the growing conditions found in situations bearing little resemblance to their local climate and will achieve success with many such 'foreign' plants.

If novice gardeners follow these stages, they will save both money and heartache and, from the very beginning, will enjoy the pleasures of growing flourishing annuals and perennials.

When purchasing annuals the choice usually lies between buying a seedling tray of seedlings or a packet of seeds. Highly bred and hybridised annuals such as the latest impatiens and petunias are best bought in seedling trays as seedlings. Many require expert handling during infancy and this is best left to those with the right equipment and knowledge. Yet the home gardener can achieve pleasing results by buying seeds designed for the home market.

Open-pollinated annuals are valued for their ability to self-sow. These are fleeting easy care plants of tremendous charm which, if conditions suit their needs, have the grace to reappear year after year often choosing the most impossible of situations and often making a success of their chosen situation. The seeds of open-pollinated annuals are easily bought, stored and grown.

Be careful when buying plants, and only choose happy, healthy specimens.

🌿 Outstanding Open-pollinated Annuals 🌿

Adonis aestivalis	Gilia capitata
Agrostemma githago	Lathyrus odorata
Ammi majus	Myosotis alpestris
Anchusa capensis	Nicotiana sylvestris
Cynoglossum amabile	Nigella damascena
Eschscholzia californica	Papaver rhoeas

When buying the seeds, inspect the packaging and the use-by date stamp. Those which have been hermetically sealed into foil packs should last for years but their deterioration will begin as soon as the packet is opened. Those packaged in paper or stored at home are best sown within 12 months of their purchase.

Many annuals can be bought either as seedlings or seeds and many gardeners, nervous of using seeds, stick with seedlings, thereby missing much of the

A colorful hanging basket placed in the lattice work makes a charming addition to a courtyard or patio.

Many annuals and perennials grow wonderfully well in containers. This glorious display of lobelia proves that!

joy provided by the old-fashioned, easy-care, open-pollinated annuals.

Perennials should always be bought from reputable growers who take pride, among other things, in endowing their plants with the correct names and cultivation notes.

Plants bearing the name of a particular cultivar should always be propagated using vegetative methods—division, cuttings or tissue culture. Plants produced using these methods will automatically grow true to their parents' appearance. Odd self-sown descendants may prove charming and thrifty but they should not be given the name of their parental cultivar as these wildlings rarely replicate their parents' characteristics.

The lists provided by out of town growers who provide mail order services are also well worth inspection by plant enthusiasts. Their advertisements are to be found in reputable gardening magazines.

If possible when buying from suburban nurseries or supermarkets buy soon after the plants have arrived. Many so-called 'bargains' will have been exposed to unsuitable overcrowded conditions for too long, and are pot bound and diseased. Only buy what look, at least superficially, like healthy happy plants.

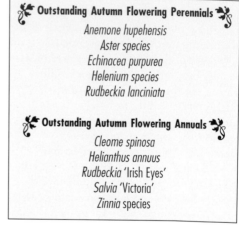

> **Outstanding Autumn Flowering Perennials**
> *Anemone hupehensis*
> *Aster species*
> *Echinacea purpurea*
> *Helenium species*
> *Rudbeckia lanciniata*
>
> **Outstanding Autumn Flowering Annuals**
> *Cleome spinosa*
> *Helianthus annuus*
> *Rudbeckia 'Irish Eyes'*
> *Salvia 'Victoria'*
> *Zinnia species*

Planting, maintenance and nurture

Prepare and plant well and you will save yourself a heap of trouble. Many seeds can be sown directly into the soil, and others do better if they are first nurtured in containers.

Raising seedlings

To raise happy, healthy plants in containers, it is important to use a good soil mix. It should be open and friable, and, of course, well-drained. Some coarse sand, and some mushroom or other garden compost should be added. There are also very good seed-raising mixtures available from nurseries and garden centers.

Sprinkle the seeds over the surface of a shallow container, such as a seedling tray, and then lightly cover the seeds with a little seed-raising mixture. Covering the container with a sheet of glass or plastic ensures that moisture loss is kept to a minimum. Now place the container in a warm spot. Don't forget to moisten the soil.

The seeds will soon germinate; but do not be in a hurry to prick out the seedlings and plant into the garden. Now is a good time to give the seedlings a light dusting of fungicide. When they have grown a little larger, gently pick the seedlings up by their leaves—not the stem—loosening the soil if necessary. They are then ready to be planted straight into a decorative pot for the balcony or verandah, or straight into the garden bed.

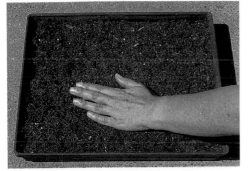

Step 1: fill the seed tray with a good soil mix.

Step 2: sprinkle the seeds over the surface of the soil.

Step 4: cover with glass or plastic.

Step 3: cover the seeds with a little seed-raising mixture.

Step 5: remove the cover when the seedlings have germinated.

Gently loosen the soil around the seedling before transplanting.

Make the holes larger than the seedling's root mass.

Place the seedling in the hole, firm it down and water immediately.

Tray-grown seedlings should be carefully separated and planted into a fine, well-prepared soil in holes at least twice the size of their existing root mass. Purpose designed slow-release granules can be added to the holes prior to planting. The little plants should be watered immediately and kept evenly moist during the early stages of their establishment. The young growth of seedlings is the favored fare of snails and slugs and the wise gardener acts accordingly. (Tomorrow morning almost always proves too late.)

Seed beds

If you want to raise many seedlings, a seed bed is probably the best way of going about it. Find a warm, sheltered location in the garden, ensure that drainage is efficient, and check that the soil is suitable. Sandy soils need the added moisture of compost; clay soils need to have some coarse sand added. Dig the bed over, adding fertilizer. Seedlings in the garden will need protection from direct sunlight. Shade cloth or some other light covering suspended on a frame is quite suitable.

Dig a hole slightly larger than the root base, separate the seedlings and place gently into the prepared hole. Some seeds are very small and stick together and an even distribution may be easier to obtain if the seeds are first dusted with talcum powder.

Water the seedlings well. The seed bed will need protection from snails, slugs and birds, and should never be allowed to dry out completely or kept in an over-soggy condition during the early stages of plant growth. If the seedlings look overcrowded a few can be pulled out and discarded. When the seedlings are large enough to transplant into the garden, carefully separate the plants, and gently place into the garden bed. Water well.

Preparing garden beds

To ensure strong growth and maximum flowering, prepare your garden beds soundly. If the area to be planted has not been dug over before, it is a good idea to

To prepare the garden bed, fork over the soil and add compost.

Rake over the soil to ensure a smooth, even surface.

double dig. This means that the topsoil, say to a fork's depth, is weeded and put aside and the soil under this layer is dug over to the depth of a fork. Humus, such as well-rotted manure, or compost can be added to this layer to help break up heavy clay particles or to add moisture-retentive qualities to sandy soils. The result should be a loose easily worked substance. This double digging is particularly beneficial to perennials which may be left in the same position for some years.

Sow the seeds, cover with a fine layer of soil, and gently firm down.

Replace the top layer of soil and prepare this surface in accordance with your planting needs. If planting perennials, a dressing of well-rotted manure or compost or a complete fertilizer can be added while roughly digging the soil over; if hardy annual seeds are to be sown directly into the soil in temperate areas, this top layer needs to be well dug over to remove any clods, then raked evenly to ensure a smooth, even surface.

Then check that water drains away quickly and freely. If there is any doubt dig a deep hole and fill it with water. If water is still visible the following morning then the drainage should be attended to before planting. Most soggy problems can be improved with the simple addition of coarse sand, small stones or some similar gritty material. If the problem persists the addition of an agricultural drain should be considered.

Problem soils, both clay and sandy soils, will benefit if well-rotted compost, as much as can be obtained, is deeply dug through the bed and when worms are encouraged to take up residence.

Generally speaking a neutral soil with a pH level between 6.5 and 7.0 will prove satisfactory for the ordinary nurture of annuals and perennials. If there are any doubts a testing kit can be purchased. An acid soil (one with a pH level falling below 6.5) can be treated with lime, dolomite and/or egg shells. An alkaline soil, or one where a lack of trace elements is suspected needs the help of a professional. (Once sulphur was added to alleviate this problem but this is no longer considered a wise move as it may damage worms and microorganisms.)

While the bed is in this initial pre-planting phase it may be wise to check the ways in which extra water can be provided during dry spells, bearing in mind that hand-held hoses and sprinklers waste water, encourage mildews and molds and often flatten small plants. A drip system is the usual domestic choice and, while the bed is bare, the layout can be checked so that an even deep delivery can be achieved. Many gardeners prefer micro-jets, such as those in the Plassay system, to achieve this deeper delivery.

If this initial preparation is done thoroughly it will be years before deep digging need be done again. Any further nutrition can be laid on the soil's surface and the work of conveying it down to the roots left to worms and water.

These mature seedlings are ready to be planted.

Pack the soil around the plants and water immediately.

In many areas the local climate determines when and if seeds can be planted directly into the ground. If a late frost is a possibility, a much greater success rate is ensured if seeds are sown in a greenhouse or on a warm, weather-proof verandah or similar sheltered spot. This guarantees that the seedlings are ready to be transplanted as soon as weather permits.

Annuals are grown from seed each season, but there are various ways to propagate perennials. Many can be grown from seed, however it usually takes longer for blooms to form. If established crowns or rhizomes are divided, new plants, true to form, are generally established more quickly and often produce flowers the following season.

For gardeners in all climatic zones, annuals provide welcome displays of color, especially in early spring, while perennials put on a color parade at least once a year, often as a bonus to distinctive foliage. What's more, perennials pay handsome dividends, providing the gardener with a source of plant material with which to experiment with design and color combinations each season.

🌿 Outstanding Winter Flowering Perennials 🌿
Erysimum mutabile
Felicia amelloides
Helleborus species
Iris unguicularis
Tagetes lemmonii

🌿 Outstanding Winter Flowering Annuals 🌿
Senecio crudentus
Papaver nudicaule
Primula malacoides
Primula obconica
Viola × *wittrockiana*

Planting perennials

Dig a hole about three times the depth and width of the container. At the bottom of the hole, make a small hump, and add a few slow-release granules of purpose-designed fertiliser. Then ease the plant from its container; slightly loosen the roots; spread them over the hump; and refill the hole steadying the plant as you go. The level at which the plant material meets the soil's surface should be the same as it was when the plant was in its container. Gently firm the soil and water gently but thoroughly. Do not apply liquid feed at this point.

Ideally perennials are planted while dormant and just before their seasonal growth spurt. However many perennials are container grown and sold while in flower. These can be planted while flowering provided adequate after care is given. However, if conditions are demanding or the plant looks in any way stressed, it will be wise to trim the plants and to remove all the flowering stems. If there are any doubts cherish the plant in its container until the appropriate season.

Mail order plants should be exposed to the light and air as soon as they arrive and allowed a small period of rest and recuperation before being planted.

Plants which prove to be pot bound should be soaked for a few hours and the roots spread with care before they are planted.

Some perennials will prove to have been grown in soil very different to the local soil. These should have all the existing soil gently washed from the roots prior to planting and may take a little longer than usual to adjust to their new environment. A hormone designed to stimulate root growth may assist.

Some perennials dislike root disturbance, and should be planted into their prepared holes gently and carefully. Paeonies are an example.

Water and watering

Most garden plants have been bred or selected for growth in places where the precipitation is evenly distributed throughout the growing season and many will prove unable to survive without help from a hose when grown in drier climates and under the usual, crowded, garden conditions.

A watering regime should be carefully thought through if plants are to put their roots down and thrive and the gardener is to maintain a sensible lifestyle. Wastage through evaporation will be minimised if water is applied during the cooler night hours and applied directly to the soil through some form of drip system. A timer will also minimise wastage. One or two deep soakings every week should be sufficient and is infinitely preferable to daily squirtings from hand-held hoses. Such squirtings will save plant lives but such rescue remedies rarely lead to lush, long term, good health.

The problems associated with artificial watering have led to a growing interest and enthusiasm for wild gardens and gravel gardens where suitable species are planted, nurtured for a few weeks and then permitted to do or die without further help or hindrance from the gardener.

Mulch and nutrition

Perennial beds are usually treated to an annual top dressing of well-rotted organic mulch. (Raw wood shavings, eucalyptus leaves, pine chips and pine needles are not recommended. The contents of the compost bin, mushroom compost, straw or any proprietary compost designed for use with perennials are recommended.) The purpose of this mulch is to suppress weeds, to conserve water and to supply nutrition. The mulch should be spread around the plants in spring or late winter before growth begins and/or in autumn when the plants are tidied up and prepared for dormancy and their next season of growth. If the soil is healthy the worms will take the nutrients down to the plants' roots. Many gardeners get superb results when using a good mulch — one which contains a little animal matter and a lot of vegetable matter — as the sole supplier of plant nutrition.

In places where the growing season is prolonged a second flowering or prolonged flowering may a possibility. In such conditions the usual mulch can be supplemented with slow release, purpose-designed granules and/or the occasional light liquid feed half way through the season.

Fine water-conserving nutritional mulches are also used with annuals.

They should be dug through the bed prior to planting and, in the case of seed beds, not laid on top of the soil's surface where they can form an impenetrable crust. In gravel gardens the stones themselves provide the water-preserving weed-suppressing substance and all nutritional needs must be supplied from above. A very few granules of slow-release fertiliser or the occasional light liquid feed will suffice as, generally speaking, the plants which grow and thrive in gravel gardens are modest feeders and well capable of scraping a living from a bit of dirt and a stony surface.

General maintenance

During the growing season weeds should be removed as they appear. A good mulch and some healthy top growth will prevent this chore from becoming over arduous.

Spent flowers and leaves should be cleared away as soon as they lose their visual appeal and the beds kept clear of

A well-mulched garden such as this will help to control weeds, conserve water and add nutrition.

It's easy to see that these violas have been lovingly tended.

withered or rotting vegetation.

Hybrid annuals should be cleared away as soon as their visual appeal fades. Open-pollinated annuals, if seed collection is intended, must be left until the seeds have set and ripened.

Some perennials will require staking. This depends on the choice of plant, the situation and the climate. Spikes of flowers like delphiniums are usually staked individually whereas mounding plants, which require support, are grown through 'mushrooms' of wire or networks of strong twigs. The trick is to provide just enough support to hold the flowering mass upright in rough weather. Too little by way of support and the plants may go down like dominoes. Too much and a flower bed will look messy. In situations where massive plant support is required many people prefer to use sticks, twigs and natural string rather than multi-hued metal and/or plastic contraptions.

Some flowering perennials (and petunias and impatiens) benefit from a minor mid-season cut back. All perennials which enjoy a period of summer growth are cut back as winter approaches and flower production ceases. Those which have grown over-large or are becoming scraggy in the center are dug up and divided in such a way as to reduce the mass and then replanted. Excess and poor or decaying material is conveyed to the compost heap. When the winter comes a perennial bed should look somewhat bare, neat and clean, and allow space for the winter flowering perennials such as hellebores to spread their decorative leaves and flowers.

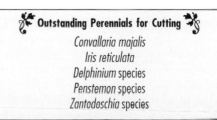

Outstanding Perennials for Cutting

Convallaria majalis
Iris reticulata
Delphinium species
Penstemon species
Zantodoschia species

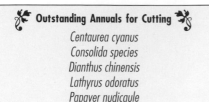

> ### 🌿 Outstanding Annuals for Cutting 🌿
>
> *Centaurea cyanus*
> *Consolida species*
> *Dianthus chinensis*
> *Lathyrus odoratus*
> *Papaver nudicaule*

In spring, when the summer flowering perennials emerge from their hibernation, the new shoots will need protection from snails and slugs. The fresh new growth of annuals certainly will. The foliage of some annuals and perennials is also prone to attack by caterpillars. If applied regularly, a simple, harmless pyrethrum spray or powder should control the problem and will be most effective if the undersides of the leaves are also coated with the mixture.

In sub-tropical climates where there is no prolonged humidity the popular perennials and annuals of colder climates can prove successful. Some will bloom in winter and die back in summer, in which case the seasonal maintenance program is reversed.

Division and propagation
Division
Large well-established perennials can (and should) be lifted and divided with a sharp clean knife while dormant in winter. In areas with hard winter frosts, it is often better to leave dividing until late winter or very early spring, in order to lessen the exposure of the young divisions to severe cold.

Each subdivision should be composed of clean-looking healthy-looking roots and a few shoots. These subdivisions can be planted directly back into the garden or potted up and cherished for future use.

The process of lifting and dividing winter or early spring flowering peren-

nials is exactly the same but is usually performed just after the plants have flowered.

Cuttings
Many perennials and a few of the so-called annuals, including petunias, nasturtiums, and wall flowers, can be grown from soft cuttings. A mature-looking shoot of manageable size can be taken. This 'cutting' or 'heel' can then be dipped into a hormone mixture designed for soft cuttings (this is not an essential procedure) and 'planted' into a pot filled with a free draining propagating mix. While these cuttings are taking root they must not be exposed to extremes of temperature or allowed to become over-dry or over-wet. Purpose-designed home propagators are available but many home gardeners develop their own ingenious methods of maintaining an even temperature and moisture level.

Plants propagated by these two methods will probably bloom in their first season and will be exact clones of

When taking soft cuttings, be sure to take a mature-looking shoot, and plant it in a good propagating mix.

The seemingly careless habit of *Erigeron karvinskianus* adds real character to this small courtyard.

their parent plant. Plants grown from seed may present in a variety of shapes and shades and have characteristics which vary from that of the parent plant. Many perennials when grown from seed do not bloom in their first year of garden growth.

Seed collection and propagation

Seeds to be collected for propagation should be allowed to remain with the parent plant until the pod is on the verge of bursting and the seeds are ripe. The easiest way to collect the seeds is by cutting the stems so that the pods, with their burden of seeds, fall directly into a container. The seeds are then removed from the pods, spread on a tray, and sun dried for a few days in a still spot. They can then be packaged, labelled and stored in a dry place. Seed grown plants do not necessarily grow true to the parent plant's appearance.

Design, placement and usage

Whether the intention is to recreate a grand English border, a cottage garden, a wild or gravel garden, to adorn a doorway or to fill a few gaps, a little forethought and planning will go a long way towards achieving a satisfactory and attractive planting. For example a deciduous plant, which looks fabulous when in flower, may leave a huge hole in the vegetation for many months and, while this may be of little account in a large garden, in a smaller one it can prove an eyesore. And no matter how much a particular plant may be desired, if the situation is unfavorable the gardener should consider the time and money it will take to nurture this favored plant.

Annuals and perennials can be used in a variety of ways either to enhance an existing design or to make and hold the design itself. Commercially produced annuals are used (petunias in sunny spots and impatiens in shady ones) when the designer seeks to establish bright blocks of color or when an entrance is perceived to be in need of some form of welcoming decoration. At the height of their glory these bright flowers can add to both structure and color. However as their flowering season is usually followed by a season of bare earth, some gardeners prefer to use evergreen perennials such as agapanthus, aquilegias, anigozanthos, arthropodiums, hellebores, liriopes, libertias and sisyrinchiums. In comparison to the well-known annuals, these plants may have shorter, less flamboyant flowering periods, but their decorative foliage is always there to hold the eye and carry the design. It is all a matter of choice and of knowing exactly what one is hoping to achieve—and for how long.

Herbaceous borders

Herbaceous borders are the apotheosis of gardening with perennials. These borders are usually arranged on a north/south axis and are either backed by a wall or hedge or paired on either side of a path. While they are a challenge to design they are less demanding of time than might be imagined, provided the gardener has a clear idea of expected plant behaviour in their particular situation.

In Britain, the home of grand herbaceous borders, the fabulous flowery display is of limited duration—two to three months at most. But the border is usually designed so that one grouping of plants succeeds another as the season progresses. In milder climates the intention is often to have something on show throughout the year and these flower borders often appear sparser than a classic British border in full flower.

In herbaceous borders perennials are arranged in a harmonious manner and identical plants are usually planted together in groups of three, five or seven. Taller plants are placed behind the shorter ones in borders which can only be viewed from one side, and along the spine in borders which are visible from all sides. Plants which display upright spikes of flowers are placed in contrast to those with mounding forms.

Great attention is given to harmonious color arrangements and to the way in which the foliage of one grouping will enhance the appearance of its near neighbors. Recognised color schemes include those which follow a segment of the colors found in the rainbow. For example the chosen theme might be scarlet, yellow, orange and bronze; or ruby-red, hot-pink, purple and sapphire blue; or lavender, silver, pink and mauve. The tonal strengths are co-ordinated and contrasted too. For example ruby-red, purple and sapphire-blue when diluted become the softer silvery shades of pale-pink, mauve lavender and baby-blue. Often, to provide visual focus, small flicks of clear scarlet or white are used to break the harmony of these careful schemes. Purists do not advocate the use of annuals in herbaceous borders but many gardeners fill the gaps created when some plant has failed to live up to expectations with annuals.

These borders in their classic form are beyond the scope of most gardeners but they are worth some study as many of their characteristics can be copied in smaller gardens and to great effect. The adoption of a harmonious color scheme for example will do much to give a small garden a spacious well-integrated feeling. Attention to the visual relationship between foliage and flower will add to its charm and architecture. And the grouping or massing of plants will prevent spotty over-busy effects.

Cottage gardens

The arrangement of annuals and perennials in modern cottage gardens is more relaxed. The easy going intention is to create an abundant flowery garden where nature has gone slightly out of control. Perennials are usually established as single plants and, if they spread beyond their allotted space, all well and good. Open-pollinated annuals are used to great effect with half their charm coming, as the years pass, from the random placements which only a plant can find for itself. A single packet of mixed open-pollinated seeds will soon give a 'cottage' effect.

Sometimes a slight air of formality is introduced with a formal planting on either side of a front path, or through a balanced arrangement of containers near a doorway. However, in general, the joy in cottage gardening comes from the abundance of flowers and fruit rather than from carefully controlled plant arrangements.

Gravel gardens

In gravel gardens plants which enjoy poor soils, good drainage and sunlight (gravel can get horribly stained when used in damp shady spaces) are planted and allowed and encouraged to come and go as they will. Some gardeners cover the entire garden with gravel; others combine paving stones with gravel. Some prefer to cover much of the surface with tough spreading low-

The joy in cottage gardening comes from the abundance of colorful flowers and fruit.

growing evergreen plants such as gazania and osteospermum while yet others prefer a more flexible open arrangement in which some of the gravel can always be seen. In these open arrangements more upright plants such as *Valeriana officinalis, Linaria purpurea, Knautia macedonica* and verbascums are used. Open-pollinated annuals are also permitted to find the odd niche.

The trick in a gravel garden is to pull out unwanted plants as soon as they appear in such a way as to give an uncontrolled natural impression.

Wild gardens

In wild gardens annuals and/or perennials are established in great drifts and waves and allowed to get on with the job of decorating the scenery. Usually the mass is arranged so that it follows and enhances the natural contours of the land. Sometimes a single easy-care species, usually one with a long flowering season, such as coreopsis, is relied on to adorn a large area. Wild gardens are usually low maintenance gardens with a single season of splendor. Yet a little ingenuity can provide decorative effects throughout the year. In cold climates, for example, frosted seed heads can prove enormously decorative.

Small suburban gardens

The design and plant arrangements in small suburban gardens can reflect any of these recognised styles. It is all a matter of picking up on few basic and appropriate design characteristics and, as always, matching the plants to the local conditions and climate. However, in small suburban gardens it is more usual and often just as effective to use annuals and perennials to add color, to fill gaps and to provide structure as and when they are required. A single row of

Because it can tolerate heat, salt air and poor soil, *Pericallis* × *hybrida* is a popular garden annual.

agapanthus, arthropodiums, evergreen day lily or liriope when used to edge a wall, fence or garden subdivision will do much to give the area a sophisticated spacious-looking trim and will enhance any existing architectural features.

Some final points

Some annuals are described as 'frost hardy annuals'. This does not necessarily indicate that these plants will perform over several years but that their seeds can be sown in autumn. If these plants are true annuals they will then die after flowering in the common way. The term 'hardy plant' refers to frost hardy plants and not to a plant's capacity to withstand drought or heat.

Poor drainage and hot humidity are as big a danger to annuals and perennials when grown in a warm temperate climates as frost is in colder climates.

Generally speaking plants with gray or

Left: The successful combination of elegant delphiniums and ever-reliable impatiens creates the ambience in this garden niche.

Wallflowers can be in bloom for months, and add vibrancy to any sized garden.

silvery leaves are well-adapted to hot sun-scorched situations.

Mark the place as perennial plants retreat into dormancy. It is all too easy to forget the position of a precious plant and to put a spade through it.

Most of the popular ornamental perennials and annuals bloom during the warmer months. However many of those described as 'summer blooming' will adapt their life cycle in the sub-tropics and bloom during the sunny but cooler winter months.

Every gardener must take on the responsibility of not introducing invasive plants to a neighborhood. What will or will not prove invasive in a particular area is beyond the scope of this book. Enquire at the relevant government department, such as the Department of Conservation, and be observant and be vigilant—if only for your own sake.

A

Abelmoschus moschatus 'Pacific Orange Scarlet'

Acaena 'Blue Haze'

ABELMOSCHUS

This is a genus of around 15 species from tropical Africa and Asia. They are annuals, biennials or short-lived perennials with tough bark (sometimes used for fiber) and maple-like leaves. The hibiscus-like flowers occur in shades of yellow, pink, orange or red. Several species make attractive ornamentals and the vegetable okra or gumbo (*A. esculentus*) is grown for its edible young pods.

Cultivation

They are mostly grown as summer annuals, requiring fertile, well-drained soil, a sheltered position in full sun, and plentiful water. Propagate from seed in spring. Rust disease can be a problem: spray with a fungicide.

Abelmoschus moschatus
Musk mallow

Some of this variable Asian species are used for fiber and the seeds (musk seeds) yield oils and fats (ambrette) used medicinally and in perfumery. The whole plant has a slight musky smell. The hairs on the leaves are often bristly and the large flowers are typically pale yellow with a purple eye. Ornamental cultivars have a range of flower colors, including 'Pacific Orange Scarlet' with red flowers. *Zones 8–12*.

ACAENA

Around 100 species make up this genus of low-growing evergreen perennials from the southern hemisphere. They have thin, creeping stems or buried rhizomes that bear at intervals tufts of small pinnate leaves with toothed margins. Flowers are insignificant, green or purple-brown, in dense stalked heads or spikes, and are followed by small dry fruit with barbed hooks. Acaenas make good rock garden plants. Some more vigorous species are regarded as weeds.

Cultivation

These tough plants thrive in exposed places and poor soil, but do demand good drainage and summer moisture. Propagate from seed or by division.

Acaena 'Blue Haze'

Thought probably to be a form of *Acaena magellanica*, from the southern Andes of South America and subantarctic islands, this vigorous creeper can spread to an indefinite size, the stems rooting. The crowded leaves with roundish, toothed leaflets are an attractive pale blue-gray, and in summer it sends up 4 in (10 cm) high purplish flowerheads followed in fall (autumn) by red-spined fruit. A useful ground cover, it will spill over rocks or retaining walls. *Zones 7–10*.

Acanthus mollis

Acanthus spinosus

ACANTHUS
Bear's breeches

Around 30 species of perennials and shrubs make up this genus. The deeply lobed and toothed leaves of *Acanthus mollis* and *A. spinosus* have lent their shape to the carved motifs seen on Corinthian columns. Only the more temperate perennial species have been much cultivated. They have erect spikes of bracted, curiously shaped flowers, which appear in spring and early summer.

Cultivation

Frost hardy, they do best in full sun or light shade. They prefer a rich, well-drained soil with adequate moisture. Watch for snails and caterpillars. Propagate by division in fall (autumn), or from seed.

Acanthus mollis

This species is somewhat variable, the form grown in gardens having broader, softer leaves and taller flowering stems than most wild plants. It is more of a woodland plant than other acanthuses, appreciating shelter and deep, moist soil. The large leaves are a deep, glossy green and rather soft. Flower spikes can be over 6 ft (1.8 m) tall, the purple-pink bracts contrasting with the crinkled white flowers. Spreading by deeply buried rhizomes, it can be hard to eradicate. *Zones 7–10.*

Acanthus spinosus

This eastern Mediterranean species has large leaves that are deeply divided, the segments having coarse, spine-tipped teeth. In summer it sends up flower spikes to about 4 ft (1.2 m) high; the individual flowers and bracts are similar to those of *A. mollis. Zones 7–10.*

ACHILLEA
Yarrow, milfoil, sneezewort

There are about 85 species of *Achillea* from the temperate northern hemisphere. Foliage is fern-like and aromatic. Most species bear masses of large, flat heads of tiny daisy flowers from late spring to fall (autumn) in shades of white, yellow, orange, pink or red. They suit massed border plantings and rockeries. This genus is named after Achilles, who, in Greek mythology, used the plant to heal wounds.

Cultivation

These hardy perennials tolerate poor soils, but do best in sunny, well-drained sites in temperate climates. They multiply rapidly by deep rhizomes and are easily propagated by division in late winter or from cuttings in summer.

Achillea 'Coronation Gold'

This vigorous hybrid cultivar originated as a cross between *Achillea clypeolata* and *A. filipendulina*. It has luxuriant grayish green foliage and flowering stems up to 3 ft (1 m) tall with large heads of deep golden yellow in summer and early fall (autumn). *Zones 4–10.*

Achillea 'Moonshine'

A cultivar of hybrid origin, this plant bears pretty flattened heads of pale sulfur yellow to bright yellow flowers throughout summer. It has delicate, feathery, silvery gray leaves and an upright habit, reaching a height of 24 in (60 cm). Divide regularly in spring to promote strong growth. *Zones 3–10.*

Achillea 'Coronation Gold'

Achillea 'Moonshine'

Achillea tomentosa
Woolly yarrow

Native to southwestern Europe, this is a low, spreading plant with woolly or silky-haired, finely divided gray-green leaves and flowerheads of bright yellow on 12 in (30 cm) stems. Tolerating dry conditions and hot sun, it is excellent in the rock garden or as an edging plant. *Zones 4–10.*

ACONITUM
Aconite, monkshood, wolfsbane

The 100 or so species of this genus from the northern hemishpere are renowned for the virulent poisons contained in the sap. From ancient times until quite recently they were widely employed for deliberate poisoning. The poison has also been used medicinally in controlled doses. The flowers are mostly in shades of deep blue or purple or less commonly white, pink or yellow, with 5 petals of which the upper one bulges up into a prominent helmet-like shape.

Cultivation

Monkshoods prefer deep, moist soil and a sheltered position, partly shaded if summers are hot and dry. Propagate by division or from seed.

Aconitum napellus
Aconite, monkshood

Of wide distribution in Europe and temperate Asia, this is also the monks-

Achillea tomentosa

hood species most widely grown in gardens. The stems are erect, to 4 ft (1.2 m) or so high, with large leaves divided into very narrow segments and a tall, open spike of deep blue to purplish flowers. A vigorous grower, it likes damp woodland or stream bank conditions. *Zones 5–9.*

ACTINOTUS

There are 11 species in the Australian genus *Actinotus*. In the structure of their flowerheads, members of this genus mimic those of the daisy (composite) family, but they belong to the carrot (umbellifer) family. Leaves and flowerheads are both felted with dense hairs which help *Actinotus* species reduce moisture loss in a dry climate and grow in poor, scarcely water-retentive soils.

Cultivation

They demand light shade, a mild climate and good drainage. Plants are usually treated as biennials. Propagate from seed or cuttings in spring or summer.

Actinotus helianthi
Flannel flower

This biennial or short-lived, evergreen shrub grows from 12 in–3 ft (30–90 cm) high with a spread of 24 in (60 cm). It has deeply divided gray-green foliage. Furry erect stems appear in spring and summer, topped by star-like flowerheads which consist of a cluster of pink-

Actinotus helianthi

stamened, greenish florets surrounded by flannel-textured dull white bracts with grayish green tips. *Zones 9–10.*

ADONIS

This genus consists of 20 species of annuals and perennials from Europe and cooler parts of Asia. The name comes from the Greek hero Adonis, beloved of Aphrodite, when red flowers were said to have sprung from drops of his blood when he was killed by a boar. Leaves are mostly finely divided, the top ones on each stem forming a 'nest' on which the single bowl-shaped flower rests.

Cultivation

Adonis require a cool climate with warm dry summers. They grow best in a sheltered spot in full sun, and in moist, fertile soil with a high humus content. Propagate from fresh seed or by division of clumps.

Aconitum napellus

Adonis vernalis

Agapanthus praecox subsp. *orientalis*

Agapanthus 'Loch Hope'

Adonis vernalis

This European perennial species has very narrow, almost needle-like, finely divided leaflets. Its 12- to 20-petalled, bright yellow flowers are large, up to 3 in (8 cm) across, and open in early spring. Both this species and *A. annua* have been used medicinally, but are now regarded as too toxic for general use. *Zones 3–9.*

AGAPANTHUS
African lily, agapanthus, lily-of-the-Nile

Native to southern Africa, these strong-growing perennials have fine foliage and showy flowers produced in abundance over summer. Arching, strap-shaped leaves spring from short rhizomes with dense, fleshy roots. Flowers are shades of blue (white in some cultivars) in many flowered umbels, borne on a long erect stem, often 3 ft (1 m) or more tall.

Cultivation

Agapanthus enjoy full sun but tolerate some shade, and will grow in any soil as long as they get water in spring and summer. Remove spent flower stems and dead leaves at winter's end. Propagate by division in late winter, or from seed in spring or fall (autumn).

Agapanthus 'Loch Hope'

A late-flowering agapanthus, this cultivar grows to a height of 4 ft (1.2 m) and has abundant, large dark violet blue flowerheads. *Zones 9–11.*

Agapanthus praecox

This is the most commonly grown of the 10 species. Its glorious starbursts of lavender-blue flowers appear in summer, and its densely clumped evergreen foliage is handsome in the garden all year round. It is also available in white. *Agapanthus praecox* subsp. *orientalis* has large dense umbels of blue flowers. It prefers full sun, moist soil and is marginally frost hardy. *Zones 9–11.*

Agastache foeniculum

Ageratum houstonianum

AGASTACHE

This genus of some 20 species of perennials is from China, Japan and North America. Most are upright with stiff, angular stems clothed in toothed-edged, lance-shaped leaves. Heights range from 18 in–6 ft (45 cm–1.8 m) tall. Upright spikes of tubular, 2-lipped flowers develop at the stem tips in summer. Flowers are usually white, pink, mauve or purple with the bracts that back the flowers being of the same or a slightly contrasting color.

Cultivation

They like moist, well-drained soil and a sunny spot. Hardiness varies, but most tolerate occasional frosts to 20°F (–7°C). Propagate from seed or cuttings.

Agastache foeniculum
syn. *Agastache anethiodora*
Anise hyssop

This 18 in–4 ft (45 cm–1.2 m) tall, soft-stemmed North American species makes a clump of upright stems with 3 in (8 cm) leaves. Often treated as an annual, it is primarily grown for the ornamental value of its purple flower spikes. The anise-scented and flavored foliage is used to make a herbal tea or as a flavoring. *Zones 8–10.*

AGERATUM
Floss flower

While best known for the annual bedding plants derived from *Ageratum*

houstonianum, this genus includes some 43 species of annuals and perennials mostly native to warmer regions of the Americas. They are clump-forming or mounding plants up to 30 in (75 cm) tall with felted or hairy, roughly oval to heart-shaped leaves with shallowly toothed or serrated edges. The flowerheads are a mass of fine filaments, usually dusky blue, lavender or pink and crowded in terminal clusters.

Cultivation

They are best grown in full sun in moist, well-drained soil. Regular deadheading prolongs flowering. Propagate by spring-sown seed, either raised indoors in containers or sown directly in the garden.

Ageratum houstonianum

Native to Central America and the West Indies, this annual ageratum is popular as a summer bedding plant. It is available in tall (12 in [30 cm]), medium (8 in [20 cm]) and dwarf (6 in [15 cm]) sizes and forms clumps of foliage with fluffy flowers in an unusual dusky blue. Pink and white forms are also available. *Zones 9–12.*

AGROSTEMMA

Two or possibly more species of slender annuals from the Mediterranean region belong to this genus. One is a weed of crops in Europe, but is still a pretty plant with large rose-pink flowers and is sometimes used in cottage gardens. Distinctive features are the long silky hairs on the leaves and the calyx consisting of 5 very long, leaf-like sepals radiating well beyond the petals.

Cultivation
They are frost hardy, preferring full sun and well-drained soil. Thin young plants to about 10 in (25 cm) spacing. Propagate from seed sown in early spring or fall (autumn).

Agrostemma githago
Corn cockle
This fast-growing showy annual reaches a height of 24–36 in (60–90 cm), making it ideal for planting at the back of an annual border. It has a slender, few-branched, willowy habit with long narrow leaves in opposite pairs. Broadly funnel-shaped pink flowers appear on long hairy stalks from late spring to early fall (autumn). *Zones 8–10.*

Ajuga reptans 'Atropurpurea'

Ajuga reptans

AJUGA
Bugle
About 50 species of low-growing annuals and perennials make up this genus, which ranges through Europe, Asia, Africa and Australia, mainly in cooler regions. Rosettes of soft, spatulate leaves lengthen into spikes of blue, purple or pink (rarely yellow) 2-lipped flowers. In most perennial species the plants spread by runners or underground rhizomes. They make attractive ground covers.

Cultivation
These are frost-hardy, trouble-free plants requiring moist soil and shelter from strong sun, though the bronze and variegated forms develop best color in sun. Propagate by division.

Ajuga reptans
European bugle, common bugle, blue bugle
The commonly grown ajuga spreads by surface runners, making a mat of leafy rosettes only 2–3 in (5–8 cm) high and indefinite spread. In spring it sends up spikes of deep blue flowers, up to 8 in (20 cm) high in some cultivars. The most familiar versions are: 'Atropurpurea' syn. 'Purpurea' which has dark purple to bronze leaves; 'Burgundy Glow', with cream and maroon variegated leaves; 'Multicolor', with white, pink and purple leaves; and 'Variegata', with light green and cream leaves. *Zones 3–10.*

Agrostemma githago

ALCEA
Hollyhock

Native to Turkey and the eastern Mediterranean, hollyhocks were originally called holy hock or holy mallow; it is said that plants were taken to England from the Holy Land during the Crusades. There are about 60 species in the genus. They bear flowers on spikes which may be 6 ft (1.8 m) or more high; 'dwarf' cultivars grow to 3 ft (1 m) tall.

Cultivation

They are frost hardy but need shelter from wind, benefiting from staking in exposed positions. They prefer sun, a rich, heavy well-drained soil and frequent watering in dry weather. Propagate from seed. Rust disease can be a problem; spray with fungicide.

Alcea rosea
syn. *Althaea rosea*
Hollyhock

This biennial or perennial has tall spikes of flowers which appear in summer and early fall (autumn). Colors range from pink, purple, cream to yellow; they can be either single, flat circles 4 in (10 cm) across, or so lavishly double that they are like spheres of ruffled petals. Foliage is roundish and the plants may be as much as 10 ft (3 m) tall, erect and generally unbranched. The Chater's Double Group of cultivars have peony-shaped, double flowers. *Zones 4–10.*

Alcea rosea

ALCHEMILLA
Lady's mantle

There are some 300 species of herbaceous perennials in this Eurasian genus, as well as a few alpine species in Australia and New Zealand. They form clumps of palmate or rounded, lobed, gray-green leaves often covered in fine hairs. Branched inflorescences of tiny yellow-green flowers develop in summer. Their sizes range from 6–30 in (15–75 cm) tall and wide. Many species have styptic and other medicinal properties.

Cultivation

These hardy plants are easily grown in any well-drained soil in afternoon shade. Propagate from seed or by division.

Alchemilla mollis
Lady's mantle

Sometimes sold as *Alchemilla vulgaris*, this is the most widely cultivated species in the genus. It is a low-growing perennial ideal for ground covers, the front of borders or for rock gardens. It is clump-forming, growing to a height and spread of 16 in (about 40 cm). It has decorative, wavy edged leaves, and in summer, it bears masses of small sprays of greenish yellow flowers, similar to *Gypsophila*. *Zones 4–9.*

Alchemilla vetteri

This is a small species from the mountains of southwest Europe. Its flowering

Alchemilla mollis

Alpinia zerumbet

Alchemilla vetteri

Alonsoa warscewiczii

stems rarely exceed 8 in (20 cm) tall and the foliage clump is usually less than 12 in (30 cm) wide. The leaves have 7 to 9 lobes with toothed edges. *Zones 4–9.*

ALONSOA
Mask flower

This genus of some 12 species of perennials and subshrubs is found in tropical western America from Mexico to Peru. They are commonly known as mask flowers because of the fancied resemblance of the shape of the flower to a carnival mask. The flowers are usually small, but often vividly colored and open through most of the year.

Cultivation

Provided they receive some sun, mask flowers are easily grown in any free-draining soil. Propagate from seed, cuttings or by layering the stems. Only very lights frosts are tolerated.

Alonsoa warscewiczii

An evergreen perennial that in some climates is short-lived and treated as an annual, this native of Peru can develop into a 24 in (60 cm) high subshrub in a frost-free climate. It bears clusters of small vivid orange-red flowers. In suitably mild conditions these appear throughout the year. There are several cultivars with flowers in various shades of pink and orange. *Zones 9–11.*

ALPINIA
Ornamental ginger

Of Asian and Pacific origin, these plants have showy blooms. They grow from fleshy rhizomes to form large clumps. The aboveground shoots are in fact pseudostems consisting of tightly furled leaf bases. The large thin leaves form 2 rows. Although strictly speaking perennials, they do not die back and can be used in the garden like a shrub.

Cultivation

Alpinias are frost tender, but many tolerate winter temperatures not far above freezing as long as summers are warm and humid. They appreciate part-shade, a warm, moist atmosphere and rich soil. Propagate by division.

Alpinia zerumbet
syns *Alpinia nutans, A. speciosa*
Shell ginger

This evergreen, clump-forming perennial grows to around 10 ft (3 m) with a spread of 5–10 ft (1.5–3 m). It has long, densely massed stems with broad, green

Alstroemeria aurea

Alstroemeria psittacina

Alstroemeria, Ligtu Hybrid

leaves. The drooping sprays of flowers appear in spring and intermittently in other seasons, starting as waxy white or ivory buds, opening one at a time to reveal yellow lips with pink- or red-marked throats. *Zones 10–12.*

ALSTROEMERIA
Peruvian lily

These tuberous and rhizomatous plants with about 50 species are among the finest of perennials for cutting, but they do drop their petals. Erect, wiry stems bear scattered, thin, twisted leaves concentrated on the upper half, and terminate in umbels of outward-facing flowers, usually with flaring petals that are variously spotted or streaked. They flower profusely from spring to summer.

Cultivation

All grow well in sun or light shade in a well-enriched, well-drained acidic soil. Propagate from seed or by division in early spring. Although frost hardy, dormant tubers should be covered with loose peat or dry bracken in cold winters.

Alstroemeria aurea

syn. *Alstroemeria aurantiaca*
Native to Chile and the most easily grown species, this has heads of orange flowers, tipped with green and streaked with maroon. Leaves are twisted, narrow and lance-shaped. 'Majestic' and 'Bronze Beauty' have deep orange flowers; they grow to 2–3 ft (0.6–1 m) with a similar spread. *Zones 7–9.*

Alstroemeria, Ligtu Hybrids

The well-known Ligtu Hybrids first appeared in Britain in the late 1920s, when *Alstroemeria ligtu* was crossed with *A. haemantha*. They come in a range of colors from cream to orange, red and yellow, but have been overshadowed in recent years as cut flowers by other hybrid strains derived from *A. aurea*. The plants die down soon after flowering. *Zones 7–9.*

Alstroemeria psittacina

syn. *Alstroemeria pulchella*
New Zealand Christmas bell

Though native to Brazil, *Alstroemeria psittacina* gets its common name from its popularity in New Zealand, where its crimson and green flowers are borne at Christmas. The well spaced stems, about 24 in (60 cm) high, spring from tuberous roots. Easily grown in warm-temperate climates, it can spread rapidly and be difficult to eradicate. *Zones 8–10.*

AMARANTHUS

The 60 or so species of annuals and short-lived perennials in this genus from tropical and warm-temperate areas are grown for their brilliant foliage, curious flowers and adaptability to hot, dry conditions. They have large and attractively colored leaves and minute flowers borne in drooping tassel-like spikes.

Cultivation

They need a sunny, dry position with protection from strong winds, and a fertile, well-drained soil, mulched during hot weather. They are marginally frost hardy. Propagate from seed.

Amaranthus caudatus
Love-lies-bleeding, tassel flower

This species, growing to 4 ft (1.2 m) or more high, has oval, dull green leaves

Amaranthus caudatus

Amaranthus tricolor 'Joseph's Coat'

and dark red flowers in long, drooping cords, their ends often touching the ground. Flowers appear in summer through to fall (autumn). In many old gardens this plant was used to give height in the center of circular beds. *Zones 8–11.*

Amaranthus tricolor

Native to tropical Africa and Asia, this quick-growing annual has given rise to many cultivated strains, some used as leaf vegetables (Chinese spinach), others as bedding plants with brilliantly colored leaves. They are bushy annuals, reaching about 3 ft (1 m) high and 18 in (45 cm) wide. Tiny red flowers appear in summer. 'Joseph's Coat' has brilliant bronze, gold, orange and red variegated 8 in (20 cm) long leaves which retain their coloring into late fall (autumn). *Zones 8–11.*

AMMI

Six species of carrot-like perennials belong to this genus, occurring wild in the Mediterranean region, western Asia and the Canary Islands. They are fairly typical umbellifers with large, ferny basal leaves and flowering stems bearing large umbels of numerous small white flowers. *Ammi* was the classical Greek and Latin name for a plant of this type, though its exact identity is uncertain.

Cultivation

Usually treated as annuals, they are easily grown in a sheltered but sunny position in any reasonable garden soil, kept fairly moist. Propagate from seed in spring. They usually self-seed once established.

Ammi majus
Bishop's weed

Native to the Mediterranean region and western Asia, this species has become widely naturalized in other continents. It grows to about 24–36 in (60–90 cm) tall, producing a succession of large, lacy flowering heads in summer and fall (autumn). The cut flowers are sometimes sold in florists' shops. *Zones 6–10.*

AMSONIA
Blue star

This genus of around 20 species of perennials and subshrubs, native to southern Europe, western Asia, Japan and North America, grow to around 3 ft (1 m) tall and have bright to deep green, narrow, lance-shaped leaves. The flowers, borne mainly in summer, are tubular with widely flared mouths. They are carried in phlox-like heads at the stem tips.

Cultivation

Amsonias are easily grown in any moist, well-drained soil. Plant in full sun or part-shade. They are moderately to very frost hardy and generally die back to the rootstock in winter. Propagation is from seed, early summer cuttings or by division.

Amsonia tabernaemontana
Blue star, blue dogbane

This delightful perennial from northeastern and central USA has stiff stems, 24–36 in (60–90 cm) tall, which are topped by pyramidal clusters of small, star-shaped flowers of pale blue from

Ammi majus

late spring to summer, flowering along with peonies and irises. The leaves are narrow to elliptical. It needs minimal care if given a moist, fertile soil in full sun to light shade, and suits a perennial border or damp wildflower meadow. *Zones 3–9.*

ANAGALLIS
Pimpernel

The 20 or so species are low-growing, often mat-forming annuals and perennials with small, heart-shaped to elliptical, bright green leaves arranged in opposite pairs. In spring and summer small, 5-petalled flowers appear in profusion on short stems. The flowers usually arise from the leaf axils or occasionally in small racemes at the stem tips. They come in a variety of colors including pink, orange, red, blue and white.

Cultivation

Plant in full sun in any well-drained soil that does not dry out in summer. Propagate annuals from seed; perennials from seed, by division or from small tip cuttings. Some of the weedy species readily self-sow.

Amsonia tabernaemontana

Anagallis monellii

Anaphalis margaritacea

Anagallis arvensis

Anagallis arvensis
Scarlet pimpernel, common pimpernel
Widely regarded as a weed, this European native behaves as an annual, biennial or short-lived perennial depending on the climate. It is a sprawling plant with ½ in (12 mm) long, rounded, bright green leaves on stems up to 18 in (45 cm) long. Small, orange flowers appear in the leaf axils from spring to fall (autumn). *Anagallis arvensis* var. *caerulea* has brilliant deep blue flowers. *Zones 7–10.*

Anagallis monellii
syns *Anagallis linifolia, A. collina*
This Mediterranean native is grown for its brilliant blue or scarlet flowers of ½ in (12 mm) diameter, which appear during summer. This species grows to under 18 in (45 cm), with a spread of 6 in (15 cm) or more. *Zones 7–10.*

ANAPHALIS
Pearl everlasting
This genus of around 100 species of gray-foliaged perennials has narrow, lance-shaped leaves which are often clothed in cobwebby hairs attached directly to upright stems. Panicles on clusters of papery white flowerheads terminate the stems in summer or fall (autumn). Heights range from 6–30 in (15–75 cm) depending on the species. They are good cut flowers, and the foliage and flowers are just as decorative when dried.

Cultivation
Plant in light, gritty, well-drained soil in full sun. They do not like being wet but when in active growth the soil should not be allowed to dry out. Prune in winter. Propagate from seed or division.

Anaphalis margaritacea
syn. *Anaphalis yedoensis*
Pearl everlasting
Native to North America, Europe and Asia, this perennial has papery, small yellow flowers which can be dried. It has lance-shaped, silvery gray leaves and the flowers are borne on erect stems in late summer. Bushy in habit, it grows to about 24–30 in (60–75 cm) high and about 24 in (60 cm) wide. It prefers a sunny situation (but will grow in part-shade) and well-drained chalky soil. *Zones 4–9.*

Anchusa capensis 'Blue Angel'

ANCHUSA
Alkanet, summer forget-me-not

This genus consists of about 50 species of annuals, biennials and perennials. Many have a weedy habit and undistinguished foliage, but they bear flowers of a wonderful sapphire blue, which are carried in clusters over a long spring and early summer season. They suit herbaceous borders, beds and containers. The dwarf perennials suit rock gardens.

Cultivation

Frost hardy, they like a sunny spot in deep, rich, well-drained soil. In hot areas planting in part-shade helps maintain flower color. Feed sparingly; water generously. Taller species benefit from staking. Propagate perennials by division in winter, annuals and biennials from seed in fall (autumn) or spring.

Anchusa azurea
syn. *Anchusa italica*
Italian alkanet

Occurring wild around the Mediterranean, and the Black Sea, this species is an upright perennial up to 3–4 ft (1–1.2 m) high and 24 in (60 cm) wide. It has coarse, hairy leaves and an erect habit with tiers of brilliant blue flowers borne in spring to summer. Cultivars differ in their precise shade of blue: rich blue 'Morning Glory', light blue 'Opal' and the intense deep blue of 'Loddon Royalist'. *Zones 3–9.*

Anchusa azurea 'Lodden Royalist'

Anchusa capensis
Cape forget-me-not

From southern Africa, this species is biennial in cool climates, but in warm-temperate gardens it can be sown very early in spring to bear intense blue flowers in summer. It grows to 15 in (40 cm) tall and wide. 'Blue Angel' reaches a height and spread of 8 in (20 cm) bearing shallow, bowl-shaped sky-blue flowers in early summer. *Zones 8–10.*

ANDROSACE
Rock jasmine

This genus consists of around 100 species of annuals and perennials from cooler regions of the northern hemisphere. The low-growing perennials form dense mats or cushions no more than 4 in (10 cm) high. Most have light green or silvery gray, loose rosettes of foliage crowded along prostrate stems, topped with umbels of small white or pink 5-petalled flowers in spring and summer.

Cultivation

They like sunny, well-drained scree or rockery conditions with free-draining gravel-based soil and additional humus. Most are quite frost hardy. Propagate from seed, cuttings or self-rooted layers.

Androsace lanuginosa

A spreading ground-cover or mat-forming perennial from the Himalayas with small deep green leaves that appear somewhat silvery due to a covering of fine silky hairs. Only about 2 in (5 cm) high, the plants can spread rapidly to 18 in (45 cm) or more wide. Heads of light pink flowers appear profusely in summer and fall (autumn). *Zones 6–9.*

ANEMONE
Windflower

There are over 100 species of perennials in this genus and all have tufts of basal

Androsace lanuginosa

Anemone blanda 'Atrocaerulea'

leaves that are divided in palmate fashion into few to many leaflets. The starry or bowl-shaped flowers have 5 or more petals. They can be divided into the autumn flowering species with fibrous roots, such as *A. hupehensis* and *A. × hybrida*, and the tuberous and rhizomatous types, usually spring flowering, which include the ground-hugging *A. blanda* and *A. nemorosa*. Replace tuberous-rooted types every 1–2 years. They are widespread in temperate regions.

Cultivation

Most are frost hardy and do well in rich, moist yet well-drained soil in a lightly shaded position. Propagate from seed planted in summer or divide established clumps in early winter.

Anemone blanda

This delicate-looking tuberous species is frost hardy. Native to Greece and Turkey, it grows to 8 in (20 cm) with crowded tufts of ferny leaves. White, pink or blue star-shaped flowers appear in spring. It self-seeds freely and, given moist, slightly shaded conditions, should spread into a beautiful display of flowers. Popular cultivars include the large-flowered 'White Splendour'; 'Atrocaerulea', with deep blue flowers; and 'Radar' with white-centered magenta flowers. *Zones 6–9.*

Anemone coronaria St Brigid Group

Anemone coronaria
Wind poppy, florist's anemone

This frost hardy species dies back to small woody tubers; these are sold in packets, the plants being treated almost as annuals. They grow to about 10 in (25 cm) high, and the poppy-like flowers range in color from pink to scarlet, purple or blue. The St Brigid Group has double flowers. It is excellent as a cut flower. *Zones 8–10.*

Anemone hupehensis
Japanese wind flower

This species from central and western China (long cultivated in Japan), can be almost evergreen in milder climates where, if conditions suit, it may spread and provide good ground cover, producing its single white to mauve flowers on tall, openly branched stems during early fall (autumn). *Anemone hupehensis* var. *japonica* is taller and has more petals than the wild Chinese plants. It includes 'Prinz Heinrich' (Prince Henry) with 10 or more deep rose-pink petals, paler on the undersides. Most of the cultivars ascribed to this species are now placed under *Anemone* × *hybrida*. *Zones 6–10.*

Anemone × hybrida

These popular hybrids have flowers in all shades from white to deepest rose,

the petals numbering from 5 to over 30. They generally lack fertile pollen. The robust plants may reach heights of 5 ft (1.5 m) in flower. There are over 30 cultivars, including 'Honorine Jobert' with pure white, 6–9-petalled flowers and dark green leaves. *Zones 6–10.*

ANGELICA

This genus of 50 or so northern hemisphere species has a bold palm-like leaf structure. The bunches of pale green flowers on tall stems have a pleasant aroma.

Cultivation

They prefer moist, well-drained, rich soil in sun or shade. Angelica will self-sow or can be propagated from seed.

Angelica archangelica

A fast-growing, robust biennial, this species was valued for centuries for its medicinal uses—to relieve toothache, to dispel 'phrenzies of the head', and to protect against plague. The young stems are used, and are most familiar as a candied green garnish for sweet dishes. It grows to 6 ft (1.8 m). Cut back flowerheads to ensure leaf production. It has deeply divided, bright green leaves and umbels of small flowers in late summer, and does best in filtered sunlight. Protect from strong winds. *Zones 4–9.*

Anemone × hybrida 'Honorine Jobert'

Angelica archangelica

Anigozanthos 'Regal Claw'

Anigozanthos manglesii

Anigozanthos Bush Gems Series, 'Bush Gold'

ANIGOZANTHOS
Kangaroo paw

These evergreen Western Australian perennials have unique bird-attracting tubular flowers, the outsides coated with dense shaggy hairs and opening at the apex into 6 'claws', the whole resembling an animal's paw. Foliage is grass-like, and species can range in height from 1–6 ft (0.3–1.8 m). Flowers come in many colors including green, gold, deep red and orange-red.

Cultivation

They prefer warm, very well-drained sandy or gravelly soil and a hot, sunny, open position. Water well during dry seasons. Most tolerate light frosts and drought. Propagate by division in spring or from fresh seed. Plants are often affected by ink disease, a fungus which blackens the foliage.

Anigozanthos Bush Gems Series

The best of the kangaroo paws for their resistance to ink disease, the Bush Gems hybrids are mostly of compact size, with flowers ranging from yellow, gold and green through to orange, red and burgundy. 'Bush Heritage' is a cultivar of 12–20 in (30–50 cm) high with flowers of burnt terracotta and olive green. 'Bush Twilight' has prolific flowers in muted orange, yellow and green tones. 'Bush Gold' has golden yellow flowers. *Zones 9–11.*

Anigozanthos manglesii
Red-and-green kangaroo paw

This striking plant has blue-green, strap-like leaves. Flowers are a deep green, contrasting vividly with a red base and stem, and appear mainly in spring. Flowering stems are 18–36 in (45–90 cm) high and the plant has a spread at the base of about 18 in (45 cm). Unfortunately this spectacular species is difficult

Anthemis cretica

Anthemis tinctoria

to cultivate, being very susceptible to ink disease as well as summer root rot. *Zones 9–10.*

Anigozanthos 'Regal Claw'

One of the many striking cultivars with parents listed as *Anigozanthos preissii* and *A. flavidus*, 'Regal Claw' is a dwarf plant with flowers of orange with a red felted overlay. *Zones 9–11.*

ANTHEMIS

There are 100 or so species of this genus of annuals and perennials. Belonging to the larger daisy family, the flowerheads have the typical daisy shape and are generally white, cream or yellow with distinctive contrasting disc florets. Most species have somewhat aromatic, finely dissected foliage in shades of green or silver gray, which makes them ideal in the mixed border or rockery.

Cultivation

They flower best in full sun and like well-drained soil. The perennials can be short-lived and often become untidy, but cutting back after flowering ensures a more shapely plant. They are easily replaced by cuttings taken in summer or by division in fall or spring. Annual species can be grown from seed.

Anthemis cretica

A mound-forming perennial from southern Europe and Turkey, often with a gray down on its leaves, this species has white flowerheads with yellow discs held on solitary stems up to 12 in (30 cm) high during the spring and summer months. *Zones 5–9.*

Anthemis tinctoria
Dyer's chamomile, golden marguerite

Native to Europe and western Asia, this is a very hardy, easily grown perennial that is covered in late spring and summer with a dazzling display of daisy flowers above fern-like, crinkled green leaves. The plant mounds to as much as 3 ft (1 m) high if supported on a rockery or a bank. The flowers of this species were once used to make a yellow dye. The cultivar 'E. C. Buxton' has subtle soft yellow blooms blending beautifully with the fine foliage. *Zones 4–10.*

ANTIRRHINUM
Snapdragon

The resemblance of snapdragon flowers to the face of a beast was noted by the ancient Greeks, who called them *Antirrhinon*, nose-like. In French they are *gueule de loup*, wolf's mouth, and in German and Italian the name means lion's mouth. The genus consists of about 40 species, most from the western Mediterranean region but with a few from western North America. They include annuals, perennials and evergreen subshrubs. The garden snapdragon (*A. majus*) is a perennial but many treat it as an annual.

Cultivation

They prefer fertile, well-drained soil in full sun. Propagate from seed.

Antirrhinum hispanicum

This short-lived perennial from Spain is a very pretty miniature species, 10 in (25 cm) tall with flowers about half the size of the garden snapdragon. Mauve-pink is its only color. *Zones 7–10.*

Antirrhinum hispanicum

Antirrhinum majus

Antirrhinum majus
Garden snapdragon

This bushy short-lived perennial bears showy flowers from spring to fall (autumn). The many named cultivars, usually grown as annuals, have a spread of 12–18 in (30–45 cm) and range from tall: 30 in (75 cm); to medium: 18 in (45 cm); to dwarf: 10 in (25 cm). Treat garden snapdragons as annuals—they rarely flower well after the first year, and old plants often succumb to the fungus, antirrhinum rust. Deadhead to prolong flowering and pinch out early buds to increase branching. The Coronette Series of F1 hybrids exemplifies some of the qualities plant geneticists are injecting into their breeding programs. These include tolerance of bad weather, extra large blooms on heavy spikes and uniformity from seedling stage. Two popular cultivars of *A. majus* are 'Flower Carpet' and 'Madame Butterfly'. *Zones 6–10.*

AQUILEGIA
Columbine

These clump-forming perennials have spurred, bell-shaped—single and double forms—flowers in a varied color range, and fern-like foliage. Some make good cut flowers, and the dwarf and alpine species make good rock-garden plants. They flower mostly in late spring and early summer, and look best in bold clumps.

Cultivation

Frost hardy, they prefer a well-drained light soil, enriched with manure, and a sunny site protected from strong winds. In cold climates columbines are perennials and need to be cut to the ground in late winter. Propagate by division or from seed in fall (autumn) and spring; many of them self-seed readily.

Aquilegia canadensis
American wild columbine
This native of eastern North America produces masses of nodding, red and yellow flowers with medium-length spurs, on 18–24 in (45–60 cm) stems in late spring and early summer. It tolerates full sun, provided there is plenty of moisture. It also tolerates heat if some shade is provided. *Zones 3–9.*

Aquilegia 'Crimson Star'
These long-spurred aquilegias usually face their flowers upwards, in contrast to the pendent flowers of the short-spurred granny's bonnets. The nectar spurs, which in other aquilegias normally match the color of the petals of which they are a prolongation, match the crimson of the sepals in this cultivar. *Zones 3–10.*

Aquilegia McKana Hybrids
The McKana Hybrids are derived chiefly from *Aquilegia caerulea*, *A. chrysantha* and *A. formosa*. They bear flowers in a variety of colors in late spring and early summer. Whatever the color of the sepals, the 5 petals that carry the spurs are usually white or yellow. Pinching off spent flowers will prolong the season. The plants grow to 3 ft (1 m) or more. *Zones 3–10.*

Aquilegia vulgaris
Granny's bonnets, columbine
This European columbine grows to 3 ft (1 m) high with a spread of 18 in (45 cm)

or more. On long stems from the center of a loose rosette of gray-green foliage, it bears funnel-shaped, short-spurred flowers, typically dull blue in wild plants but ranging through pink, crimson, white and purple in garden varieties. 'Nora Barlow' has curious double flowers, with many narrow, greenish sepals and pink petals. *Zones 3–10.*

Aquilegia vulgaris 'Nora Barlow'

Aquilegia canadensis

Aquilegia McKana Hybrid

Aquilegia 'Crimson Star'

Arabis caucasica

Arabis blepharophylla

ARABIS
Rock cress

Over 120 species make up this northern hemisphere genus of annuals and perennials, the latter mostly evergreen. Although some can reach as much as 3 ft (1 m) in height, species grown in gardens are dwarf, often mat-forming perennials suited to the rock garden, dry walls and crevices. They spread by short rhizomes, producing crowded tufts of spatula-shaped leaves. Short sprays of delicate, 4-petalled flowers are held above the foliage in spring and summer.

Cultivation

They grow best in very well-drained soil in a sunny position. Propagation is from seed or from cuttings taken in summer, or by division.

Arabis blepharophylla
California rock cress

This is a moderately frost-hardy species native to California, where it grows at low altitudes. Forming a compact clump 4–6 in (10–15 cm) high, it has tufts of toothed green leaves that extend into short, leafy spikes of pink to purple flowers during spring. It is best planted in a rockery or crevice where it will not be overrun. Most commonly available is the cultivar 'Frühlingzauber' ('Spring Charm'), with rich, rose-purple flowers. *Zones 7–10.*

Arabis caucasica
syn. *Arabis albida*
Wall rock cress

This tough, evergreen perennial is sometimes used to overplant spring-flowering bulbs. It forms dense clusters of thick foliage up to 6 in (15 cm) high with a spread of 18 in (45 cm). In spring it has white flowers on loose racemes above gray-green leaf rosettes. There are various forms of *Arabis caucasica* such as 'Pinkie', *A. c.* var. *brevifolia* and double-flowered forms such as 'Flore Pleno' (syn. 'Plena'). *Zones 4–10.*

ARCTOTIS
syns *Venidium,* × *Venidio-arctotis*
African daisy

The stems and leaves of this South African genus of about 50 species of annuals and evergreen perennials, are coated in matted downy hairs, giving them a gray-green or silvery gray color. The flowers are typical of the daisy family. They need the sun to open fully, and colors range from creamy yellow through orange to deep pinks and claret reds. Growth habit varies from compact and shrubby to prostrate.

Cultivation

Given plenty of space in full sun and well-drained, sandy soil, arctotises may be used as bedding plants or to cover a large area of dry bank. Propagate from seed or cuttings.

Arctotis Hybrid, 'Apricot'

Arctotis fastuosa

Arctotis fastuosa
syn. *Venidium fastuosum*
Cape daisy, monarch of the veld
This adaptable perennial can be treated
as an annual in colder regions. It will
grow 24 in (60 cm) high, with silvery
green, lobed leaves and glistening
orange flowerheads with purple zones at
the base of each of the many ray petals
and a black central disc. It is a colorful
choice for a sunny position in the
garden. *Zones 9–11.*

Arctotis Hybrids
These plants are grown as annual
bedding plants in frost-prone areas but
will overwinter in milder climates.
Growing to a height and spread of
around 18 in (45 cm), they have gray,
lobed leaves that are quite downy
beneath. In summer and fall (autumn)
they produce a long succession of showy
blooms, to 3 in (8 cm) across in a very
wide range of colors, often 2-toned.
'Gold Bi-Color', 'Apricot', 'Dream Coat'
and 'Wine' are among the more popular
named hybrids. *Zones 9–11.*

ARENARIA
Sandwort
This genus consists of some 160 species
of mainly mound-forming or ground
cover perennials, some of which become
shrubby with age. They are widespread
in the northern hemisphere, with a few
southern hemisphere species too. The
plants commonly develop a dense mass

Arenaria montana

of fine stems clothed with tiny, deep
green or gray-green leaves and small,
usually white, flowers in spring or
summer. The flowers may be borne
singly or in small clusters.

Cultivation
They are easily grown in any moist,
well-drained soil in full sun. They are
ideal rockery or tub plants and are
generally very frost hardy. Propagate
from seed, self-rooted layers or small tip
cuttings.

Arenaria montana
This species from southwest Europe is
larger than most arenarias in both leaves
and flowers. It has gray-green leaves up
to 1¹/₂ in (35 mm) long and mounds to
about 6 in (15 cm) tall. Its flowering
stems tend to be rather upright and
extend slightly above the foliage clump.
The abundant flowers are pure white
with yellow-green centers. *Zones 4–9.*

ARGEMONE
Prickly poppy

This genus of 29 species of poppy-like plants from North and Central America, Hawaii and the West Indies tend to be upright growers, many reaching 4 ft (1.2 m) or more tall, with strong stems and lobed leaves. In many species the stems, leaves and flowerbuds are a pale blue-gray and are covered in sharp prickles. The flowers, mainly yellow or orange, are usually 6-petalled and appear throughout the warmer months. Several species have become troublesome weeds of crops.

Cultivation

They are easily grown in any well-drained soil in full sun. Propagate from seed. Some species self-sow and become invasive.

Argemone mexicana

This annual species is native to Mexico and nearby areas of the Caribbean but has spread widely through warmer parts of the world as a weed of crops and waste ground. It has prickly, white-marked, grayish green leaves and fragrant, yellow, poppy-like flowers about 2 in (5 cm) wide appearing in summer. It has an erect habit, growing to 3 ft (1 m) high. *Zones 8–11.*

Argemone mexicana

ARGYRANTHEMUM
Marguerite, Paris daisy

The 22 species in this Macronesian genus of evergreen subshrubs tend to be upright, rarely over 3 ft (1 m) tall, and bushy with deeply lobed or divided, bright green to blue-green leaves. From spring to fall (autumn) in cool climates but mainly in winter–spring in warmer climates the bushes are covered in daisies in white and a wide range of pink and yellow shades.

Cultivation

They like any light, well-drained soil in full sun. They grow well near the sea. Cut back either in late winter or late summer to encourage fresh growth. Propagate from seed or cuttings.

Argyranthemum frutescens

syn. *Chrysanthemum frutescens*
Although the true species, a 3 ft (1 m) tall, white-flowered shrub from the Canary Islands, is now rarely cultivated, most of the commonly seen garden cultivars are classified under this name though many may in fact be hybrids with other species. There are numerous cultivars with a huge range of flower forms and sizes in a range of colors. Some notable examples include 'Bridesmaid', 'California Gold', 'Harvest Gold', 'Jamaica Primrose', 'Little Rex', 'Margaret', 'Pink Lady', 'Rising Sun', 'Silver Leaf', 'Snow Man', 'Tauranga Star' and 'Weymouth Pink'. *Zones 8–11.*

Argyranthemum frutescens

ARMERIA
Thrift, sea pink

This genus of about 35 species of low-growing, tufted, early summer-flowering perennials is found in a wide variety of environments in temperate Eurasia, Africa and the Americas—from salt marshes and storm-swept headlands of the seashores to alpine meadows. The plants have crowded, narrow, mostly evergreen leaves, usually forming a dense mound, and small flowers crowded into globular heads, each atop a slender stalk.

Cultivation

They suit rock gardens or borders and prefer exposed, sunny positions and rather dry soil with good drainage. They are generally frost hardy. Propagate from seed or cuttings.

Armeria maritima
Common thrift, sea pink

Native around much of the northern hemisphere and consisting of many wild races, thrift was in cultivation as early as 1578. Growing to 4 in (10 cm) high and spreading to 8 in (20 cm), it has a mound-like mass of narrow, dark green leaves, and dense flowerheads of small, white to pink flowers are produced in spring and summer. Most *Armeria* cultivars are derived from this species. 'Vindictive' has vibrant rose-pink flowers. 'Alba' has small white flowers. *Zones 4–9.*

Armeria maritima

ARTEMISIA
Wormwood

This large genus of some 300 species of perennials and shrubs is native to temperate regions of the northern hemisphere, many from arid and semi-arid environments. They have decorative foliage which is often aromatic and sometimes repellent to insects; in many species it is coated with whitish hairs. It makes an attractive addition to a flower border. The small yellowish flowerheads are not showy. There are both evergreen and deciduous species.

Cultivation

Mostly quite frost hardy, they prefer an open, sunny situation with light, well-drained soil. Prune lightly in spring. Propagate from cuttings in summer or by division in spring.

Artemisia ludoviciana
syn. *Artemisia purshiana*
Western mugwort, white sage

Native to western North America and Mexico, this rhizomatous species has lance-shaped, sometimes coarsely toothed leaves, which are densely white-felted beneath and gray- to white-haired above. Bell-shaped, grayish flowerheads are produced in summer. A spreading, invasive species, it reaches a height of 4 ft (1.2 m) and is very frost hardy. 'Valerie Finnis', with its jagged margined leaves, is a popular cultivar. *Zones 4–10.*

Artemisia ludoviciana 'Valerie Finnis'

Arthropodium cirratum

Aruncus dioicus

ARTHROPODIUM

The ungainly name *Arthropodium* is from the Greek and means having a jointed foot, referring to the way the footstalk of each flower has a joint in the middle. Of this genus of a dozen or so perennials from Australasia, only 2 or 3 are seen in gardens, the most ornamental being the New Zealand renga renga, *Arthropodium cirratum*.

Cultivation

They are essentially plants of warm-temperate climates; in cool areas they need a sheltered spot in fertile, well-drained soil. Propagate from seed or by division.

Arthropodium cirratum
Renga renga lily

This New Zealand species bears graceful sprays of starry white flowers on a 24 in (60 cm) stem above tufts of broad, handsome leaves in late spring. It looks a little like a hosta and is a good substitute in the hot-summer climates in which hostas languish. The Maori made use of the fleshy roots in medicine. *Zones 8–10.*

ARUNCUS
Goat's beard

There are 3 species in this genus of rhizomatous perennials, occurring widely over temperate and subarctic regions of the northern hemisphere. Their appearance is like the giant astilbe, with ferny basal leaves up to 3 ft (1 m) long and summer plumes of tiny cream flowers in 8–18 in (20–45 cm) long, pyramidal panicles carried on wiry stems that hold them well above the foliage.

Cultivation

They are best grown in sun or part-shade in moist, humus-rich, well-drained soil around edges of ponds. Goat's beard is very frost hardy and is propagated from seed or by division.

Aruncus dioicus

syns *Aruncus sylvestris, Spiraea aruncus*
A graceful, woodland perennial, this clump-forming plant produces a mass of rich green, fern-like foliage and arching plumes of tiny, greenish or creamy white flowers in summer. It grows 6 ft (1.8 m) tall and 4 ft (1.2 m) wide. Cut flowering stems back hard in fall (autumn). 'Kneiffii' reaches about 3 ft (1 m) and has cream-colored flowers. *Zones 3–9.*

ASPERULA
Woodruff

There are around 100 species of annuals, perennials and subshrubs in this Euro-

Asperula arcadiensis

Asphodeline lutea

pean and Asian genus. Most are densely foliaged mat- or tuft-forming perennials with tiny, narrow leaves arranged in whorls of 4 or more on fine stems. In spring and summer the plants may be smothered in tiny flowers, usually white, pale pink, sometimes yellow. Most spread by underground runners and a few woodland species grow to around 24 in (60 cm) high, with larger, bright green leaves.

Cultivation
They generally do best in rockery conditions with gritty, well-drained soil in full sun. Propagate from seed, from small rooted pieces removed from the clump, or by division.

Asperula arcadiensis
This perennial Greek species makes a woody based tuft of foliage up to 6 in (15 cm) high. The narrow leaves are gray and downy, $1/2$ in (12 mm) or so long. The tiny flowers are pink to pale purple. *Zones 5–9.*

ASPHODELINE
Jacob's rod
This is a genus of some 20 species of biennial and perennial lilies, from the Mediterranean region and Asia Minor. They have thick, fleshy roots, from which sprout narrow, grassy to spear-shaped leaves that are usually bright green, sometimes with a bluish tint. Stiffly upright flower spikes up to 5 ft

(1.5 m) tall develop in summer. They carry large numbers of star-shaped yellow, white or pale pink flowers on the upper half of the stem.

Cultivation
These frost hardy plants are easily grown in any well-drained soil in full sun. Propagate from seed or by division in winter or early spring.

Asphodeline lutea
Asphodel, king's spear
A native of the Mediterranean region eastward from Italy, this fragrant, frost-hardy plant can grow to 5 ft (1.5 m). Tufts of narrow, glossy leaves appear below spear-like stems bearing spikes of yellow, star-shaped flowers. The plants should be kept moist before the flowering period in spring. *Zones 6–10.*

ASPHODELUS
When Tennyson's lotus eaters 'rested weary limbs at last on beds of asphodel', it was the plant now known as *Asphodelus albus* on which they probably reclined— the name asphodelus goes back to the ancient Greeks. The genus consists of 12 species of fleshy-rooted annual and

perennial lilies. They have basal tufts of narrow, grass-like leaves and 6-petalled, starry, white, green or pink flowers borne along stiff, upright stems. Spring and summer are the main flowering seasons.

Cultivation
Most will tolerate moderate frosts. They require reasonably sunny, warm, dry summer conditions and prefer a light, sandy, humus-rich soil with good drainage. Propagate by division immediately after flowering or from seed.

Asphodelus albus
Native to Europe and North Africa, *Asphodelus albus* has thick, fleshy roots and sword-shaped leaves up to 24 in (60 cm) long. The 12–36 in (30–90 cm) tall flower stems bear pinkish brown striped, white flowers along most of their length in spring, those at the base opening first. The variable bracts—white or brown—are especially noticeable before the star-shaped flowers open. *Zones 5–10.*

ASTELIA
This genus of some 25 species of rhizomatous, evergreen perennials has a scattered distribution around the southern hemisphere including the Falkland Islands, Mauritius, Réunion, southeastern Australia and New

Zealand. The bold, sword-shaped leaves are arranged in rosettes or tufts and the plants vary in stature from about 2 in (5 cm) to about 8 ft (2.4 m). Habitats vary from alpine bogs to temperate rainforests. Inconspicuous flowers are often hidden by foliage but in many species are followed by showy clusters of berries.

Cultivation
They are easily grown in moist, peaty, well-drained soil in full sun or part-shade. Propagate from seed or by division.

Astelia chathamica
From the remote Chatham Islands, this is the most striking of the 13 New Zealand species, with bright, almost metallic, silvery leaves. It forms a dense foliage clump up to 5 ft (1.5 m) high with a spread of up to 6 ft (1.8 m). The tiny flowers are followed by bright orange berries on female plants. These plants do best in full sun. *Zones 9–10.*

ASTER
Michaelmas or Easter daisy, aster
This genus of perennials and deciduous or evergreen subshrubs contains over

Astelia chathamica

Asphodelus albus

250 species, ranging in height from miniatures suitable for rock gardens to 6 ft (1.8 m) giants. Showy, daisy-like flowerheads are usually produced in late summer or fall (autumn) in a wide range of colors, including blue, violet, purple, pink, red and white, all with a central disc of yellow or purple.

Cultivation

They prefer sun (or part-shade in hot areas) in a well-drained soil. Keep moist, and shelter from strong winds. Cut the long stems down to ground level and tidy the clumps when the flowers have faded. Propagate by division in spring or late fall, or from softwood cuttings in spring. Divide plants every 2 to 3 years.

Aster alpinus

This clump-forming plant, native to the European Alps, is usually about 6–12 in (15–30 cm) high and spreading to 18 in (45 cm), and bears large, violet-blue, daisy flowers with yellow centers from late spring until mid-summer; foliage is dark green. It is a popular rock garden plant and is fully frost hardy. 'Trimix' grows to 8 in (20 cm) and has flowers that are a tricolor mix of pink, blue and white. *Zones 3–9.*

Aster alpinus

Aster amellus
Italian aster

In its typical form, the Italian aster, a native of eastern Europe and also Turkey, grows to 18–24 in (45–60 cm). It has oblong basal leaves that can be somewhat hairy and erect stems which can become floppy if grown in too much shade. It is especially disease resistant. The large, fragrant flowerheads are pink and purple-blue, while popular cultivars are stronger in color and include 'King George', with deep violet flowers. *Zones 4–9.*

Aster ericoides
Heath aster

The specific name means 'with leaves like those of Erica', the heath genus, and

Aster ericoides 'White Heather'

Aster amellus 'King George'

indeed this American species has small, narrow leaves, at least on the upper stems. With flowering stems rising up to 3 ft (1 m) high from tufted basal shoots towards mid-summer and into fall (autumn), it provides a lovely display of massed, small, white flowerheads as does one of its more compact cultivars, 'White Heather'. *Zones 4–10.*

Aster novae-angliae
New England aster

Originally native over a wide area of the eastern and central USA, this species is represented in cultivation by many cultivars, showing much variation in form and color of blooms. Vigorous clumps of mostly vertical, 3–5 ft (1–1.5 m) stems are likely to lean with the weight of large, loose clusters of daisies, making staking necessary. Cultivars include the late-blooming, clear pink 'Harrington's Pink'; the rose-pink, mildew-resistant 'Barr's Pink'; and the cerise 'September Ruby'. *Zones 4–9.*

ASTILBE
False spiraea

The 14 species in this genus of summer perennials have basal tufts of ferny,

Aster novae-angliae 'Barr's Pink'

compound leaves. Pointed, plume-like panicles of tiny, white to pink or red flowers rise above the foliage. Most usual in cultivation are the *Astilbe × arendsii* hybrids, though there are many recent hybrid cultivars of different parentage. The name 'spiraea' was mistakenly attached to this genus when they were introduced to England in the 1820s.

Cultivation

They need a lightly shaded place with rich, leafy soil that never dries out, though they do not like being flooded. Cooler climates suit them best. They make good cut flowers and indoor plants. Propagate by division in winter.

Astilbe 'Straussenfeder'

Bred in Germany, 'Straussenfeder' grows to 3 ft (1 m) tall, with decorative leaves and distinctive flowering panicles with drooping branches, the blooms rose pink. The name is German for 'ostrich feather'. *Zones 6–10.*

Astilbe 'Straussenfeder'

ASTRANTIA
Masterwort

All 10 species of this genus, an unusual member of the carrot family, are herbaceous perennials that occur in mountain meadows and woodlands of Europe and western Asia. They have delicate flowerheads surrounded by a collar of pointed bracts, carried on wiry stems above clumps of deeply toothed, lobed foliage of soft mid-green.

Cultivation

They prefer moist, fertile, woodland conditions, or near the edges of streams or ponds. As long as the roots are kept moist they will tolerate full sun, indeed the variegated species color much better in sun. In a suitable position they will build up clumps. Propagate by division in early spring or from seed.

Astrantia major

Native to central and eastern Europe, this species has deeply lobed, palmate leaves forming a loose mound of foliage 18 in (45 cm) tall from which rise nearly bare stems to 24 in (60 cm) or more, each topped by intricately formed, soft pink or white, daisy-like flowerheads, surrounded by petal-like bracts in the same colors. The flowers are produced almost throughout summer. 'Rosea' is slightly taller, with blooms of rich rose pink. *Zones 6–9.*

AUBRIETA
Rock cress

These mountain flowers make carpets of color at the front of flowerbeds, or down retaining walls. Not very tall—6 in (15 cm) or so at most—they will happily sprawl to several times their height and in spring cover themselves with 4-petalled flowers, mainly in shades of purple. The plants most often seen in gardens are hybrids mainly derived from *Aubrieta deltoidea*. The genus name honors the French botanical painter Claude Aubriet (1668–1743).

Cultivation

They are easy to grow in cool-temperate climates (flowering is erratic in warm ones), in fertile, well-drained soil. They are short lived and cuttings should be taken in summer every 3 or 4 years. They are also propagated by division of the rhizomatous rootstock.

Aubrieta deltoidea

Native to southeastern Europe and Turkey, this compact, mat-forming perennial has greenish gray leaves and

Aubrieta deltoidea

Astrantia major

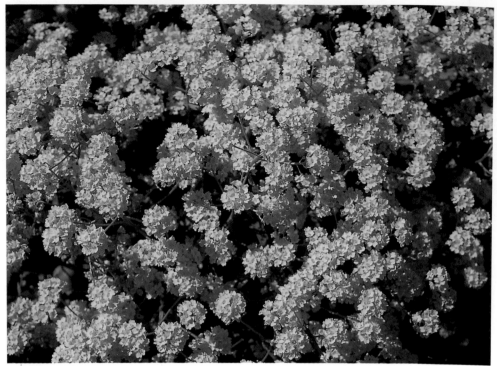

Aurinia saxatilis

masses of starry, mauve-pink flowers borne over a long period in spring. The species itself is now rare in gardens, most cultivated aubrietas being hybrids now known collectively as *Aubrieta* × *cultorum*, though they are often listed as *A. deltoidea*. *Zones 4–9.*

AURINIA

This is a genus of 7 species of biennials and evergreen perennials native to Europe, Turkey and the Ukraine. They are mainly small, spreading, mound-forming plants. The leaves are initially in basal rosettes, mostly fairly narrow. They bear elongated sprays of tiny yellow or white flowers in spring and summer.

Cultivation

Plant in light, gritty, well-drained soil in full sun. They suit rockeries, rock crevices or dry-stone walls. Most species are frost hardy and are propagated from seed or small tip cuttings; they will self-sow in suitable locations.

Aurinia saxatilis
syn. *Alyssum saxatile*
Basket of gold, yellow alyssum
This commonly grown species has hairy, gray-green leaves, and forms rather loose mounds to 10 in (25 cm) high. It is smothered in bright yellow flowers in spring and early summer. It is very popular as a rockery or wall plant. There are a number of cultivars, including 'Argentea' with very silvery leaves; 'Citrina' with lemon-yellow flowers; 'Gold Dust', up to 12 in (30 cm) mounds with deep golden-yellow flowers; and 'Tom Thumb', a 4 in (10 cm) high dwarf with small leaves. *Zones 4–9.*

Baptisia australis

Begonia fuchsioides

BAPTISIA
False indigo
Baptisia is a genus of 20–30 species of pea-flowered perennials from eastern and central USA. The common name arises from the former use of some species by dyers as a substitute for true indigo (*Indigofera*). Most are shrubby in habit, and the leaves are divided into 3 leaflets like a clover. The blue, purple, yellow or white pea-flowers are borne in terminal spikes over summer.

Cultivation
They prefer full sun and neutral, well-drained soil. They are not bothered by frost, or very dry conditions in summer. They should not be transplanted or disturbed. Propagation is from seed in fall (autumn) or by division.

Baptisia australis
False indigo
This summer-flowering perennial is attractive in both flower and foliage. The leaves are blue-green and form a loose mound up to about 4 ft (1.2 m) high and 3 ft (1 m) across. The lupin-like flowers are borne on erect spikes from early to mid-summer and are an unusual shade of purplish blue. The seed pods can be dried for indoor decoration. *Zones 3–10.*

BEGONIA
There are over 1,500 known species of begonias. From tropical and sub-tropical areas they have beautifully colored and textured foliage and showy flowers. Mostly evergreen, they have usually asymmetrical leaves of rather brittle and waxy texture. Begonias are divided into a number of classes depending on growth habit and type of rootstock. Cane-stemmed begonias are erect growers, with usually pendent clusters of flowers; shrubby begonias have a more closely branched habit; winter-flowering begonias bear profuse and colorful flowers that peak in winter; rhizomatous begonias are a large and varied class, with leaves arising directly from creeping, knotty rhizomes—they include the Rex begonias with colorfully variegated leaves; and the tuberous begonias, which die back to tubers in winter and bear large, often double flowers in summer.

Cultivation
Many of the cane-stemmed, winter-flowering, shrubby and rhizomatous types can be grown outdoors in frost-free climates. As indoor plants they need standard potting mix with peat moss or leafmold added. Grow in bright to moderate light, with good ventilation and above-average humidity. Tuberous begonias need special treatment: tubers must be forced into growth in early spring at 65°F (18°C) in peat moss or sphagnum, and kept in a cool, well-ventilated greenhouse for the flowering season. After flowering, plants die back

Begonia scharffii

Begonia Semperflorens cultorum Group

and tubers are lifted in mid-fall (mid-autumn) and stored dry. Propagate from tubers in the case of tuberous begonias. Propagate other begonias from stem or leaf cuttings, or by division of rhizomes, or from seed.

Begonia fuchsioides
This shrubby Venezuelan begonia has small, crowded, oval leaves, flushed pink on new growths. Small coral-red to pale pink flowers are borne in numerous short sprays over a long season from fall (autumn) to spring. Suitable for outdoor use, it grows to 3 ft (1 m) tall with an erect, closely branched habit and gracefully drooping branchlets. *Zones 10–12.*

Begonia scharffii
syn. *Begonia haageana*
This shrub-like begonia from Brazil grows to 24 in (60 cm) tall with a sprawling habit and has hairy stems and leaves. The large, olive-green leaves have pointed tips and are red-veined on the undersides. The flowers, pinkish white with pink-red hairs at the base like a beard, are produced throughout the year. *Zones 10–12.*

Begonia Semperflorens-cultorum Group
Bedding begonia, wax begonia
These dwarf, shrubby begonias are often grown as bedding annuals, for example, 'Ernst Benary', or for borders, and are also popular as potted plants. Freely branching plants with soft, succulent stems, they have rounded, glossy green leaves (bronze or variegated in some cultivars). The flowers are profuse, opening progressively at the branch tips over a long summer and early fall (autumn) season (most of the year in warmer climates). The numerous cultivars include singles and doubles in colors of bright rose pink, light pink, white or red. Pinch out growing tips to encourage bushy growth. *Zones 9–11.*

BELAMCANDA
This genus, native to southern and eastern Asia and belonging to the iris family, contains only 2 species. The plants are perennials but of weak growth and short lived, with flattened fans of thin-textured leaves arising from thin rhizomes. Slender flowering stems terminate in a few rather small flowers with 6 narrow petals; these are followed by seed pods which split widely to reveal rows of shiny black seeds, like small berries, which are popular for dried flower arrangements.

Cultivation
These plants need sunshine and rich, well-drained soil. Water well in summer. In cold climates dormant plants need protection from heavy frosts. Propagate by division or from seed, which should be sown every second or third year.

Belamcanda chinensis
Leopard lily, blackberry lily

This 24–36 in (60–90 cm) tall plant has something of the habit of an iris but the summer flowers do not look like irises. Up to 2 in (5 cm) across, they come in a range of colors from cream to yellow, apricot or deep orange-red, usually with darker spotting, hence the common name leopard lily. The seed pods open to reveal tight clusters of seeds resembling the fruitlets of a blackberry, hence their other common name. *Zones 8–11.*

BELLIS
Daisy

This genus consists of 15 species of small perennials from Europe and western Asia. *Bellis* is from the Latin *bellus* which means 'pretty' or 'charming', while the English 'daisy' is a corruption of 'day's eye', arising from the way the flower closes up at night, opening again to greet the sunrise. The plants form rosettes with small oval to spoon-shaped leaves; each rosette produces a succession of flowerheads on individual stalks in shades of white, pink, blue or crimson.

Cultivation

While daisies are perennial in cool-temperate climates, it is usual to treat them as annuals or biennials, sowing seed in fall (autumn). They thrive in any good garden soil in sun or part-shade. Propagate from seed or by division.

Bellis perennis
English daisy, common daisy

This daisy has become widely natural-ized in temperate parts of the world. The flowerheads, appearing from late winter to early summer, are white with golden centers and pale purplish undersides. The garden strains mostly have double flowerheads of red, crimson, pink or white, all with a gold center. The Pomponette Series daisies are popular bedding plants and cut flowers; they have neat hemispherical flowerheads 1½ in (35 mm) wide with curled petals, on stems up to 10 in (25 cm) high, in mixed colors. *Zones 3–10.*

BERGENIA

Consisting of 6 or 7 species of rhizo-matous, semi-evergreen perennials, from near-Arctic areas to warm temperate Asia, this genus is characterized by large, paddle-shaped leaves, arising from the ground on short stalks to form loose clumps. Large clusters of flowers — mostly pale pink, but also white and dark pink — are borne on short, stout stems in winter and spring.

Bellis perennis

Belamcanda chinensis

Cultivation

Bergenias make excellent ground cover and rockery plants, thriving in sun or shade and tolerant of exposed sites as well as moist ground. Water well in hot weather and remove spent flowerheads to prolong flowering. Propagate by division in spring after flowering.

Bergenia cordifolia
Heartleaf saxifrage

Native to Siberia's Altai Mountains, this tough perennial has crinkly edged, more or less heart-shaped leaves up to 8 in (20 cm) wide, and produces panicles of drooping purple-pink flowers on 12–15 in (30–38 cm) stems in late winter and early spring. The plant is long flowering and the leaves remain green in winter. 'Purpurea' has magenta-pink flowers and leaves tinged purple. *Zones 3–9.*

Bergenia × schmidtii

Arguably the most vigorous and most widely planted bergenia, this old hybrid between *Bergenia ciliata* and *B. crassifolia* has large, rounded, fleshy, dull green leaves. Set among the foliage are rose-pink blooms on stalks up to 12 in

(30 cm) long. The main flush of flowers occurs in late winter and early spring, frosts often damaging the blooms, though it often flowers sporadically at other times. It makes a fine ground cover, and adapts well to warm-temperate humid climates. *Zones 5–10.*

BLANDFORDIA
Christmas bells

This is an eastern Australian genus of 4 species of grassy leafed perennials with deeply buried corm-like rhizomes. Beautiful, waxy red or red-and-yellow flowers appear around Christmas in the southern hemisphere (early summer). The plants are long lived, with tough, narrow basal leaves in sparse to dense tufts, from which arise one to several stiff flowering stems, bearing near the top semi-pendent, bell-shaped flowers.

Cultivation

They are prone to root-rot and are sensitive to nutrient imbalances. Plant in moist, peaty soil in full sun or light shade. Keep consistently moist. They tolerate light frosts. Propagate by division or from seed. Seedlings develop

Bergenia cordifolia

Bergenia × schmidtii

Boltonia asteroides

Blandfordia grandiflora

slowly, taking 2 or more years to flower; divisions also may be quite slow to re-establish.

Blandfordia grandiflora

syn. *Blandfordia flammea*
This colorful species is the one most prized for cut flowers. Its leaves are narrow and rather rigid, and flowering stems are 24–36 in (60–90 cm) tall, carrying 3 to 10 flowers; these are up to 2¹/₂ in (6 cm) long, flared toward the mouth, and vary from deep pinkish red to red with yellow tips or sometimes pure yellow, always with a thin waxy bloom that enhances the flower's heavy substance. *Zones 9–11.*

BOLTONIA
False chamomile

This is a genus of 8 species of perennial daisies, which have, in recent years, become popular as background plants for perennial borders and as cut flowers. Over winter they die back to a clump of simple, narrow leaves. In late spring, tall flowering stems begin to develop and by late summer they carry hundreds of small daisies in shades of white, pink, lilac, violet or purple.

Cultivation

They like moist, well-drained soil in any sunny position. However, they are prone to mildew from late summer. Frost hardy, they are propagated from seed or cuttings or by division.

Boltonia asteroides

This is the best known boltonia in gardens. The flowering stems may be as much as 8 ft (2.4 m) tall, with the flowerheads ranging in color from white through pale pink to mauve. 'Snowbank' is a white-flowered selection with stems growing up to 6 ft (1.8 m) tall. *Boltonia asteroides* var. *latisquama* differs in its larger flowerheads, which are in shades of mauve or purple. *Zones 4–9.*

BORAGO

The 3 species in this European genus of annuals and short-lived perennials are generally erect with rather coarse growth and covered with bristly hairs. They form clumps of lance-shaped basal leaves that develop in spring into branched, leafy flowering stems. By late spring the plants bear semi-pendulous, starry purple-blue or white flowers. The flowers are a rich source of nectar and are popular with beekeepers.

Cultivation

They like any light, moist, well-drained soil in full sun. Usually they are propagated from seed, which often self-sows, so plants may become invasive. Seed of the annual species can be sown in late winter for an early crop.

Brachycome iberidifolia 'Blue Star'

Borago officinalis

Borago officinalis
Borage

This annual herb has cucumber-flavored leaves and purplish blue star-shaped flowers. The plant grows to around 30 in (75 cm) high with clusters of flowers in spring and summer. Young leaves are used raw in salads and cool drinks or cooked with vegetables. The edible flowers have long been used to decorate salads. *Zones 5–10.*

BRACHYCOME

syn. *Brachyscome*
Native to Australia, the low-growing annuals and evergreen perennials of this genus are attractive ground cover or rockery plants. Many of the perennials are mound-forming, spreading by underground runners and having finely divided, soft, fern-like foliage. They bear a profusion of daisy-like flowerheads in shades of blue, mauve, pink and yellow.

Cultivation

They require a sunny situation and a light, well-drained garden soil. Many are moderately frost hardy and some will tolerate coastal salt spray. Do not over-water. Pinch out early shoots to encourage branching and propagate from ripe seed or stem cuttings or by division in spring or fall (autumn).

Brachycome multifida 'Break O' Day'

Brachycome iberidifolia
Swan River daisy

This daisy is a weak-stemmed annual, long grown as a bedding or border plant, that grows to a height and spread of around 12 in (30 cm), sometimes taller. It has deeply dissected leaves with very narrow segments. Small, fragrant, daisy-like flowerheads, normally mauve-blue but sometimes white, pink or purple, appear in great profusion in summer and early fall (autumn). 'Blue Star' is a cultivar with massed small mauve to purple-blue flowers. *Zones 9–11.*

Brachycome multifida

This perennial species is a charming ground cover in warm-temperate climates, though it is not long lived. It grows about 4–6 in (10–15 cm) high and spreads to about 18 in (45 cm). The mauve-pink flowerheads bloom for weeks in late spring and summer. It likes sunshine and perfect drainage. 'Break O' Day' is a selected form with finer leaves, profuse mauve-blue flowers and a very compact habit. *Zones 9–11.*

Brachycome 'Sunburst'

A low-growing, sometimes short-lived, perennial which makes a good ground cover, or can be grown from hanging baskets. The flowers, bright yellow on opening and fading to cream, are borne in spring, summer and fall (autumn). The plant grows 8–12 in (20–30 cm) with a spread of 15–19 in (40–50 cm) and is mat-forming. Hardy in most situations, it requires sunlight and a free draining sandy soil. Trim little and often. *Zones 9–11.*

Bracteantha bracteata

Brachycome 'Sunburst'

BRACTEANTHA
syn. *Helichrysum*
Strawflower, everlasting daisy

This Australian genus consists of 7 species of annuals and perennials, until recently classified under *Helichrysum*. They differ from true helichrysums in their large, decorative flowerheads carried singly or a few together at the end of the flowering branches, each consisting of golden-yellow to white bracts of straw-like texture surrounding a disc of tiny yellow or brownish florets. The leaves are often downy on their undersides, or can be very sticky in some species.

Cultivation

Plant in moist, well-drained soil in full sun. Provided they are not waterlogged, most species will tolerate light to moderate frosts. Propagate annuals from seed and perennials from seed or tip cuttings.

Bracteantha bracteata
syn. *Helichrysum bracteatum*

This annual or short-lived perennial has an erect habit and grows to a height of around 3 ft (1 m). It has weak, hollow stems, thin green leaves and from summer to early fall (autumn) bears golden-yellow blooms at the branch tips. Some more spreading, shrubby perennial plants from eastern Australia, which may be recognized as distinct species, have been named as cultivars, including

Bracteantha bracteata 'Dargan Hill Monarch'

the popular 'Dargan Hill Monarch', with rich yellow blooms up to 3 in (8 cm) across. *Zones 8–11.*

BROWALLIA
Bush violet

This genus of 6 species of bushy annuals and evergreen perennials, is native to tropical South America and the West Indies. They are densely foliaged with a compact habit, soft stems and simple, strongly veined, deep green leaves. The flowers, carried singly in the leaf axils, come in shades of blue, purple or white.

Cultivation

In cool climates browallias are grown as conservatory plants or as summer annuals. In frost-free climates they grow well outdoors in moist, humus-rich, well-drained soil in a warm, part-shaded, sheltered position. Propagate the annuals from seed in spring, the perennials from seed or tip cuttings.

Browallia speciosa

This shrubby perennial Colombian species grows to around 30 in (75 cm) tall and wide with leaves up to 4 in (10 cm) long. Its flowers are purple-blue to deep purple. There are many cultivars, with flowers in all shades of blue and purple as well as white. 'Blue Troll' is a 12 in (30 cm) dwarf with masses of blue flowers; 'White Troll' is similar with white flowers. 'Marine Bells' has deep indigo flowers. *Zones 9–11.*

Browallia speciosa

BRUNNERA

This is an eastern European genus of 3 species of perennials. They form clumps of heart-shaped to rather narrow basal leaves on long stalks. Leafy, branched flowering stems bear panicles of tiny 5-petalled purple or blue flowers in spring and early summer. There are forms with white flowers and variegated foliage.

Cultivation

They prefer humus-rich, moist soil with a leafy mulch and a position in dappled shade. They are cold hardy and in suitable conditions will self-sow and naturalize. Propagate from seed, by removing small rooted pieces or by taking cuttings of the soft spring shoots.

Brunnera macrophylla
Siberian bugloss

The small violet flowers of this species resemble forget-me-nots (to which they are related); they are held on slender stems 18–24 in (45–60 cm) tall above the mounds of heart-shaped leaves. When the flowers appear the new leaves grow to their full length of 4–6 in (10–15 cm). Clumps spread slowly underground but self-seed readily, making excellent ground cover. *Zones 3–9.*

Brunnera macrophylla

Bulbinella hookeri

Bulbinella floribunda

BULBINELLA

Six species of this southern hemisphere genus are endemic to New Zealand and the remainder of its 20 or so species are native to southern Africa. They are fleshy-rooted perennial lilies with broad, thin leaves and crowded spikes of golden yellow flowers terminating the long, hollow stems. Some of the larger South African species make excellent cut flowers. The alpine species are much smaller but not so easily grown.

Cultivation

They need moist, humus-rich soil that never dries out entirely in summer. Sun or semi-shade is best. Most species are at least slightly frost hardy and are propagated from seed or by dividing established clumps. Plant the fleshy roots with the root-crown at soil level.

Bulbinella floribunda
Cat's-tail

This South African plant bears 24–36 in (60–90 cm) tall flower stalks from late winter to mid-spring. Each stalk is topped with a broad spike crammed with tiny orange-yellow flowers and terminating in tight green buds. Long, narrow basal leaves appear in winter, forming a large tangled clump. The plant dies back in summer and fall (autumn). It is excellent as a long-lasting cut flower. *Zones 8–10.*

Bulbinella hookeri

Found in the subalpine grasslands of both the main islands of New Zealand, this species has very narrow, grassy leaves and develops into a thick clump of foliage. The flower stems are around 24 in (60 cm) tall, half of which is the densely packed spike of $^1/_4$ in (6 mm) wide flowers. *Zones 8–10.*

CALCEOLARIA
Ladies' purse, slipper flower, pocketbook flower

Gardeners who know this genus only as gaudy 'slipper flowers' may be surprised to learn that it contains upward of 300 species, ranging from tiny annuals to herbaceous perennials, scrambling climbers and woody shrubs. They are native to South America and Mexico, and all share the same curious flower structure, with a lower lip inflated like a bulbous slipper. Flower colors are mainly yellows and oranges, often with red or purple spots.

Cultivation

Calceolarias vary greatly in cold hardiness. When grown outdoors they prefer a shady, cool site in moist, well-drained soil with added compost. Provide shelter from heavy winds. Propagate from seed or softwood cuttings in summer or late spring.

Calceolaria, Herbeohybrida Group

These are the popular florists' calceolarias. They are soft-stemmed, compact, bushy biennials often treated as annuals, producing in spring and summer blooms in a range of bright colors from yellow to deep red and so densely massed they almost hide the soft green foliage. Innumerable named varieties have appeared over the years,

Calceolaria, Herbeohybrida Group

and they are now mostly sold as mixed-color seedling strains and series. Marginally frost hardy, they can be used for summer bedding but do not tolerate very hot, dry weather. The normal height is 12–18 in (30–45 cm) but dwarf strains can be as small as 6 in (15 cm). *Zones 9–11.*

CALENDULA
Marigold

St Hildegard of Bingen (1098–1179) is said to have dedicated *Calendula officinalis* to the Virgin Mary and named the flowers Mary's gold, or marigold. In the Middle Ages marigolds were considered a remedy for smallpox, indigestion and 'evil humors of the head', and even today the marigold is a favorite of herbalists. The genus consists of 20-odd species of bushy annuals and evergreen perennials from the Canary Islands, Iran and the Mediterranean. They have aromatic leaves and daisy-like, orange or yellow flowers.

Cultivation

Calendulas are mostly fairly frost-hardy plants and like well-drained soil of any quality in sun or part-shade. Prolong flowering with regular deadheading. Propagate from seed, and watch for aphids and powdery mildew.

Calendula officinalis, Pacific Beauty Series

Calendula officinalis
Pot marigold, English marigold

Long valued for its medicinal qualities, this species is known in gardens only by its many cultivars and seedling strains, popular winter- and spring-flowering annuals that remain in bloom for a long time. There are tall and dwarf forms, all of bushy habit, the tall growing to a height and spread of 24 in (60 cm) and the dwarf to 12 in (30 cm). All have lance-shaped, strongly scented, pale green leaves and single or double flowerheads. The Pacific Beauty Series has double flowers in a number of different colors including bicolors. *Zones 6–10.*

CALLISTEPHUS
China aster

This genus contains just one annual species—a flower with summer blooms in shades from white to pink, blue, red and purple. The flowerheads can be either yellow-centered single daisies or fully double. The doubles can have petals that are plume-like and shaggy, more formal and straight or very short.

Cultivation

It is usually sown in spring to flower during summer, but it is usual to make successive sowings to prolong blooming time. It grows in any climate, from the coolest temperate to subtropical. Give it sunshine and fertile, well-drained soil, and do not plant it in the same bed 2 years in a row—this guards against aster wilt, a soil-borne fungus.

Callistephus chinensis
syn. *Aster chinensis*

This erect, bushy, fast-growing annual from China has oval, toothed, mid-green leaves and long-stalked flowerheads. There are many seedling strains available, ranging from tall, up to 36 in (90 cm), to dwarf, about 8 in (20 cm). Stake tall cultivars and remove spent flowers regularly. *Zones 6–10.*

CALTHA

There are about 10 species of moisture-loving perennials in this genus of the ranunculus family, all occurring in cold marshlands and alpine bogs of the cool-temperate zones in both northern and southern hemispheres. They have cup-shaped, white or yellow flowers and kidney- or heart-shaped leaves, and spread by thick rhizomes. They often come into leaf and flower very early, appearing from beneath melting snow.

Cultivation

These frost-hardy plants prefer full sun

Callistephus chinensis

Caltha palustris 'Monstrosa'

Campanula 'Burghaltii'

and rich, damp soil. Propagate by division in fall (autumn) or early spring, or from seed in fall. Watch for rust fungus, which should be treated with a fungicide.

Caltha palustris
Marsh marigold, kingcup

Occurring widely in temperate regions of the northern hemisphere, this semi-aquatic or bog plant is sometimes grown for its attractive flowers. It is deciduous or semi-evergreen with dark green, rounded leaves and glistening buttercup-like, golden-yellow flowers borne from early spring to mid-summer. It grows to a height and spread of 18 in (45 cm). The cultivars 'Monstrosa' and 'Flore Pleno' both have double flowers, while *Caltha palustris* var. *alba* has single white flowers with yellow stamens. *Zones 3–8.*

CAMPANULA
Bellflower, bluebell

This genus includes about 250 species of showy herbaceous plants, mostly perennials but a few annual or biennial, from the temperate northern hemisphere. Flowers are mostly bell-shaped but some are more tubular, urn-shaped or star-shaped, and come mainly in shades of blue and purple with some pinks and whites.

Cultivation

They are useful for rockeries, borders

Campanula glomerata 'Superba'

and hanging baskets. All like a moderately rich, moist, well-drained soil. They grow in sun or shade, but flower color remains brightest in shady situations. Propagate from seed in spring (sow seed for alpines in fall (autumn), by division in spring or fall, or from basal cuttings in spring. They are very frost hardy to frost tender.

Campanula 'Burghaltii'

This cross between *Campanula latifolia* and *C. punctata* has interesting flowers, up to 3 in (8 cm) long and amethyst purple in the bud stage opening to pale gray-mauve. Rhizomes do not creep to any great degree. It grows to a height of about 24 in (60 cm). *Zones 4–9.*

Campanula lactiflora 'Pritchard's Variety'

Campanula portenschlagiana

Campanula glomerata
Clustered bellflower

This variable species is found through-out Europe and temperate Asia. The violet-blue flowers are grouped in almost globular clusters on 10–15 in (25–38 cm) tall stems in early summer and again later if the spent flower stems are removed. 'Superba' grows to 24 in (60 cm); *Campanula glomerata* var. *dahurica* is a deeper violet than the species. There are also double-flowered and white versions. *Zones 3–9.*

Campanula lactiflora
Milky bellflower

Native to the Caucasus region and eastern Turkey, this popular strong-growing perennial reaches a height of 5 ft (1.5 m) and spreads into a broad clump. The strong stems bear many narrow oval leaves. In summer it produces very large and dense panicles of bell-shaped lilac-blue flowers (occa-sionally pink or white). If the flowering stem is cut back after flowering, side shoots may bear blooms in late fall (autumn). 'Pritchard's Variety' has deep violet-blue flowers. *Zones 3–9.*

Campanula medium
Canterbury bell

This is a slow-growing, erect, biennial plant with narrow basal leaves. In spring and early summer it has stout spires up

Campanula medium

to 4 ft (1.2 m) tall of crowded, bell-shaped, white, pink or blue flowers with recurved rims and prominent large green calyces. Dwarf cultivars grow to about 24 in (60 cm), and double forms have a colored calyx like a second petal tube. Grow as border plants in part-shade. *Zones 6–10.*

Campanula portenschlagiana
syn. *Campanula muralis*
Dalmatian bellflower

Native to a small area of the Dalmatian limestone mountains of Croatia, this is a dwarf, evergreen perennial growing to a maximum height of 6 in (15 cm) with an indefinite spread. It has crowded small violet-like leaves and a profusion of small, star-shaped, violet flowers in late spring and early summer. Best suited to rockeries and wall crevices, it likes a cool, partially shaded position with good drainage. *Zones 5–10.*

Campanula rotundifolia
Harebell, Scottish bluebell

This variable species, widely distributed around the temperate northern hemi-sphere, has a hardy nature. Loose rosettes of rounded, long-stalked leaves arise from creeping rhizomes, followed by slender, wiry stems holding nodding lilac-blue to white bells during the summer months. *Zones 3–9.*

Campanula vidalii

Campanula vidalii
syn. *Azorina vidalii*
Azores bellflower

Campanula vidalii is so different from other campanulas that some botanists place it in a genus of its own *(Azorina)*. A shrubby evergreen perennial, it has crowded, narrow, fleshy leaves and bears nodding flesh pink or white bells of a waxy texture in early summer on 18 in (45 cm) tall stems. It is a garden plant for warm-temperate climates only—in cool climates it is best grown in a mildly warmed greenhouse. *Zones 9–11.*

CANNA

This genus of rhizomatous perennials consists of about 9 tropical species. The apparent aboveground stems are actually tightly furled leaf bases, rising from thick knotty rhizomes. Slender flowering stems grow up through the centers of these false stems, emerging at the top with showy flowers. Most wild species have rather narrow-petalled flowers in shades of yellow, red or purple. Colors of garden cannas range from reds, oranges and yellows through to apricots, creams and pinks. Plants range in height from 18 in (45 cm) to 8 ft (2.4 m).

Cultivation

Cannas thrive outdoors in frost-free, warm climates but if grown outside in

Campanula rotundifolia

colder areas protect the roots with thick mulch in winter. They thrive in hot weather as long as water is kept up to the roots. Cut back to the ground after flowers finish. Propagate by division.

Canna × generalis

These plants are extremely variable, ranging from dwarfs less than 3 ft (1 m) to large growers that reach 6 ft (1.8 m). Foliage is also variable and may be plain green, reddish, purple or variegated. Flowers come in either in plain single colors such as the orange-red 'Brandywine', or spotted or streaked as in the yellow and red 'King Numbert'. 'Königin Charlotte' has red flowers. 'Lenape' is a dwarf hybrid cultivar with bright yellow flowers with a red throat and brownish red spots; 'Lucifer' has yellow-edged red petals and purple-toned leaves. *Zones 9–12.*

Canna indica

syn. *Canna edulis*

Indian shot

This species grows to about 8 ft (2.4 m) tall, and in summer it bears dark red to yellow flowers with very narrow petals, followed by fleshy spined capsules containing black seeds—their hardness and smooth spherical shape allowed them to be substituted for shotgun pellets, hence the common name. Some strains, once distinguished as *Canna*

Canna indica

edulis, have been cultivated for the edible starch in their rhizomes, known as 'Queensland arrowroot'. *Zones 9–12.*

CATANANCHE
Cupid's dart

Consisting of 5 species of annuals and perennials from the Mediterranean region, the growth form of this genus of the daisy family is like a dandelion, with narrow basal leaves radiating from a root crown, and leafless flowering stems each terminating in a showy blue or yellow flowerhead. The distinctive heads have few ray florets; these are broad and flat with 5 prominent teeth at the tip of each and a darker zone at the base. The genus name is from a Greek word meaning 'love potion', indicating its use in ancient times.

Canna × generalis

Catananche caerulea

Celmisia semicordata

Cultivation
Grow in full sun in any well-drained soil. Propagate from seed or root cuttings or by division.

Catananche caerulea
Common Cupid's dart
This is popular as a cottage garden plant or it can be grown among grasses in a meadow garden. A fast-growing but usually short-lived perennial, it reaches 24 in (60 cm) in height with a spread of 12 in (30 cm). The narrow leaves are gray-green and thin, forming a dense basal clump. Lavender-blue flowerheads are borne freely throughout summer on slender, weak, leafless stems. The flowers are suitable for drying. *Zones 7–10.*

CELMISIA
Snow daisy, mountain daisy, New Zealand daisy
Sixty or so species of rhizomatous perennials and subshrubs with white daisy-like flowerheads make up this Australasian genus. These evergreens have tufts of silvery gray leaves and a profuse display of yellow-centered white flowers, mostly solitary on scaly stalks.

Cultivation
Most are true alpine plants that resent lowland conditions, but some will grow in rockeries, peat beds or scree gardens in temperate climates. Plant in full sun or part-shade in moist, well-drained, gritty, acid soil. Protect from hot sun in drier areas and from excessive moisture in cool climates. Propagate from seed in fall (autumn) or by division in late spring.

Celmisia semicordata
syn. *Celmisia coriacea*
This is native to the South Island of New Zealand. Forming with age large mounds of rosettes, the striking silvery leaves are stiff and straight, up to 18 in (45 cm) long. The white flowerheads are up to 4 in (10 cm) across, on slender stems to 15 in (38 cm) long. Generally regarded as the easiest celmisia to grow, it is more tolerant than most of heat and dry conditions but likes ample summer moisture. *Zones 7–9.*

CELOSIA
Cockscomb, Chinese woolflower
This genus of erect annuals, perennials and shrubs in the amaranthus family contains 50 or more species, but only one (*Celosia argentea*) is widely cultivated. It has evolved in cultivation into several different forms, hardly recognizable as belonging to the one species. It has simple, soft, strongly veined leaves; the variation is almost wholly in the structure of the heads of the small flowers, which have undergone proliferation and deformation in the two major cultivated races.

Celosia argentea, Plumosa Group

Centaurea cyanus

Cultivation

In cool climates celosias are usually treated as conservatory plants. They are better adapted to hot climates, withstanding the fiercest summer heat. They require full sun, rich, well-drained soil and constant moisture. Propagate from seed in spring.

Celosia argentea

syns *Celosia cristata, C. pyramidalis*
This annual can reach 3 ft (1 m) or more in height. The silvery white flowers appear in summer in dense, erect, pointed spikes with a silvery sheen. There are two strikingly different cultivar groups—the Plumosa Group, with erect, plume-like heads of tiny deformed flowers in a range of hot colors, and the Cristata Group (cockscombs), with bizarre wavy crests of fused flower stalks also in many colors. Both have been developed with a range of seedling strains, differing in height as well as size and the color of the flowerheads. *Zones 10–12.*

CENTAUREA
Cornflower, knapweed

This genus of around 450 species includes annuals, biennials and perennials. Some spiny-leafed species are troublesome weeds in some parts of the world. Apart from the common annual cornflower, some perennial species are desirable garden plants; they come in colors from white through shades of blue, red, pink, purple and yellow. The flowerheads typically have an urn-shaped receptacle of fringed or spiny bracts, from the mouth of which radiate the quite large florets, each deeply divided into 5 colored petals; smaller florets occupy the center of the head, but do not form a distinct disc.

Cultivation

Cornflowers like well-drained soil in a sunny position. Propagate from seed in spring or fall (autumn); perennials can also be divided in spring or fall.

Centaurea cyanus
Blue-bottle, bachelor's button, cornflower

One of the best known wildflowers of Europe and northern Asia, this species is also a common weed of cereal crops. It is a weak-stemmed erect annual 24–36 in (60–90 cm) tall with narrow leaves and small, untidy flowerheads that are typically a slightly purplish shade of blue. Garden varieties have been developed with larger flowers in shades of pale and deep pink, cerise, crimson, white, purple and blue, some of them dwarf and more compact. *Zones 5–10.*

Centaurea montana
Perennial cornflower, mountain bluet

From the mountains of Europe, this long-cultivated perennial species is up to 30 in (75 cm) high and has creeping rhizomes; it may form large clumps when conditions suit. The leaves are usually smooth edged and green, and the 2 in (5 cm) wide violet flowerheads, borne in early summer, are distinctive for their widely spaced florets, giving them a delicate lacy effect. *Zones 3–9.*

Centaurea macrocephala
Globe cornflower

With foliage resembling a dandelion, this perennial species is from the subalpine fields of Armenia and Turkey. In summer stout leafy stems, up to 3 ft (1 m) tall, carry yellow flowerheads

Centaurea macrocephala

Centaurea montana

about 2 in (5 cm) across with a club-like base of shiny brown bracts. *Zones 4–9.*

CENTRANTHUS
Valerian

Around 10 species belong to this genus of annual and perennial herbs, but only *Centranthus ruber* is widely planted for ornament. They make tufts of soft leaves that may be smooth edged or less commonly dissected, and the leafy, branched flowering stems bear many irregular heads of tiny tubular flowers.

Cultivation

Grow in full sun in moderately fertile, well-drained, chalk or lime soil. Dead-head regularly. Divide every 3 years. Propagate from seed or by division.

Centranthus ruber
Red valerian, Jupiter's beard, kiss-me-quick

This perennial often naturalizes on dry banks and is ideal for dry rock gardens and borders. It forms loose clumps of somewhat fleshy leaves and grows to a height of 24–36 in (60–90 cm). From late spring to fall (autumn) it produces dense clusters of small, star-shaped, deep reddish pink to pale pink flowers that last for a long time. 'Albus' has white flowers. It requires sun and good drainage and will tolerate exposed positions and poor alkaline soil. *Zones 5–10.*

Centranthus ruber

CERASTIUM

There are 60–100 species of low-growing annuals and perennials in this genus from northern temperate and arctic regions. The annuals include some common weeds of lawns, but some of the perennials are grown as ground covers or in rock-gardens. They have weak stems from a network of thin rhizomes and small leaves usually clothed in whitish hairs. The flowers are white with 5 petals.

Cultivation

Easily cultivated, some cerastiums can be invasive. All are frost hardy and like full sun and well-drained soil. Keep foliage dry in winter and in humid summer weather as the hairs on the leaves tend to retain moisture and become mildewed. Propagate by division.

Cerastium tomentosum
Snow-in-summer

A vigorous, fast-growing ground cover, this perennial suits a well-drained, hot, dry bank or rockery. It has narrow silvery gray leaves, and masses of star-shaped white flowers are borne in loose heads in late spring and summer. The foliage is dense and an effective weed suppressant. It grows to 6 in (15 cm) high and spreads indefinitely. *Zones 3–10.*

CHELONE
Turtlehead

This genus of 6 species of rather coarse but showy perennials from North America is related to *Penstemon*, which they resemble in growth habit and foliage. The name comes from the Greek *kelone* meaning a tortoise or turtle, and refers to the hooded, gaping flowers, borne in short terminal spikes. Leaves are toothed and shiny in most species.

Cultivation

They prefer moist conditions with rich soil in full sun or part-shade. Propagate by dividing clumps in early spring, from cuttings in summer or from seed in spring or fall (autumn).

Chelone obliqua
Rose turtlehead

From southeastern USA, this is the showiest of the turtleheads. Pairs of rich green leaves line 3 ft (1 m) tall vertical stems topped with short spikes of rosy-purple flowers in late summer and fall (autumn). *Zones 6–9.*

Cerastium tomentosum

Chelone obliqua

Chrysanthemum carinatum

Cimicifuga simplex

CHRYSANTHEMUM
Chrysanthemum

As now recognized by most botanists, this once large and varied genus is a shadow of its former self, reduced to a mere 5 species of annuals from Europe and North Africa. As a common name, though, 'chrysanthemum' will always be understood by gardeners to refer to the group of showy hybrid plants derived from East Asian species now classified under *Dendranthema*.

Cultivation

True chrysanthemums are easily grown annuals, requiring little more than a moist, fertile, well-prepared soil and a sunny position. They prefer coolish summers but in warmer, drier climates can be timed to bloom in winter. Propagate from seed, sown in fall (autumn) or early spring.

Chrysanthemum carinatum
syn. *Chrysanthemum tricolor*
Painted daisy, summer chrysanthemum, tricolor chrysanthemum

This spectacular annual species is from Morocco and grows to 24 in (60 cm), spreading to 12 in (30 cm) with much-divided, rather fleshy leaves and banded, multicolored flowers in spring and early summer. 'Monarch Court Jesters' comes in red with yellow centers or white with red centers, and the Tricolor Series has many color combinations. They are excellent bedding plants. *Zones 8–10*.

CIMICIFUGA
Bugbane

This genus of about 15 species of perennials in the ranunculus family is native to cooler regions of the northern hemisphere. The name means 'bug repellent', from the Latin *cimex* (bedbug) and *fugare* (to repel) reflecting an early use of one species. The branched flowering stems terminate in long, erect spikes of white, cream or pinkish flowers, the many stamens being the conspicuous part of each flower.

Cultivation

They prefer part-shade, a deep, rich soil and need regular watering. Plant rhizome divisions in spring or fall (autumn), but do not disturb the root; they flower best when established.

Cimicifuga simplex
Kamchatka bugbane

From Japan and far eastern Siberia, this species is the latest to flower of the whole genus, the flowers coming in late fall (autumn). It is also smaller, reaching a height of about 4 ft (1.2 m). The flowers are white, carried on long arching wands, and the foliage is much divided. 'Elstead' has purplish buds opening to pure white and is a very graceful plant. *Zones 3–9*.

Clarkia unguiculata

Clematis integrifolia

CLARKIA
syn. *Godetia*

This genus, allied to the evening prim-roses (*Oenothera*) and consisting of about 36 species, was named in honor of Captain William Clark, of the Lewis and Clark expedition that crossed the American continent in 1806. They are bushy annuals, undistinguished in foliage but spectacular in their short flowering season when they are covered in showy funnel-shaped flowers in various shades of pink, white and carmine. The flowers look a little like azaleas—in Germany they are called *Sommerazalee*, the summer azalea.

Cultivation
They are easily grown in full sun in any temperate climate. They prefer moist but well-drained, slightly acid soil. Propagate from seed.

Clarkia unguiculata
syn. *Clarkia elegans*
Mountain garland
This species is usually taller than its fellow-Californian *Clarkia amoena* but with smaller flowers, only 1 in (25 mm) across, often frilled and doubled. The flowers, produced at the tops of slender, reddish stems 3 ft (1 m) or more in height, have a broader color range, including orange and purple. *Zones 7–11.*

CLEMATIS
Virgin's bower, traveller's joy
The 200 or more species of mostly woody climbers in this genus are scattered throughout the world's temperate regions, but most of the popular, larger-flowered plants come from Japan and China. They climb by twisting their leaf-stalk tendrils about a support and are ideal for verandah posts, arbors, bowers and trellises. Showy bell-shaped or flattish flowers with 4 to 8 petals (*sepals* really) are followed by masses of fluffy seed heads.

Cultivation
A well-drained, humus-rich, perma-nently cool soil with good moisture retention is needed. Prune old twiggy growth in spring and propagate from cuttings or by layering in summer.

Clematis integrifolia
This herbaceous clematis is hardly recognizable as belonging to this genus, at least until it flowers. It forms a gradually expanding clump with masses of stems arising from the base each spring, each one ending in a single, nodding flower. It is normally purple-blue, deeper in the center. The stamens are creamy white and tightly packed. The flower stalks tend to flop and may need support. *Zones 3–9.*

CLEOME
Spider flower, spider plant

This genus of 150 species of bushy annuals and short-lived evergreen shrubs, from subtropical and tropical zones all over the world, is characterized by its spidery flowers with 4 petals that narrow into basal stalks, and mostly long, spidery stamens and styles.

Cultivation
Marginally frost hardy, they require full sun and fertile, well-drained soil, regular water and shelter from strong winds. Encourage taller growth by removing side branches. Propagate from seed in spring or early summer.

Cleome hassleriana
syn. *Cleome spinosa* of gardens
Native to subtropical South America, this fast-growing, bushy annual has unusual spidery flowers. An erect plant, it grows to 4 ft (1.2 m) tall with a spread of 18 in (45 cm). It has large palmate leaves and the hairy, slightly prickly stems are topped in summer with heads of airy, pink and white flowers with long, protruding stamens. Several strains are available as seed, ranging in color from pure white to purple. *Zones 9–11.*

Cleome hassleriana

CLINTONIA

Five species of woodland lilies from North America and eastern Asia make up this genus, all rhizomatous perennials with rich green smooth foliage rather like that of *Convallaria*, and erect spikes or umbels (solitary in one species) of small, starry 6-petalled flowers.

Cultivation
All species need a cool, peaty, lime-free soil and a shaded, humid position, and so are best suited to a woodland garden. Winter mulching will protect from frost. Propagate from seed or division of rhizomes.

Clintonia umbellulata
Speckled wood-lily
From eastern USA, this is one of the prettiest species with dense umbels of fragrant white flowers, often speckled green or purplish, rising on stems up to 15 in (40 cm) tall above dense patches of luxuriant foliage. The flowers appear in late spring and early summer and are followed by black berries. *Zones 4–9.*

CLIVIA
Kaffir lily
This genus of southern African lilies was named after Lady Clive, Duchess of Northumberland, whose grandfather was the famous Clive of India. She was a patron of gardening and *Clivia nobilis* first flowered in the UK in her green-

Clintonia umbellulata

houses. The genus consists of 4 species of evergreen perennials with thick, strap-like leaves springing from short rhizomes with thick roots. Flowers are borne in dense umbels and are funnel-shaped to trumpet-shaped, with 6 red to orange, sometimes green-tipped petals. They are sometimes followed by deep red, berry-like fruits.

Cultivation
They prefer a mild, frost-free climate; or a conservatory or greenhouse in colder climates. Plant in a shaded or part-shaded, position in friable, well-drained soil. Propagate by division after flowering. Seed can also be used but plants can be slow to flower.

Clivia miniata
Bush lily, fire lily
This showy species grows to about 18 in (45 cm) high. It bears clusters of broadly funnel-shaped flowers, mostly orange to scarlet with a yellow throat, usually in spring but with the occasional bloom at other times. Many cultivars have been selected over the years, including yellow and cream forms. There is a group of especially prized forms commonly called 'hybrids' with tulip-shaped, deep, rich scarlet blooms. *Zones 10–11.*

CODONOPSIS
Native to eastern Asia and higher mountains of the Malay region, this

genus allied to *Campanula* consists of about 30 species of perennials with swollen roots, some with scrambling or climbing stems, and simple, broad to narrow leaves that smell slightly un-pleasant when bruised. The flowers are pendent or nodding, basically bell-shaped but with many variations, and in many cases prettily veined.

Cultivation
Codonopsis species require a moist, cool-temperate climate and grow best in a light, well-drained soil in part or complete shade. Propagate from seed or by division with care.

Codonopsis convolvulacea
This species from the Himalayas and Western China sends up twining stems to as much as 8 ft (2.4 m) high if a suitable support is available or it may hang down a bank or wall. The broadly bell-shaped flowers are up to 2 in (5 cm) across, range in color from violet to almost white and are carried singly on long stalks at ends of lateral branches. *Codonopsis clematidea* from central Asia is very similar but has nodding flowers with purple veining. *Zones 5–9.*

CONSOLIDA
Larkspur
These annuals were often treated as species of *Delphinium*, but the consensus now is that the 40 or so species consti-

Clivia miniata

Codonopsis clematidea

Convallaria majalis

Consolida ambigua

tute a distinct genus. The name *Consolida* was bestowed in the Middle Ages because of the plants' use in the healing of wounds; they were believed to help the clotting (consolidating) of blood. Garden larkspurs are mostly derived from *Consolida ajacis*, and include many strains, mostly grown as mixed colors. They have finely divided, feather-like leaves and poisonous seeds.

Cultivation
They succeed in any temperate or even mildly subtropical climate and like full sun and rich, well-drained soil. Tall cultivars need to be staked. Propagate from seed and watch for powdery mildew.

Consolida ambigua
syns *Consolida ajacis, Delphinium consolida* The name larkspur comes from the nectar spur at the back of the flowers, hidden in the open blooms but clearly visible on unopened buds. This Mediterranean species originally had blue flowers. Present-day garden larkspurs are the result of hybridizing this species with *Consolida orientalis* to give the 'rocket larkspurs', or may be derived from *C. regalis* in the case of the 'forking larkspurs'. Blooms may be pink, white or purple and are usually double, borne mainly in summer. Some reach a height of 4 ft (1.2 m). *Zones 7–11.*

CONVALLARIA
Lily-of-the-valley
This plant spreads over the forest floor by slender underground rhizomes which at intervals send up pointed oval leaves and slender flowering stems adorned with little white bells. The red berries that follow have their uses in medicine, but they are poisonous.

Cultivation
The rhizomes should be planted in fall (autumn) in a part-shaded spot. Grow in fertile, humus-rich, moist soil. They can be potted for display indoors, then replanted outdoors after flowering. Propagate from seed or by division.

Convallaria majalis
Renowned for its glorious perfume, this beautiful plant does best in cool climates. It is low growing, 8–12 in (20–30 cm) high but of indefinite spread, with dark green leaves. The dainty white bell-shaped flowers appear in spring. Pink-flowered variants are known, collectively referred to as *Convallaria majalis* var. *rosea*, and there are several cultivars with variegated or gold foliage. *Zones 3–9.*

Convolvulus sabatius

Coreopsis grandiflora

CONVOLVULUS

Found in many temperate regions of the world, this genus of some 250 species consists mainly of slender, twining creepers (the bindweeds) and small herbaceous plants. Only a few species are shrubby, and even these are soft stemmed and renewed by shooting from the base. They have simple, thin-textured, usually narrow leaves and the flowers are like morning glories, with a strongly flared tube that opens by unfurling 'pleats'. *Convolvulus* differs from true morning glories *(Ipomoea)* in having flowers that stay open all day.

Cultivation

They adapt to most soils and exposed as well as sheltered positions, but always prefer full sun. Propagate from cuttings.

Convolvulus sabatius
syn. *Convolvulus mauritanicus*
Moroccan glory vine, bindweed, ground morning glory
This densely trailing perennial bears profuse lilac-blue flowers from spring to fall (autumn). It has slender stems that may twine around twigs, and small oval green leaves. An excellent plant for draping over walls and hanging baskets, it grows to a height of 6–8 in (15–20 cm) and spreads extensively. *Zones 8–11.*

COREOPSIS

Around 80 species of annuals and perennials from cooler or drier regions of the Americas make up this genus of the daisy family. The flowerheads, borne on slender stems mainly in summer, are mostly shades of gold or yellow, some bicolored. Leaves vary from simple and narrow, usually toothed, to deeply divided, and may be basal or scattered up the stems.

Cultivation

Both annuals and perennials prefer full sun and a fertile, well-drained soil. Propagate perennials by division of old clumps in winter or spring, or by spring cuttings. Propagate annuals from seed in spring or fall (autumn).

Coreopsis grandiflora
Tickseed
Among the easiest of perennials, this bright golden-yellow daisy provides color from late spring to mid-summer. Somewhat hairy leaves and stems form a loose mound to 12–24 in (30–60 cm) tall and wide, the flower stems rising to nearly 24 in (60 cm) or usually flopping on their neighbors. It can be treated as an annual and self-seeds freely. Cultivars of more compact habit such as 'Badengold', 'Sunray' or 'Early Sunrise' are the best choices for the well-maintained border. *Zones 6–10.*

Coreopsis lanceolata
This is a tufted perennial with long-stalked, lance-shaped basal leaves and bright golden-yellow flowerheads on leafy stems up to about 24 in (60 cm) high. It is extremely floriferous and when mass planted can make sheets of

gold in spring and early summer. Short lived, it is very free-seeding, and has become an environmental weed in parts of Australia. Double forms are sometimes grown. 'Baby Sun' is a compact long blooming cultivar about 12 in (30 cm) high. *Zones 3–11.*

Coreopsis verticillata

This perennial species produces crowded erect stems to 30 in (75 cm) tall from a tangled mass of thin rhizomes; the leaves, in whorls of 3, are divided into very narrow segments. The abundant bright yellow flowerheads are borne from late spring until fall (autumn). It does best in light soil of low fertility. 'Moonbeam' is slightly lower and more compact with lemon-yellow blooms. *Zones 6–10.*

CORYDALIS

The 300 or so species that make up this genus, allied to the fumitories (*Fumaria*),

Coreopsis verticillata 'Moonbeam'

Corydalis flexuosa

occur widely as natives in temperate regions of the northern hemispere, with a great concentration in the mountains of east Asia. The genus includes some annuals but species are mostly perennials, with basal tufts of ferny, deeply dissected leaves springing from fleshy rhizomes or tubers. The smallish tubular flowers have a short backward-pointing spur that may be curved; they are usually grouped in short spikes or clusters and come in mostly creams, yellows, pinks and purples but a few have clear blue flowers.

Cultivation

Soil should be well drained but moisture-retentive, rich in humus for the woodland species. Several species, such as *Corydalis lutea*, self-seed freely. Propagate from seed or by division.

Corydalis flexuosa

This blue-flowered species is from western China. It forms a small clump of green foliage around 12 in (30 cm) tall, from which emerge in late spring and early summer short spikes of long-spurred tubular blue flowers, each flower about 1 in (25 mm) long. It requires a cool spot in part-shade and moist soil. *Zones 5–9.*

Coreopsis lanceolata 'Baby Sun'

Corydalis lutea
Yellow corydalis

The most easily cultivated species, this native of Europe's southern Alps region is widely naturalized in temperate climates around the world. A rhizomatous perennial, it makes broad clumps or mounds of fresh green foliage, to about 12 in (30 cm) high, and is dotted from spring to fall (autumn) with short sprays of soft yellow flowers. It often self-seeds in wall crevices or moist chinks in rockeries. In a woodland garden it makes an attractive ground cover. *Zones 6–10.*

COSMOS
Mexican aster

This genus of annuals and perennials contains 25 species native to warmer parts of the Americas but mostly to Mexico. They have erect but weak, leafy stems and the leaves are variously lobed or deeply and finely dissected. The flowerheads, on slender stalks terminating branches, are daisy-like with showy, broad ray-florets surrounding a small

Corydalis lutea

disc; they range in color from white through pinks, yellows, oranges, reds and purples to deep maroon.

Cultivation

They are moderately frost hardy and in cold climates need protection in winter. They need a sunny spot with protection from strong winds, and well-drained soil that is not over-rich. Mulch with compost and water well in hot weather. Propagate annuals from seed in spring or fall (autumn), perennials from basal cuttings in spring.

Cosmos atrosanguineus
Black cosmos, chocolate cosmos

A tuberous-rooted, clump-forming perennial growing to 24 in (60 cm) in height and spread, the unusual black cosmos has long-stalked, very dark maroon flowerheads that have a chocolate scent, most noticeable on warm days. It flowers from summer to fall (autumn). The leaves are rather few-lobed and tinged dull purplish. It normally dies back in fall and requires fairly dry soil if the rootstock is not to rot; alternatively the roots can be lifted and stored for the winter like dahlias. *Zones 8–10.*

Cosmos atrosanguineus

Cosmos bipinnatus 'Sea Shells'

Cosmos bipinnatus

Cosmos bipinnatus
Common cosmos, Mexican aster

This feathery-leafed annual reaches
5–6 ft (1.5–1.8 m) in height with showy
daisy-like flowerheads in summer and
fall (autumn), in shades of pink, red,
purple or white. Taller plants may need
staking. Newer strains are usually more
compact and can have double flowers
and striped petals. 'Sea Shells' has
usually pink, sometimes crimson or

white flowerheads with edges of ray-
florets curled into a tube. *Zones 8–11.*

CRAMBE

This genus, related to *Brassica*, consists
of 20 species of annuals and perennials,
ranging in the wild from central Europe
to central Asia, and parts of Africa. They
have large, cabbage-like basal leaves
that are shallowly to very deeply lobed,
and large panicles of small, 4-petalled
white flowers with a somewhat cabbage-
like smell.

Cultivation

Mostly very frost hardy, they will grow
in any well-drained soil and prefer an
open, sunny position, although they will
tolerate some shade. Propagate by
division in early spring or from seed
sown in spring or fall (autumn).

Crambe cordifolia
Colewort

From the Caucasus region, this spectacular perennial has lobed leaves up to

about 18 in (45 cm) long and almost as wide, forming a broad but untidy rosette. The stout, much-branched flowering stem bursts into a cloud of small, white, starry flowers, the whole measuring 4 ft (1.2 m) across with a total height of 6 ft (1.8 m). It is very deep rooted and will produce numerous offsets. *Zones 6–9.*

CYNARA

A genus of 10 species of perennials, thistle relatives of statuesque proportions from the Mediterranean, they grown both for their large silvery gray, deeply divided leaves and their thistle-like flowerheads. It includes the globe artichoke and the cardoon, both of which have edible parts, in one the immature flowerheads and in the other, the leaf stalks.

Cultivation

Grow in full sun in a fertile well-drained soil. To be seen to best advantage they need plenty of space. Propagation is from seed by offsets that are formed around the crown.

Cynara cardunculus
Cardoon

Resembling its relative the globe artichoke, the cardoon produces broad, fleshy, edible leaf stalks in a similar manner to celery. It also makes a fine ornamental, towering up to 8 ft (2.4 m) high with coarse gray stems and leaves and multiple large mauve flowerheads. Most often grown from offsets, seed may be started indoors and planted out after all danger of frost has passed. Space plants 5 ft (1.5 m) apart in rows in well-drained, humus-rich soil. Leaf stalks can be blanched by enclosing them in cardboard tubes. Harvest stems by slicing under the crown through the roots. *Zones 6–10.*

Crambe cordifolia

Cynara cardunculus

Cynoglossum amabile

CYNOGLOSSUM

This genus of 55 species of annuals, biennials and perennials occurs in most temperate regions of the world. All are frost hardy and have a long flowering period. They are related to the common forget-me-not, which many resemble.

Cultivation

All species need a fertile but not too rich soil; if over-nourished the plants tend to flop over. Propagation is from seed sown in fall (autumn) or spring or, in the case of perennial species, by division.

Cynoglossum amabile
Chinese forget-me-not

This upright annual or biennial, growing to a height of about 20 in (50 cm) has dull green hairy lanceolate leaves and flowers in racemes, generally blue although white and pink forms can occur. Flowers are produced in spring and early summer. *Cynoglossum amabile* self-seeds very readily. The popular cultivar 'Firmament' has pendulous sky-blue flowers.
Zones 5–9.

D

Dahlia × *hortensis* 'Bishop of Llandaff'

Dahlia, Waterlily or nymphaea-flowered (Group 4) 'Gerrie Hoek'

Dahlia, Semi-cactus (Group 9) 'Bandaris'

DAHLIA

This genus of about 30 species, native from Mexico to Colombia, has had a big impact on gardens. Of this number only 2 or 3 species were used to create the thousands of named varieties available. So many different flower forms have been developed that the hybrids are classified into about 10 different groups, determined by the size and type of their flowerheads.

Cultivation

Dahlias are not frost resistant so in cold climates lift the tubers each year and store in a frost-free place to be split and replanted in spring. Most prefer a sunny, sheltered position in well-fertilized, well-drained soil. Feed monthly and water well when in flower. Propagate bedding forms from seed, others from seed, cuttings from tubers or by division.

Dahlia × *hortensis* 'Bishop of Llandaff'

Peony-flowered dahlias, which are kept as a separate group in some countries, usually have one or two rows of flat petals with a center which can be open or partly covered by small twisted petals, such as 'Bishop of Llandaff' with its brilliant scarlet blooms above its beautiful deep burgundy leaves. *Zones 8–10.*

Dahlia, Waterlily or nymphaea-flowered (Group 4)

These fully double-flowered dahlias have slightly cupped petals that have a more than passing resemblance to their namesakes, the waterlilies. The overall effect is of a flattish flower. 'Cameo' has white flowers with a cream base; 'Gerrie Hoek' has pink waterlily flowers on strong stems and is popular as a cut flower. *Zones 8–10.*

Dahlia, Semi-cactus (Group 9)

This group of fully double-flowered dahlias have long, narrow rolled petals giving the flowers a spidery look. 'So Dainty' is a miniature with golden

Delphinium, Belladonna Group

bronze and apricot flowers; 'Brandaris'
is a medium form with soft orange and
golden yellow flowers; 'Hayley Jane' is a
small form with purplish pink flowers
and white bases; and 'Salmon Keene' has
large salmon pink to golden flowers.
Zones 8–10.

DELPHINIUM

This genus of 250 or so species ranges
from self-seeding annuals or dwarf
alpine plants up to statuesque perennials
that exceed 8 ft (2.4 m) in height. Nearly
all start as a tuft of long-stalked basal
leaves, their blades divided into 3 to 7
radiating lobes or segments. The tufts
elongate into erect, sometimes branched
flowering stems bearing flowers with a
backward-pointing nectar spur. Recognized groups include the Belladonna,
Elatum and Pacific hybrids.

Cultivation

Very frost hardy, most like a cool to cold
winter. They prefer full sun with shelter
from strong winds, and well-drained,
fertile soil. Apply a liquid fertilizer at
2–3 weekly intervals. Propagate from
cuttings or by division.

Delphinium, Belladonna Group

These frost-hardy perennials (*Delphinium
elatum × D. grandiflorum*) have an

Delphinium cardinale

upright, loosely branching form. Their
widely-spaced blue or white flowers are
single or sometimes semi-double and
borne on loose spikes ranging in height
up to 4 ft (1.2 m). They bloom in early
and late summer. Propagate by division
or from basal cuttings in spring.
Zones 3–9.

Delphinium cardinale
Scarlet larkspur

This short-lived upright perennial to 6 ft
(2 m) tall is native to California and
Mexico. It has finely divided leaves and
bears slender loose spikes of small,
single red flowers with yellow centers in
summer. Provide a rich, moist soil and a
little shade. *Zones 8–9.*

Delphinium grandiflorum
syn. *Delphinium chinense*
Butterfly delphinium, Chinese delphinium
Native to China, Siberia, Japan and
Mongolia, this tufted perennial grows to
a height of 18 in (45 cm) and a spread of
12 in (30 cm). The leaf segments are
divided into narrow lobes. It bears large
bright blue flowers over a long period in
summer. It is fully frost hardy. 'Azure
Fairy' is a pale blue-flowering form;
'Blue Butterfly' has bright blue flowers.
Zones 3–9.

Delphinium, Pacific Hybrid 'Black Knight'

Delphinium grandiflorum 'Blue Butterfly'

Delphinium, Pacific Hybrids
These short-lived perennials are usually
grown as biennials. They are stately
plants to 5 ft (1.5 m) or more in height
with star-like single, semi-double or
double flowers of mostly blue, purple or
white, clustered on erect rigid spikes.
Cultivars include 'Astolat', a perennial
with lavender-mauve flowers with dark
eyes; 'Black Knight', with deep rich
purple flowers with black eyes;
'Guinevere' with pale purple flowers
with a pinkish tinge and white eyes; and
'Summer Skies' with pale sky-blue
flowers. *Zones 7–9.*

DENDRANTHEMA
This genus of about 20 species of upright
perennials was previously included in
the genus *Chrysanthemum*. It has a
distribution from Europe to central and
eastern Asia. They are very popular
temperate region flowers. With continuous hybridization the flowerheads have
diversified in size, shape and disposition
of the florets in the blooms. There are 10
main groups of classification based largely
upon floral characteristics. All but a few
flower in mid- to late fall (autumn).

Cultivation
Dendranthema are generally frost hardy,
though some forms may be somewhat
frost tender. Grow in a sunny position in
a well-drained slightly acidic soil,
improved with compost and well-rotted
manure. Propagate from seed, by
division or cuttings.

Dendranthema × grandiflorum
syns *Chrysanthemum indicum, C.
morifolium*
Florists' chrysanthemum
This hybrid is the parent of hundreds of
cultivars. It is a vigorous subshrub to
5 ft (1.5 m) tall with thick, strongly
aromatic lobed leaves to 3 in (8 cm) in

length with a gray felted underside. The single blooms have yellow centers and spreading ray florets in white, yellow, bronze, pink, red or purple. There are numerous cultivars of various shapes and sizes and new ones are being raised annually. 'Elizabeth Shoesmith' bears large deep pink to purple flowers; 'Flame Symbol' has burnt orange double flowers; 'Yellow Symbol' has bright golden yellow blooms. *Zones 4–10.*

DIANELLA
Flax lily

This genus of small-flowered lilies is named after Diana, Roman goddess of hunting. It consists of 25 to 30 species of evergreen, clump-forming perennials from Australia, New Zealand and the Pacific Islands. They are mostly under 3 ft (1 m) tall and are alike in their long leaves and sprays of small, deep or bright blue flowers in spring and early summer. The flowers are followed by long-lasting, bright blue berries.

Cultivation

They prefer sun or part-shade and a moderately fertile, humus-rich, well-drained, neutral to acidic soil. Propagate

Dianella tasmanica

by division, or rooted offsets, or from seed in spring and fall (autumn).

Dianella tasmanica

Native to southeastern Australia, including Tasmania, this species spreads from underground rhizomes and sends up arching, strap-like leaves that can be up to 4 ft (1.2 m) long and 1½ in (35 mm) wide. Nodding, star-shaped, bright blue or purple-blue flowers are borne in branching sprays up to 3 ft (1 m) tall in spring and early summer, followed by glossy, deep blue berries. *Zones 8–10.*

DIANTHUS
Carnation, pink

This large genus consists of some 300 species. Much hybridizing has created several different groups of pinks and carnations bred for specific purposes. Border Carnations are annual or perennial plants up to 24 in (60 cm). Perpetual-flowering Carnations are often disbudded leaving only the top bud to develop. American Spray Carnations are treated like perpetuals except that no disbudding is carried out. Malmaison Carnations are so-called because of their supposed resemblance to the Bourbon rose 'Souvenir de la Malmaison'. Other groups are the Modern Pinks and the Old-fashioned Pinks. Finally comes the Alpine or Rock Pinks used mostly in rock gardens.

Dendranthema × grandiflorum

Dianthus chinensis 'Strawberry Parfait'

Dianthus, Modern Pink 'Doris'

Dianthus barbatus

Cultivation

Dianthus species like a sunny position, protection from strong winds, and well-drained, slightly alkaline soil. Propagate perennials by layering or from cuttings in summer; annuals and biennials from seed in fall (autumn) or early spring. Watch for aphids, thrips and caterpillars, rust and virus infections.

Dianthus barbatus
Sweet William

A slow-growing, frost-hardy perennial usually treated as a biennial, sweet William self-sows readily and grows to a height of 18 in (45 cm) and spread of 6 in (15 cm). The crowded, flattened heads of fragrant flowers range from white through pinks to carmine and crimson-purple and are often zoned in two tones. They flower in late spring and early summer and are ideal for massed planting. The dwarf cultivars, about 4 in (10 cm) tall, are usually treated as annuals. *Zones 4–10.*

Dianthus chinensis
Chinese pink, Indian pink

This Chinese annual has a short, tufted growth habit, and gray-green, lance-shaped leaves. In late spring and summer it bears masses of single or double, sweetly scented flowers in shades of pink, red, lavender and white. It is slow growing to a height and spread of 6–12 in (15–30 cm), and is fully frost hardy. 'Strawberry Parfait' has single pink flowers, lightly fringed with deep red centers. *Zones 7–10.*

Dianthus, Modern Pinks

These are densely leafed, mound-forming perennials derived from crosses between cultivars of *Dianthus plumarius* and *D. caryophyllus.* They have gray-green foliage and many erect flowering stems, each carrying 4 to 6 fragrant, single to fully double flowers in shades of white, pink or crimson, often with dark centers and with plain or fringed petals. Most are 12–18 in (30–45 cm) tall with a spread of 18 in (45 cm) and flower from late spring until early fall

Dianthus, Old-fashioned Pink 'Pink Mrs Sinkins'

Diascia rigescens

Dianthus superbus 'Rainbow Loveliness'

(autumn); some are clove-scented. 'Doris' is a scented, pale pink double with deep pink center. *Zones 5–10.*

Dianthus, Old-fashioned Pinks

These are tuft-forming perennials that grow to 18 in (45 cm) high. In late spring and early summer they bear single to fully double, clove-scented flowers in colors varying from white, through pale pink and magenta to red, often fringed and with contrasting centers. 'Mrs Sinkins' has pure white shaggy flowers prone to split at the calyx; it is highly perfumed. 'Pink Mrs Sinkins' is a pale pink form of 'Mrs Sinkins'. *Zones 5–9.*

Dianthus superbus

This species is a loosely tufted perennial sometimes as much as 3 ft (1 m) high. The rich purple-pink fragrant flowers, produced singly or in pairs through summer, have petals deeply divided

giving flowers a loosely fringed appearance. It has been used in producing garden hybrids and is better known as a parent of the Loveliness Strain which includes 'Rainbow Loveliness', with deeply fringed single flowers of mauve and pink shades carried on slender stems in spring. *Zones 4–10.*

DIASCIA
Twinspur

This is a genus of about 50 species of delicate, long-blooming perennials from South Africa, popular in rockeries and borders and in containers. They bear terminal racemes of flat, generally pink flowers with double nectar spurs on the back, and have erect or prostrate stems with toothed, mid-green leaves.

Cultivation

Full sun is best, with afternoon shade in hot areas; most are frost hardy, but they dislike humidity. A fertile, moist but well-drained soil and regular summer watering are vital. Propagate from seed in fall (autumn), or cuttings in fall, to overwinter in a cool greenhouse.

Diascia rigescens

This vigorous twinspur has a sprawling form with dense 6–8 in (15–20 cm) spikes of pink flowers at the upturned ends of each stem; clumps may be 24 in (60 cm) across. It flowers nearly all summer if faded flower spikes are removed. *Zones 8–10.*

Diascia 'Rose Queen'

This South African plant, often grown as an annual in harsh winter climates, is a tough floriferous perennial in milder climates. It forms a loose bushy mat of fine mid-green foliage and covers itself with a froth of rose-pink flowers during the warmer months. It grows to a height and spread of about 12 in (30 cm). Use to edge a border, in a gravel garden or as an underplanting for roses. *Zones 8–10.*

DICENTRA
Bleeding heart

This genus consists of about 20 species of annuals and perennials admired for their feathery leaves and the graceful carriage of their flowers, although they do not grow or flower well without a period of winter chill. The flowers,

Diascia 'Rose Queen'

Dicentra formosa

pendent and heart-shaped, come in red, pink, white, purple and yellow. They flower from mid-spring into early summer. From Asia and North America, they are usually found in woodland and mountainous areas.

Cultivation

Mostly quite frost hardy, dicentras love humus-rich, moist but well-drained soil and some light shade. Propagate from seed in fall (autumn) or by division in late winter.

Dicentra formosa
syn. *Dicentra eximia*
Western bleeding heart

This spreading plant grows to about 18 in (45 cm) high with a spread of 12 in (30 cm). Dainty pink and red flowers appear on slender arching stems through-out spring and summer. *Zones 3–9.*

Dicentra spectabilis
Bleeding heart

This popular garden perennial grows 24–36 in (60–90 cm) tall with a spread of 18–24 in (45–60 cm). Pink and white heart-shaped flowers on long arching stems appear in late spring and summer. After flowering, the foliage usually dies down to the ground. 'Alba' is a pure white form with green-yellow markings and pale green leaves. *Zones 2–9.*

Dicentra spectabilis 'Alba'

DICTAMNUS
Burning bush

The Book of Exodus tells how God spoke to Moses on Mount Sinai from a bush that burned yet was not consumed by the fire. Gardeners insist that it must have been *Dictamnus albus*, the only species in its genus and indigenous to the Mediterranean and temperate Asia. In still, warm conditions so much aromatic oil evaporates from the leaves that if you strike a match near it the vapor ignites and the bush is engulfed in flame, but so briefly that it is not damaged.

Cultivation

This perennial needs full sun and fertile, well-drained soil. It resents disturbance. Propagate from fresh seed in summer.

Dictamnus albus
syn. *Dictamnus fraxinella*
Burning bush, dittany, gas plant

This herbaceous, woody-stemmed perennial bears early summer spikes of fragrant, star-shaped, white, pink or lilac flowers with long stamens. It grows to 3 ft (1.2 m) tall with a spread of 36 in (90 cm) and has glossy light green leaves. It is quite frost hardy. *Dictamnus albus* var. *purpureus* (syn. *D. a.* var. *rubra*) bears purple-pink flowers with purple veins. *Zones 3–9*.

Dictamnus albus

DIETES
Fortnight lily

Native to southern Africa and to Lord Howe Island off eastern Australia, this genus contains 6 species of evergreen rhizomatous perennials with attractive, iris-like flowers. The flowers usually last only for a day but new buds open over a long period in spring and summer. They have leathery, erect, sword-like leaves which form large clumps.

Cultivation

Fortnight lilies thrive in part-shade or full sun, and prefer humus-rich, well-drained soil that does not dry out quickly. Marginally frost hardy, they are tough enough to serve as low hedges and, once established, self-seed readily. Propagate from seed in spring or fall (autumn) or by division in spring.

Dietes bicolor
syn. *Moraea bicolor*

Sometimes called the Spanish iris, though it is neither an iris nor Spanish (it comes from South Africa), *Dietes bicolor* has pale green sword-shaped basal leaves and pale yellow flowers that appear from spring to summer. Each of the 3 larger petals has a central brown mark. It grows to around 36 in (90 cm) in height. *Zones 9–11*.

Dietes bicolor

Dietes iridioides

Digitalis purpurea

Dietes iridioides

syns *Dietes vegeta, Moraea iridioides*
This species has branching, wiry stems
that carry white, iris-like flowers with
central yellow marks. It grows to a
height of 4 ft (1.2 m) and a spread of
12–24 in (30–60 cm), forming dense
clumps of basal leaves in a spreading
fan. Its preferred habitat is in semi-
shade under tall, open trees. *Zones 8–11.*

DIGITALIS
Foxglove
These 22 species of biennials and
perennials, some of them evergreen, bear
tall spikes of tubular, 2-lipped flowers
which come in many colors including
magenta, purple, white, cream, yellow,
pink and lavender. The medicinal
properties of digitalis have been known
since ancient times, and it is still used in
the treatment of heart ailments.

Cultivation
Marginally to fully frost hardy, they
grow in most sheltered conditions,
preferring cool climates in part-shade
and humus-rich, well-drained soil. Cut
flowering stems down to the ground
after spring flowering to encourage
secondary spikes. Propagate from seed
in fall (autumn) or by division.

Digitalis × mertonensis

Digitalis × mertonensis
A hybrid of *Digitalis grandiflora* and *D.
purpurea*, this frost-hardy perennial
forms a clump about 36 in (90 cm) tall
and 12 in (30 cm) wide. Summer
flowering, it bears spikes of tubular, pink
to salmon flowers above a rosette of soft,
hairy, oval leaves. Divide after flowering. *Zones 4–9.*

Digitalis purpurea
The common foxglove is a short-lived,
frost-hardy perennial with an upright
habit, a height of 3–5 ft (1–1.5 m) and a

Dimorphotheca pluvialis

spread of 24 in (60 cm). The flowers are purple, pink, rosy magenta, white or pale yellow, above a rosette of rough, oval leaves. All parts of the plant are poisonous. Many seedling strains are available, grown as bedding annuals, the Excelsior Hybrids in mixed colors being very popular. *Digitalis purpurea* f. *albiflora* has pure white flowers sometimes lightly spotted brown inside. *Zones 5–10*.

DIMORPHOTHECA
African daisy, Cape marigold
These 7 species of annuals, perennials and evergreen subshrubs from South Africa have colorful, daisy-like flowers from late winter. Related to the genus *Osteospermum*, they are useful for rock gardens and borders.

Cultivation
They need an open sunny situation and fertile, well-drained soil; they are salt tolerant. The flowers only open in sunshine. Deadheading prolongs flowering. Propagate annuals from seed in spring and perennials from cuttings in summer. Watch for fungal diseases in summer rainfall areas.

Dimorphotheca pluvialis
syn. *Dimorphotheca annua*
Rain daisy
This bedding annual produces small flowerheads in late winter and spring that are snow white above, purple

Dodecatheon meadia

beneath, with brownish purple centers. Low growing, it reaches 8–12 in (20–30 cm) in height with a similar spread. *Zones 8–10*.

DODECATHEON
Shooting star
The shooting stars (about 14 species) are western North America's equivalent to Europe's cyclamens and, like them, they are perennials and related to the primrose. Most are rosette-forming and grow to about 15 in (38 cm) high, with pink or white flowers. They have swept-back petals and protruding stamens.

Cultivation
Fully frost hardy, they prefer part-shade in moist, well-drained acidic soil. Most require a dry dormant summer period after flowering. Propagate from seed in fall (autumn) or by division in winter.

Dodecatheon meadia
This is the best-known species, bearing white, rose pink or cyclamen pink, nodding flowers. It has primula-like, clumped rosettes of pale green leaves, and ranges from 6–18 in (15–45 cm) high with a spread of 18 in (45 cm). It was named for English scientist Richard Mead (1673–1754), a patron of American botanical studies. *Zones 3–9*.

Doronicum pardalianches

DORONICUM
Leopard's bane

The 35 species of herbaceous perennials that make up this genus extend from Europe through western Asia to Siberia. Species have attractive, bright yellow daisy-like flowers which are produced in spring and summer above fresh bright green foliage. Most species make attractive border plants of restrained habit and are also good as cut flowers.

Cultivation

Doronicums will cope with a range of habitats, but prefer a moisture-retentive but not wet soil, high in humus; part-shade or morning sun is preferred but never heavy dark shade. Propagate from seed or by division.

Doronicum columnae 'Miss Mason'

This is a large-flowered selection with blooms about 3 in (8 cm) across in mid- to late spring. Its bright yellow daisies are held well above its heart-shaped leaves on stems up to 24 in (60 cm) tall. *Zones 5–9.*

Doronicum pardalianches
syn. *Doronicum cordatum*
Leopard's bane

Doronicum pardalianches is a spreading, clump-forming perennial to 3 ft (1 m) tall and wide. The oval basal leaves, to 5 in (12 cm) long, have heart-shaped bases. Bright yellow daisy-like flowers are borne on slender, branching stems from late spring to mid-summer. *Zones 5–9.*

DOROTHEANTHUS
Ice plant, Livingstone daisy

A genus of about 10 species of succulent annuals from South Africa, these mat-forming plants bear masses of daisy-like flowers in bright shades of red, pink, white or bicolored with dark centers in

Doronicum columnae 'Miss Mason'

summer. They are ideal for borders and massed displays.

Cultivation
Marginally frost hardy, they like well-drained soil in a sunny position. Dead-head to prolong flowering. In frost-prone areas plant out after the likelihood of frost has passed. Propagate from seed.

Dorotheanthus bellidiformis
Ice plant, Livingstone daisy, Bokbaai vygie
This small succulent annual has daisy-like flowerheads in dazzling shades of yellow, white, red or pink in summer sun; flowers close in dull weather. It grows to 6 in (15 cm) tall and spreads to 12 in (30 cm) and has fleshy light green leaves to 3 in (7 cm) long with glistening surface cells. *Zones 9–11.*

DORYANTHES
The 2 species of *Doryanthes* are large evergreen perennials indigenous to the east coast of Australia. Somewhat resembling agaves in growth habit, they have loose rosettes of sword-shaped leaves and bear large red flowers with spreading petals, at the end of very tall stalks. Although requiring up to 10 years to bloom, they are popular in warm-climate public gardens.

Cultivation
Frost tender, they do best in full sun or part-shade in warm, frost-free conditions in light, humus-rich, well-drained soil. Water well during the growing season. Propagate from seed or by division.

Doryanthes excelsa
Gymea lily
The larger and more common of the 2 species, *Doryanthes excelsa* is one of the largest lilies in the world. The large rounded head of deep red, torch-like flowers is borne terminally on a stem that can reach 20 ft (6 m) tall, arising from a rosette of sword-shaped leaves that can spread to about 8 ft (2.4 m) wide. It makes a spectacular feature plant for the large garden. *Zones 9–11.*

Doryanthes excelsa

Dorotheanthus bellidiformis

Doryanthes palmeri

This species forms a dense rosette of lance-shaped, bright green leaves up to 10 ft (3 m) long. The flower stalk, up to 18 ft (5 m) tall, carries numerous scarlet, funnel-shaped flowers with white throats arranged along the upper part of the stalk and appear in spring. *Zones 9–11.*

DRYAS

Mountain avens

A genus of 3 species from alpine and Arctic regions of the northern hemisphere, *Dryas* species make dense mats of evergreen foliage somewhat like tiny oak leaves; these often turn dark bronze in winter. Although the foliage and stems hug the ground, the showy flowers and seed heads sit up well above them.

Cultivation

Completely cold tolerant they may be less than satisfactory in warm climates. They make attractive rock garden or ground cover plants and are also useful between paving slabs. Grow in full sun or part-shade in a well-drained, humus-rich soil. Propagate from seed or cuttings.

Dryas octopetala
Mountain avens

This lovely alpine plant can make evergreen mats up to 4 in (10 cm) tall in flower with a spread exceeding 3 ft (1 m). The pure white flowers, 1½ in (4 cm) across and with a boss of golden stamens in the center, are produced in late spring and early summer and followed by equally ornamental fluffy silver seed heads. *Zones 2–9.*

Dryas octopetala

Doryanthes palmeri

E

Echinops ritro

Echinacea purpurea

ECHINACEA
Coneflower

The 9 coneflower species, all native to the USA, share their common name with their cousins the rudbeckias. They are clump-forming plants with thick edible roots. The daisy-like flowerheads are usually mauve-pink or purple, with darker and paler garden forms available. The dried root and rhizome of *Echinacea angustifolia* and *E. purpurea* are used in herbal medicine and allegedly increase the body's resistance to infection.

Cultivation

Very frost hardy, they like full sun and fertile soil. Divide them only to increase stock, otherwise leave them alone and mulch each spring. Deadhead regularly. Propagate by division or from root cuttings from winter to early spring.

Echinacea purpurea
syn. *Rudbeckia purpurea*
Purple coneflower

This showy, summer-flowering perennial has dark green, lance-shaped leaves and large, daisy-like, rosy purple flowers with high, orange-brown central cones. The flowerheads are borne singly on strong stems. Of upright habit, it grows

to 4 ft (1.2 m) tall and spreads about 18 in (45 cm). 'Robert Bloom' has dark pink flowers with orange-brown centers; 'White Swan' has large, pure white flowers with orange-brown centers. *Zones 3–10.*

ECHINOPS
Globe thistle

This genus, related to thistles, contains some 120 species of erect perennials, biennials and annuals, found in Europe, Asia and tropical Africa. The cultivated species make bold additions to mixed or herbaceous borders and many are used in dried flower arrangements. The foliage is usually gray-green and thistle-like. The ball-shaped flowerheads can be blue, blue-gray or white, and up to 2 in (5 cm) in diameter. Most cultivated species grow to about 4 ft (1.2 m).

Cultivation

They are usually fully frost hardy and heat tolerant, requiring a sunny aspect with a well-drained soil of any quality. Cut them to the ground in fall (autumn) or early winter. Propagate by division or from seed.

Echinops ritro

This perennial is a useful plant for the herbaceous border, and its globe-like, spiky flowers can be cut and dried for winter decoration. It has large, deeply cut, prickly leaves with downy under-

Echium plantagineum

Echium vulgare

sides, silvery white stems and round, thistle-like, purplish blue flowerheads in summer. Of upright habit, it grows 30 in (75 cm) tall and wide. *Zones 5–10.*

ECHIUM

Indigenous to the Mediterranean, Canary Islands, western Europe and Madeira, the 40 or so species of annuals, perennials and shrubs in this genus have spectacular bright blue, purple or pink flowers in late spring and summer. The hairy leaves form rosettes at the bases of the flowering stems. They look best in mixed borders; ingestion of the plants can cause stomach upsets.

Cultivation

Very frost hardy to frost tender, they require a dry climate, full sun and a light to medium, well-drained soil. Prune gently after flowering. Propagate from seed or cuttings in spring or summer. In mild climates they self-seed readily.

Echium plantagineum
syn. *Echium lycopsis*

This annual or biennial to 24 in (60 cm) and native to warm, dry areas of Europe, produces a basal rosette of bristly leaves up to 6 in (15 cm) long. The flower stems produced in late spring and summer form a panicle of rich blue-purple, occasionally red flowers. This is an attractive bedding plant but it tends to self-seed in dry climates; in southern Australia it has become a notorious weed known as Paterson's curse. *Zones 9–10.*

Echium vulgare
Viper's bugloss

This spectacular European biennial to 3 ft (1 m) tall has erect leafy stems. The funnel-shaped flowers, borne in spikes or panicles, are usually a rich violet, although white and pink forms exist. A dwarf form is available with white, blue, pink or purple flowers. *Zones 7–10.*

EPILOBIUM
syn. *Chamaenerion*
Willow herb

This is a large genus of about 200 species of annuals, biennials, perennials and subshrubs in the evening primrose family, widely distributed throughout the temperate and cold zones of both hemispheres. Most species are invasive, but some are valued for their pretty deep pink or white flowers, which are produced over a long period from summer to fall (autumn).

Cultivation

Plant in sun or shade in moist, well-drained soil. They are mostly quite frost hardy. Remove spent flowers to prevent seeding. Propagate from seed in spring or fall (autumn), or from cuttings.

Epilobium angustifolium
syn. *Chamaenerion angustifolium*
Fireweed, Rose Bay willow herb

This is a tall, vigorous perennial to 5 ft (1.5 m) found throughout the northern and mountainous parts of Eurasia and North America, most widespread in areas that have been recently burned or logged. Drifts of rose-pink flowering spikes are produced in late summer. It will spread indefinitely unless confined by pruning or containing the root system and self-seeds freely. *Zones 2–9.*

Epilobium canum subsp. canum
syn. *Zauschneria californica*
Californian fuchsia

The common name refers both to the species' Californian origin and to its flowers, which are indeed like the related fuchsias. These are bright red, appearing in terminal spikes on erect, slender stems in late summer and early fall (autumn). This evergreen shrub is highly variable and grows 12–24 in (30–60 cm) tall and 3–6 ft (1–1.8 m) wide. It needs only occasional water and is hardy to around 15°F (–9°C). *Zones 8–10.*

EPIMEDIUM
Barrenwort

This genus of about 40 species comes mainly from temperate Asia with a few species extending to the Mediterranean. A useful low-growing perennial for shady situations, the barrenworts produce delightful sprays of delicate, often spurred flowers in late spring or early summer just above the foliage. Slowly spreading to form a broad mound or mat, they serve well as ground covers or in rockeries.

Cultivation

Frost hardy, most tolerate dry conditions, especially in the shade. All prefer woodland conditions and well-drained soil. Propagate from ripe seed or by division in fall (autumn).

Epilobium canum subsp. canum

Epilobium angustifolium

Epimedium × versicolor

This hybrid of *Epimedium grandiflorum* and *E. pinnatum* is a carpeting perennial to 12 in (30 cm) high and wide. The green, heart-shaped leaves are tinted reddish when young. Clusters of pendent pink and yellow flowers with red spurs are produced in spring. 'Sulphureum' has sulfur-yellow flowers and reddish bronze-tinted young foliage. As summer advances it turns green, then russet again in fall (autumn). *Zones 5–9.*

ERANTHIS
Winter aconite

From Europe and temperate Asia, these 7 species of clump-forming perennials have the ability to naturalize under deciduous trees. They flower in late winter and early spring. The short-stemmed, yellow, buttercup-like flowers are surrounded by a ruff of green leaves.

Cultivation

Very frost hardy, they like full sun or part-shade. Slightly damp conditions during the summer dormancy and an alkaline, well-drained soil are conducive to good growth and plentiful flowers. Propagate from seed or by division.

Eranthis hyemalis

Native to Europe, this ground-hugging perennial with knobbly tubers grows to a height of 3 in (8 cm). The yellow, cup-shaped flowers are borne above a ruff of lobed leaves. *Zones 5–9.*

EREMURUS
Foxtail lily, desert candle

There are 50 or so species in this Asian genus. Their dramatic flower spikes, each of which can contain hundreds of flowers in pale shades of white, yellow or pink, rise to well over head height. Foliage is luxuriant but low so the flower stems rise almost naked, which makes them all the more imposing.

Cultivation

In the wild these cool- to cold-climate plants are protected from the winter cold by a thick blanket of snow; in milder climates they need a winter mulch to ensure the soil does not freeze. They also need sun and a well-drained soil. Propagate from fresh seed or by division.

Eranthis hyemalis

Epimedium × versicolor 'Sulphureum'

Erigeron 'Charity'

Eremurus × *isabellinus,* Shelford Hybrid

Eremurus × *isabellinus,* **Shelford Hybrids**

These frost-hardy perennials have lofty spikes of close-packed flowers. They produce rosettes of strap-like leaves and in mid-summer each crown yields spikes of blooms with strong stems and hundreds of shallow cup-shaped flowers in a wide range of colors including white, pink, salmon, yellow, apricot and coppery tones. 'Shelford Desert Candle' is a pure white form. They grow to about 4 ft (1.2 m) in height with a spread of 24 in (60 cm). *Zones 5–9.*

ERIGERON
Fleabane

This large genus of about 200 species of annuals, biennials and perennials, some evergreen, occurs throughout the world's temperate regions. Some were believed to repel fleas. The mainly erect stems are capped by masses of pink, white or blue, daisy-like flowers and suit borders or rock gardens. They flower between late spring and mid-summer.

Erigeron foliosus

Cultivation

Frost hardy, they prefer a sunny position sheltered from strong winds and moderately fertile, well-drained soil. Do not allow to dry out during the growing season. Cut back immediately after flowering. Some erigerons can become invasive. Propagate from seed or by division in spring.

Erigeron 'Charity'

This perennial cultivar produces a profusion of pale lilac-pink flowers with yellowy green centers over a long period in summer. Clump forming, it grows to a height and spread of about 24 in (60 cm) and may require support. *Zones 5–9.*

Erigeron foliosus

This clump-forming species grows to about 8 in (20 cm) in flower and comes

Erodium pelargoniiflorum

Erigeron karvinskianus

from western North America. Its leaves are narrow-oblong and reduce in size up the stem. The flowers are usually blue with a yellow center. *Zones 5–9.*

Erigeron karvinskianus
syn. *Erigeron mucronatus*
Mexican daisy, Santa Barbara daisy, fleabane daisy
This scrambling or mound-forming perennial from Mexico and Central America makes an informal ground cover and in mild climates will bloom profusely throughout the year. The small flowers open white, fading to various shades of pink and wine red. It grows to about 15 in (38 cm) tall with an indefinite spread, and has lax stems and narrow, often lobed, hairy leaves. It can be quite invasive in mild climates, and is considered a weed in New Zealand. *Zones 7–11.*

ERODIUM
Heronsbill
This is a cosmopolitan genus of about 60 species of annuals and perennials in the geranium family. The evergreen leaves are often finely divided, and the 5-petalled flowers are quite like those of the true geranium though generally smaller. They are mostly low-growing, clumping plants and are best suited for ground cover, rock gardens or for cracks in a stone wall.

Cultivation
Frost hardy, they prefer full sun, doing well in warm, dry regions. Soil must be well drained and not too fertile. Propagate from cuttings or from seed.

Erodium pelargoniiflorum
Native to Turkey, this mound-forming, tufted perennial is ideal for rock gardens or alpine houses, reaching a height of about 12 in (30 cm). It has prostrate, woody stems and heart-shaped, lightly lobed, green leaves. Umbels of white, purple-veined flowers are produced from late spring to fall (autumn). It is prone to aphid infestation. *Zones 6–9.*

ERYNGIUM
Sea holly
Mostly native to South America and Europe, these 230 species of biennials and perennials are members of the same family as the carrot, and have spiny collared flowerheads that usually have a bluish metallic sheen. They flower over a long period in summer and may be cut before they fully open, and dried for winter decoration. The spiny margins of the strongly colored, thistle-like bracts that surround the central flower give rise to the common name 'holly'.

Cultivation
Mostly frost hardy, they need sun, good drainage and sandy soil. Propagate

species from fresh seed; selected forms by root cuttings in winter or by division in spring.

Eryngium bourgatii

This striking herbaceous perennial from the eastern Mediterranean has basal leaves that are leathery, gray-green and silver veined. Its flower spikes rise up to 30 in (75 cm) tall and support numerous blue or gray-green flowers surrounded by silvery spiny bracts. 'Othello' is a compact form that produces shorter flowers on strong, thick stems. *Zones 5–9.*

Eryngium giganteum

Eryngium bourgatii

Eryngium giganteum
Miss Willmott's ghost

This short-lived, clump-forming perennial grows to a height of about 3–4 ft (1–1.2 m) and spreads about 30 in (75 cm). The leaves are heart-shaped and mid-green, and it bears large, rounded, blue or pale green thistle heads surrounded by silvery bracts. It dies after its late summer flowering but if conditions are good its seeds will thrive. *Zones 6–9.*

ERYSIMUM
syn. *Cheiranthus*
Wallflower

Some of the 80 species of annuals and perennials in this genus are suitable for rock gardens, such as 'Orange Flame'; others fit nicely into the border. Short-lived species are best grown as biennials. Some are fine winter–spring-flowering plants, while some flower all winter or all year in very mild regions. The older types are sweetly scented, while the newer cultivars have no fragrance but bloom well over a long season.

Cultivation

Mostly frost hardy, they like a well-drained, fertile soil in an open, sunny position. Cut back perennials after flowering so only a few leaves remain on each stem. Propagate from seed in spring or cuttings in summer.

Erysimum × allionii
syn. *Cheiranthus × allionii*
Siberian wallflower

This slow-growing but short-lived hybrid is a bushy evergreen suitable for rock gardens, banks and borders. It has toothed, mid-green leaves and bears bright yellow or orange flowers in spring, putting on a dazzling display for a long period. It reaches a height and spread of 12–18 in (30–45 cm). *Zones 3–10.*

Erysimum bicolor

syn. *Cheiranthus mutabilis*
This shrub from the Canary Islands and Madeira grows to 3 ft (1 m) high and has narrow, lance-shaped leaves. In spring the flowers open pale yellow and age to a purplish color. It is marginally frost hardy. *Zones 9–11*.

Erysimum 'Golden Bedder'

syn. *Cheiranthus* 'Golden Bedder'
This is one of the color forms of the Bedder Series, bred for compact shape and available in shades from cream through yellow to orange and red. They can flower for months, often starting in winter in mild climates. *Zones 8–10*.

ESCHSCHOLZIA
California poppy

This genus from western North America was named by botanist/poet Adalbert von Chamisso (1781–1838) in honor of his friend, Johan Friedrich Eschscholz. It is a genus of 8 to 10 annuals and perennials with deeply dissected leaves. They bear yellow to orange poppy-like flowers that close up in dull weather, and capsular fruits.

Cultivation

Species thrive in warm, dry climates but will tolerate quite severe frosts. They do not like transplanting so should be sown directly where they are to grow. Grow in poor, well-drained soil. Propagate from seed sown in spring.

Eschscholzia caespitosa

This fast-growing, slender, erect annual bears cup-shaped, solitary yellow flowers 1 in (25 mm) wide in summer and early fall (autumn). It has bluish green leaves and reaches a height of 6 in (15 cm). *Zones 7–10*.

Erysimum × allionii

Eschscholzia caespitosa

Erysimum 'Golden Bedder'

Erysimum bicolor

Eschscholzia californica

Etlingera elatior

ETLINGERA

This is a genus of about 57 species of tall, rhizomatous perennials with cane-like stems and linear or lance-shaped leaves, found from Sri Lanka to New Guinea. Small flowers surrounded by waxy, colorful bracts are borne in torch-like clusters at the tops of leafless stems arising from the rhizome.

Cultivation

Frost tender, these tropical plants need a moist, humus-rich soil in full sun or part-shade with a minimum temperature of about 64°F (18°C). Indoors they need warmth, high humidity and lots of water during the summer. Propagate from seed or by division.

Etlingera elatior

syns *Nicolaia elatior, Phaeomeria speciosa*
Torch ginger

This is a magnificent plant from Indonesia for the tropical garden only. The oblong leaves to 3 ft (1 m) long are borne on 20 ft (6 m), bamboo-like leaf stalks. In spring a cluster of small, white-to gold-rimmed, scarlet flowers is embedded in a waxy, pyramid-like cone of pink-edged, bright red bracts, sometimes opening to 10 in (25 cm) across. The inflorescence is borne on a 5 ft (1.5 m) leafless stem. *Zones 11–12.*

EUCOMIS
Pineapple lily

The 15 species of pineapple lily, all deciduous and native to southern Africa, bear spikes of small, star-shaped flowers with crowning tufts of leaves resembling a pineapple. They grow from enlarged bulbs, and the basal rosette of glossy foliage is rather bulky—these are substantial border plants in their own right. The Xhosa people used the bulbs, boiled into a poultice, as a cure for rheumatism.

Eschscholzia californica

This short-lived perennial, the official floral emblem of California, has cup-shaped flowers that open out from gray-green feathery foliage into vivid shades of orange, though cultivated strains have extended the color range to bronze, yellow, cream, scarlet, mauve and rose. It flowers in spring with intermittent blooms in summer and fall (autumn); the flowers close on cloudy days. It grows to 12 in (30 cm) high. *Zones 6–11.*

Eucomis bicolor

Cultivation

Marginally frost hardy, they prefer warm-temperate climates in full sun in moist, well-drained soil; they dislike water during the dormant winter months. Where frost may reach the bulbs, winter indoors in pots. Propagate from seed or by division.

Eucomis bicolor

This summer-flowering bulb bears spikes of green or greenish white flowers with purple-margined petals; these are topped by a cluster of leaf-like bracts. It grows to 18–24 in (45–60 cm) tall and 24 in (60 cm) wide. *Zones 8–10.*

EUPATORIUM

This genus contains about 40 species of perennials and subshrubs, mainly from the Americas but a few from Asia and Europe. Only a few are cultivated for their large terminal panicles of small flowerheads, which come in white or shades of purple, mauve or pink.

Cultivation

Mostly quite frost hardy, they need full sun or part-shade and moist but well-drained soil. Prune lightly in spring or after flowering. Propagate from seed in spring, from cuttings in summer or by division in early spring or fall (autumn).

Eupatorium megalophyllum

syn. *Bartlettina megalophylla*

Mist flower

A native of Mexico, this species grows to a height of 5 ft (1.5 m) and spreads—

Eupatorium megalophyllum

branching at the ground—to 6 ft (1.8 m). In spring it bears dramatic, wide heads of lilac flowers. The very large leaves, up to 10 in (25 cm) long and 8 in (20 cm) wide, are dark green and velvety on the upper surface and paler on the underside. Immature stems are covered in fine purple hairs. It will not survive even the mildest of frosts. *Zones 10–11.*

EUPHORBIA

Milkweed, spurge

This genus has close to 2,000 species, among them annuals, herbaceous perennials, shrubs and numerous succulent species. The flowers of all species are almost identical in structure. They consist of only a stigma and a stamen, always green, and usually carried in small clusters. Many species have showy bracts. Mainly tropical and subtropical, the genus also includes many temperate species. All euphorbias have milky sap which is corrosive to sensitive areas of the skin.

Cultivation

They like sun or part-shade in moist, well-drained soil. Cold tolerance varies depending on the species; the more highly succulent species are generally frost tender. Propagate from cuttings in spring or summer, allowing succulent species to dry and callus before placing in barely damp sand, by division or from seed.

Euphorbia characias

This is a sun-loving, frost-hardy sub-shrub usually up to 3 ft (1 m) or so. It likes a sunny, well-drained site and where happy, will self-seed. It has deep brown nectaries giving a brown spot in the center of each yellow-green bract. *Euphorbia characias* subsp. *wulfenii* (syn.

E. wulfenii) has blue-green leaves densely clothing the erect stems, which in spring are topped by dome-like chartreuse flowerheads. *Zones 8–10.*

Euphorbia griffithii

This perennial from the eastern Himalayas, which grows to a height of 3 ft (1 m), produces small, yellow flowers surrounded by brilliant orange bracts in summer. The lanceolate, green leaves have prominent pinkish midribs and turn red and yellow in fall (autumn). 'Fireglow' produces orange-red floral bracts in early summer. *Zones 6–9.*

Euphorbia marginata
Snow on the mountain, ghostweed

Native to central areas of North America, this bushy annual makes an excellent foil for brighter flowers. It has pointed oval, bright green leaves, sharply margined with white, and broad, petal-like white bracts surrounding small flowers in summer. It is fairly fast growing to about 24 in (60 cm) tall with a spread of about 12 in (30 cm), and will endure cold conditions. *Zones 4–10.*

Euphorbia characias

Euphorbia griffithii 'Fireglow'

Euphorbia myrsinites

This trailing species is only 6–8 in (15–20 cm) tall but spreads to over 24 in (60 cm) wide. Blue-green, oval leaves spiral around the stems, each stem ending in a rounded flowerhead of soft chartreuse in spring. It is excellent in a rock garden or at the top of a low wall. It ranges in the wild from southern Europe to central Asia. It self-seeds readily and will tolerate frost, poor soil, heat and dry conditions. *Zones 5–10*.

Euphorbia polychroma

syn. *Euphorbia epithymoides*

Cushion spurge

Native to central and southern Europe, this frost-hardy, clump-forming peren-nial is grown for its heads of bright chrome-yellow flowers produced from spring to summer. It has softly hairy, deep green leaves and a rounded, bushy habit, reaching a height and spread of about 18 in (45 cm). 'Major' has yellow-ish green flowers in loose clusters. *Zones 6–9*.

EUSTOMA

syn. *Lisianthus*

Belonging to the gentian family, this genus consists of 3 species of annuals, biennials and perennials. Japanese plant breeders extended the pastel color range to white, pale blue and pink as well as the original violet, and also developed double-flowered strains. Any unopened buds on the spray develop beautifully in water, so these give pleasure for an extended period.

Cultivation

Usually regarded as frost tender, they like in any warm-temperate climate. Give them sun, perfect drainage and fertile soil; they rarely perform well after their first year. Propagate from seed in spring or from cuttings in late spring or summer.

Euphorbia myrsinites

Euphorbia marginata

Euphorbia polychroma

Eustoma grandiflorum

Eustoma grandiflorum
syn. *Lisianthus russellianus*
Prairie gentian, Texas bluebell, lisianthus
Native to America's Midwest from
Nebraska to Texas, this biennial's
flowers last up to 3 weeks in water after
cutting. It has gray-green leaves and 2 in
(5 cm) wide, flared, tulip-like flowers in
colors of rich purple, pink, blue or white.
Of an upright habit, the plant is slow
growing to a height of 24 in (60 cm) and
spread of 12 in (30 cm). *Zones 9–11.*

EXACUM
This genus also belongs to the gentian
family; it consists of about 25 species of
annuals, biennials or perennials, with
mostly yellow, white, blue or purple
flowers that are often broadly cup-shaped
or flat. Only one species, *Exacum affine*,
has become widely cultivated, a miniature from the hot dry island of Socotra
just off the horn of Africa at the mouth
of the Red Sea; it is grown as an indoor
plant, and has a neat shrub-like growth
habit and long succession of flowers.

Cultivation
They can only be grown outdoors in
warm, frost-free climates, where they do
best in a sunny position in rich, moist

Exacum affine

but well-drained soil. Indoors they like
diffused sun and a night temperature not
below 50°F (10°C). Propagate from seed
in early spring.

Exacum affine
Persian violet, German violet
This showy miniature has shiny, oval
leaves and bears a profusion of small,
5-petalled, saucer-shaped, usually purple-
blue flowers with yellow stamens
throughout summer. A biennial usually
treated as an annual, it grows to a height
and spread of 8–12 in (20–30 cm). 'Blue
Midget' grows to only half as big and
has lavender-blue flowers, while 'White
Midget' has white flowers. *Zones 10–12.*

F, G

Felicia amelloides

FELICIA
Blue daisy

This genus, which ranges from southern Africa to Arabia, consists of 80 species of annuals, perennials and evergreen subshrubs. They are sprawling plants with aromatic foliage; in mild climates they flower on and off almost all year. The daisy-like, usually blue flowerheads are borne in masses.

Cultivation

These fully frost hardy to frost tender plants need full sun and well-drained, humus-rich, gravelly soil; they do not like wet conditions. Frost-tender perennial species need protection in winter with open-ended cloches. Propagate from cuttings taken in late summer or fall (autumn) or from seed in spring.

Felicia amelloides
Blue marguerite

This bushy, evergreen subshrub has a spreading habit, growing to 24 in (60 cm) in height and twice as wide. It has roundish, bright green leaves and sky blue flowerheads with bright yellow centers borne on long stalks from late spring to fall (autumn). Frost tender, it is fast growing in temperate climates and is suitable for seaside gardens. It is often grown as an annual in cool areas. 'Santa Anita' has extra large blue flowers and 'Alba' is a white form. *Zones 9–11.*

Filipendula vulgaris

FILIPENDULA

This is a genus of 10 species of herbaceous perennials from northern temperate regions. All except *Filipendula vulgaris* occur naturally in moist waterside habitats. They have alternate pinnate leaves and erect stems bearing large panicle-like clusters of tiny, 5-petalled flowers with fluffy stamens. They do well at the back of large perennial borders and in waterside positions.

Cultivation

Fully frost-hardy, they like full sun or part-shade in any moisture-retentive but well-drained soil. Propagate from seed or by division in spring or fall (autumn). Check for powdery mildew.

Filipendula vulgaris
syn. *Filipendula hexapetala*
Dropwort

From Europe and Asia, this species reaches about 24–36 in (60–90 cm) high and has fleshy swollen roots. It has attractive, deeply cut, fern-like foliage, and showy, crowded heads of tiny white flowers; some garden varieties are pink. This species will tolerate fairly dry conditions and must have good drainage. *Zones 3–9.*

Fragaria 'Pink Panda'

Francoa sonchifolia

FRAGARIA
Strawberry

The 12 or so species in this genus from northern temperate zones and Chile are low-growing, creeping or tufted perennials. The palmate leaves have 3 toothed leaflets, and the white or pink, 5-petalled flowers appear in cymes. The strawberry is a false fruit consisting of tiny pips on a fleshy receptacle. Strawberry plants can produce fruit for 6 months, or all year round in a warm climate.

Cultivation

Grow these frost-hardy plants in beds or containers lined with straw, in free-draining, acidic soil. They need full sun or light shade and protection from wind. Propagate from seed or by runners and replant with fresh stock every few years. Botrytis can be a problem in high rainfall areas.

Fragaria 'Pink Panda'

This spreading, ground cover perennial to 6 in (15 cm) high with an indefinite spread is grown for its pretty bright pink flowers to 1 in (2.5 cm) across, which appear from late spring to fall (autumn). It rarely bears fruit. *Zones 4–10.*

FRANCOA
Maiden's wreath, bridal wreath

The 5 species of evergreen perennials that make up this genus are from Chile.

The plants form a basal rosette of wavy, lobed leaves, each with a large terminal lobe. The 5-petalled bell-shaped flowers in white, pink or red with darker markings at the base are borne in terminal, spike-like racemes in summer and early fall (autumn).

Cultivation

They are mostly frost hardy, but in very cold climates plants should be grown in a greenhouse. Grow outdoors in humus-rich, moist but well-drained soil in a sheltered sunny or part-shaded position. Water sparingly in winter. Propagate from seed or by division in spring.

Francoa sonchifolia

This species to 3 ft (1 m) tall has oblong to oval, crinkled dark green basal leaves. The pale pink flowers, spotted deep pink within, appear on erect, sparsely branched stems from summer to early fall (autumn). *Zones 7–10.*

GAILLARDIA
Blanket flower

This genus of around 30 species of annuals, perennials and biennials is native to the USA, with 2 from South America. The perennials are better suited to cool-temperate climates. All bloom for a long season from summer until the first frosts. The common name arose because the colors of the flowers resemble the bright yellows, oranges and reds of the blankets traditionally worn by Native Americans.

Cultivation
These hardy garden flowers tolerate extreme heat, cold, dryness, strong winds and poor soils. Plant in full sun in well-drained soil and stake if necessary. Propagate from seed in spring or early summer. Perennials may be divided in spring.

Gaillardia × grandiflora
These hybrids of *Gaillardia aristata* and *G. pulchella* are the most commonly grown of the blanket flowers. The plants form mounds up to 3 ft (1 m) high and wide and have narrow, slightly lobed hairy leaves. The flowerheads, 3–4 in (8–10 cm) in diameter, come in red, yellow, orange and burgundy. They are propagated by division or from cuttings to provide named cultivars. 'Kobold' ('Goblin') has compact growth to 12 in (30 cm) high and rich red flowers with yellow tips. *Zones 5–10.*

GAURA
Related to the evening primrose *(Oenothera)*, this genus of about 20 species of annuals, biennials, perennials

and subshrubs from North America are apt to be weedy, despite their showy flowers and the genus name that translates as 'gorgeous'. They have simple, narrow leaves and either racemes or panicles of flat, star-shaped, pink or white flowers.

Cultivation
They prefer full sun and light, well-drained soil. Cut ruthlessly to the ground when flowering has finished. Propagate from seed in fall (autumn) or spring, or from cuttings in summer.

Gaura lindheimeri
Native to the USA–Mexico border region, this clump-forming, long-flowering perennial is useful for backgrounds and mixed flower borders. It has loosely branched stems covered with tiny hairs, and from spring to fall (autumn) produces long sprays of beautiful flowers which open white from pink buds. It grows to 4 ft (1.2 m) in height with a spread of 3 ft (1 m). *Zones 5–10.*

GAZANIA
This African genus, named in honor of the medieval scholar Theodore of Gaza (1398–1478), consists of about 16

Gaillardia × grandiflora 'Kobold'

Gaura lindheimeri

Gazania rigens var. leucolaena

Gazania, Sunshine Hybrid

species of low-growing annuals and perennials. The leaves are long and narrow, often dark green on top and white- or silver gray-felted beneath or in some species silvery haired on both sides. The flowerheads, borne singly on short stalks, range from cream to yellow, gold, pink, red, buff, brown and intermediate shades, usually with contrasting bands or spots at the petal bases. They appear from early spring until summer. They are useful for bedding, rock gardens, pots and tubs and for binding soil on slopes.

Cultivation
Grow in full sun in sandy, fairly dry, well-drained soil. Mulch with compost and water during dry periods. Propagate by division or from cuttings in fall (autumn), or from seed in late winter to early spring.

Gazania rigens
This perennial grows to a height of 12 in (30 cm) with a similar spread. It is a mat-forming plant with crowded rosettes of mostly unlobed leaves that are green above and whitish beneath, and orange flowerheads with a black eye spot at petal bases. The leaves of *Gazania rigens* var. *leucolaena* are silvery green on both sides and the flowers are yellow; *G. r.*

var. *uniflora* has flowers that are smaller and short stalked. *Zones 9–11.*

Gazania, Sunshine Hybrids
These mat-forming perennials may be grown as annuals. The height and spread is around 8 in (20 cm) and solitary flowers, borne in summer, range in color with the disc-florets usually ringed in a darker color. *Zones 9–11.*

GENTIANA
Gentian
Occurring worldwide, mostly in alpine meadows and occasionally in woodlands, this is a genus of around 400 species of annuals, biennials and perennials; many commonly grown forms may be hybrids. Intense deep blues and sky blues are the usual flower colors, but whites, creams, yellows and even red are also found. The mostly trumpet-shaped flowers are borne from spring to fall (autumn).

Cultivation
They prefer cooler regions and well-drained, but moisture-retentive soil rich in humus. Some grow naturally in limestone soil. Plant in either sun or semi-shade. Propagate by division in spring or from fresh seed in fall. Divide fall-flowering species every 3 years in early spring, planting out in fresh soil.

Gentiana sino-ornata 'Alba'

Gentiana septemfida

Geranium 'Johnson's Blue'

Gentiana septemfida
Crested gentian

Native to mountains of western and
central Asia, this sun-loving perennial
grows about 8 in (20 cm) tall and has
paired oval leaves. The rich blue flowers
with white throats are borne in terminal
clusters of up to 8 in summer. *Zones 3–9.*

Gentiana sino-ornata

This evergreen perennial from western
China flowers in fall (autumn), bearing
deep blue trumpet flowers that are paler
at the base and banded purplish blue. It
has a prostrate, spreading habit, reaching 2 in (5 cm) tall and 12 in (30 cm)
wide. 'Alba' has white flowers. *Zones 6–9.*

GERANIUM
Cranesbill

Over 300 species of annual, biennial and
perennial geraniums, some evergreen,
grow all over the world mainly in cool-
temperate regions. They make small,
showy clumps with pink to blue or
purple and white, 5-petalled flowers.
The true geraniums or cranesbills, so-
called for the shape of their small, dry
fruitlets, are often confused with species
of the genus *Pelargonium*, also commonly
known as 'geraniums'. Symmetrical
flowers are their chief point of distinc-
tion from pelargoniums, which produce
irregularly shaped or marked flowers.
They are useful for rock gardens,
ground covers and borders. Compact
species and hybrids are also good for
containers.

Cultivation

Mostly quite frost hardy, they prefer a
sunny situation and damp, well-drained
soil. Transplant during winter. Propagate from cuttings in summer or seed in
spring, or by division in fall (autumn).

Geranium 'Johnson's Blue'

This rhizomatous perennial may be
merely a form of *Geranium himalayense*. It
has deeply divided leaves and bears cup-

Geranium maderense

Geranium phaeum

shaped lavender-blue flowers with pale centers throughout summer. It has a spreading habit, reaching 18 in (45 cm) tall and 30 in (75 cm) wide. *Zones 5–9.*

Geranium macrorrhizum

The sticky, deeply lobed leaves of this clump-forming perennial are aromatic, often turning red or bronze in fall (autumn). The flowers appear on 12 in (30 cm) stems above the foliage in spring and early summer. Flower color varies from pink or purplish to pure white. It makes an excellent ground cover for a dry, shady site. 'Album' has white petals with reddish calyces; 'Ingwersen's Variety' has pale pink flowers and smoother glossy leaves. 'Spessart' is an attractive German cultivar. *Zones 4–9.*

Geranium maderense

Native to Madeira, this short-lived, evergreen bushy perennial to 5 ft (1.5 m) tall has huge leaves for a geranium, often 12 in (30 cm) or more across, divided in a striking snowflake pattern and turning reddish in fall (autumn). Shallowly cup-shaped pinkish magenta flowers with darker centers are borne in tall panicles from late winter to late summer. Old leaves should not be

Geranium macrorrhizum 'Ingwersen's Variety'

removed too soon, as the plant props itself on them to resist wind-loosening. *Zones 9–10.*

Geranium phaeum
Mourning widow, dusky cranesbill

From Europe and western Russia, this clump-forming perennial to 30 in (75 cm) high and 18 in (45 cm) wide has soft green, densely lobed leaves. Its flowers are a deep, brownish purple with a paler center ring, borne in late spring or early summer. 'Lily Lovell' has large white flowers; *Geranium phaeum* var. *lividum* has pale pink or lilac flowers; 'Variegatum' has leaves with yellow margins and pink splotches. *Zones 5–10.*

Geranium renardii

This clump-forming perennial from the Caucasus develops into a neat mound to 12 in (30 cm) high and wide. It has lobed, circular, finely wrinkled leaves with a velvety underside. The saucer-shaped white flowers with bold purple veins are borne in early summer. *Zones 6–9*.

Geranium sanguineum
Bloody cranesbill

This European species is a low-growing perennial of around 8 in (20 cm) tall spreading by rhizomes. The dark green leaves are deeply cut into toothed lobes. Abundant cup-shaped bright magenta flowers with notched petals are produced during summer. 'Vision' is a

Geranium sylvaticum 'Album'

Geranium renardii

compact form with deep pink flowers. *Zones 5–9*.

Geranium sylvaticum
Wood cranesbill

Another well-known European species, this upright, clump-forming perennial to 30 in (75 cm) tall has deeply divided basal leaves from which arise branching stems carrying bluish purple, cup-shaped flowers with white centers from late spring to summer. 'Album' has white flowers; 'Mayflower' has rich violet-blue flowers with white centers. *Zones 4–9*.

GERBERA

This genus of around 40 perennial species is from Africa, Madagascar and Asia. The showy flowerheads, in almost every color except blue and purple, are carried on bare stems 18 in (45 cm) long. They are ideal rockery plants in frost-free climates.

Cultivation

They need full sun to part-shade in hot areas and fertile, composted, well-drained soil. Water well during summer. In the greenhouse, they require good light and regular feeding during the growing season. Propagate from seed in fall (autumn) or early spring, from cuttings in summer or by division from late winter to early spring.

Geranium sanguineum 'Vision'

Geum chiloense 'Mrs Bradshaw'

Gerbera jamesonii cultivar

Geum chiloense 'Lady Stratheden'

Gerbera jamesonii
Barberton daisy, Transvaal daisy

This decorative daisy is an excellent cut flower. From a basal rosette of deeply lobed, lance-shaped leaves, white, pink, yellow, orange or red flowerheads, up to 3 in (8 cm) wide, are borne singly on long stems in spring and summer. Florists' gerberas derive from crosses between *Gerbera jamesonii* and the tropical African *G. viridifolia*. Some have flowerheads as much as 12 in (30 cm) across, in a wide range of colors, as well as double, for example 'Brigadoon Red', and quilled forms. *Zones 8–11.*

GEUM
Avens

This genus of 50 or so herbaceous perennials is from the temperate and colder zones of both northern and southern hemispheres. Species form basal rosettes of hairy, lobed leaves and bear masses of red, orange and yellow flowers with prominent stamens from late spring until early fall (autumn), and almost all year in frost-free areas. They suit mixed herbaceous borders and rock gardens, but may require a lot of room.

Cultivation
Frost hardy, they prefer a sunny, open position and moist, well-drained soil. Propagate from seed in fall or by division in fall or spring.

Geum chiloense
syns *Geum coccineum* of gardens, *G. quellyon*
Scarlet avens

This Chilean native reaches a height of 24 in (60 cm) with a spread of 12 in (30 cm). It forms a basal rosette of deep green, pinnate leaves to 12 in (30 cm) long. The vivid scarlet, cup-shaped flowers appear in terminal panicles in summer. 'Lady Stratheden' (syn. 'Goldball') has semi-double, golden-yellow flowers. 'Mrs Bradshaw' bears rounded semi-double scarlet flowers. *Zones 5–9.*

Gilia capitata

Glaucium flavum

GILIA

From temperate western regions of North and South America, this is a genus of about 30 species of annuals, biennials and perennials in the phlox family. The basal leaves are feathery and finely divided, and erect panicles of small, funnel- to trumpet-shaped flowers, often densely clustered, appear in spring and summer.

Cultivation

Moderately to very frost hardy, gilias prefer a climate with cool wet winters and hot summers, and well-drained soils in full sun. They are sensitive to drought and heat and wilt rapidly. They may need staking on windy sites. Propagate from seed in spring directly in the spot where they are to grow when the soil has warmed up.

Gilia capitata
Queen Anne's thimbles, blue thimble flower

Native to the west-coastal ranges of Canada, the USA and Mexico, this erect, branching annual to 24 in (60 cm) high has mid-green, fern-like leaves and tiny, soft lavender blue flowers that appear in a pincushion-like mass in summer and early fall (autumn). It is a good cut flower and useful border plant. *Zones 7–9.*

GLAUCIUM
Horned poppy, sea poppy

This is one of the most distinctive genera of poppy relatives, consisting of 25 species of annuals, biennials and perennials from temperate Asia and the Mediterranean region (with one extending to Atlantic coasts). Their characteristic feature is the up to 12 in (30 cm) long, narrow seed capsule that rapidly elongates after the petals fall from the flowers. Showy flowers terminate the leafy branches and may be yellow, red or white, usually with a darker blotch at the base of each petal.

Cultivation

Fairly frost hardy, they prefer a sunny position and sandy, well-drained soil. Propagate from seed in spring or fall (autumn).

Glaucium flavum
Yellow horned poppy

This native of western and southern Europe and northern Africa occurs naturally in coastal areas and is widely naturalized elsewhere. It is a slightly hairy short-lived perennial with a basal rosette of pinnately lobed, glaucous gray-green leaves. The golden-yellow or orange flowers, to 3 in (8 cm) across, are produced in summer. *Zones 7–10.*

GOODENIA

This genus of about 170 species of perennials or shrubs is mostly found in Australia with 3 species extending to Papua New Guinea and Indonesia. Growth habit is variable but most are dwarf evergreen perennials or sub-shrubs, some with a basal rosette of leaves and well-displayed, mostly bright yellow flowers, their 5 petals spreading like fingers. Some bear flowers in various shades of pink, mauve or blue. Only a few species are cultivated and most of these make good rock garden, ground cover or container subjects.

Cultivation

Frost tender to moderately frost hardy, they require good drainage and a sunny or part-shaded position. Prune back after flowering. Propagate from seed or cuttings.

Gunnera manicata

Goodenia macmillanii
Pinnate goodenia

This small shrub with a suckering habit may reach up to 3 ft (1 m) high. It has pinnate basal leaves to 3 in (8 cm) and small lobed leaves on the stems. The fragrant flowers, borne in spring and summer, are pink with purple streaks and about 1 in (25 mm) across. *Zones 9–11.*

GUNNERA

This is a genus of around 45 species of rhizomatous perennials from temperate regions of Africa, Australasia and South America. They range in size from small, mat-forming plants to large, clump-forming plants with some of the largest leaves of any broad-leafed plants.

Cultivation

Most enjoy moist but well-aerated soil at the edge of a pond or stream. Plant in rich soil in full sun, although they may need shelter from very hot sun and wind (which can reduce the leaves to tatters). Propagate from seed in fall (autumn) or spring, or by division in early spring. Protect from slugs and snails.

Gunnera manicata
syn. *Gunnera brasiliensis*
Giant ornamental rhubarb

Native to the high mountain swamps of Brazil and Colombia, this huge plant

Goodenia macmillanii

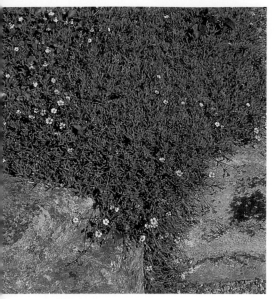

Gypsophila repens 'Rosea'

Gypsophila paniculata 'Compacta Plena'

thrives in boggy soil and is usually grown on the margins of a pond. The massive leaves quickly unfurl in spring to a width of up to 8 ft (2.4 m) on prickly stalks about 6 ft (1.8 m) high. Long spikes of greenish red flowers are borne in summer. Give the dormant crown a protective mulch of straw in winter. *Zones 7–9.*

GYPSOPHILA

Native to Europe, Asia and North Africa, there are over 100 species of these annuals and perennials, some of which are semi-evergreen. They have masses of small, dainty, white or pink flowers, often used by florists as a foil for bolder flowers or foliage. The narrow leaves are borne in opposite pairs.

Cultivation

Plant in full sun with shelter from strong winds. Fully frost hardy, they tolerate most soils but prefer deep, well-drained soil lightened with compost or peat. Cut back after flowering. Transplant when

dormant during winter. Propagate from cuttings in summer or from seed in spring or fall (autumn).

Gypsophila paniculata
Baby's breath

This short-lived perennial, mostly treated as an annual, has small, dark green leaves and sprays of tiny white spring flowers. It reaches a height and spread of 3 ft (1 m) or more. 'Bristol Fairy' has double white flowers. 'Compact Plena' has double white or soft pink flowers. *Zones 4–10.*

Gypsophila repens

This prostrate perennial has stems forming low mounds up to 8 in (20 cm) high and 18 in (45 cm) wide. It has narrow, bluish green leaves and bears panicles of star-shaped white, lilac or pale purple flowers in summer. It is an ideal plant for trailing over rocks. 'Dorothy Teacher' has abundant pale pink flowers ageing to deep pink. 'Rosea' has deep pink flowers. *Zones 4–9.*

H

Hacquetia epipactis

Hedychium coccineum

HACQUETIA
syn. *Dondia*

There is one species only in this genus: a tiny perennial from the woodlands of eastern Europe. At most it grows to 4 in (10 cm) tall, spreading slowly into a small mat. Flowers appear in spring before the leaves and the plant is usually grown in rock gardens or in small pots in collections of alpine plants. It requires a cold winter.

Cultivation
Grow in porous, gritty soil that contains leafmold or other rotted organic matter in part- or dappled shade. Keep moist. Propagate from seed sown as soon as it is ripe or by division of clumps in late winter, before flower buds appear.

Hacquetia epipactis
syn. *Dondia epipactis*

The pinhead-sized, bright yellow flowers of this species are surrounded by glossy green bracts, giving the effect of a most unusual bright green flower. Appearing straight from the ground in earliest spring, they are followed by 3-lobed

leaves. This is a most unusual and desirable plant for cooler areas. *Zones 6–9.*

HEDYCHIUM
Ginger lily

Ginger lilies are associated with the tropics because of their glamorous flowers and heady scent. Yet, of the 40 species native to southern Asia, many grow on mountains, and tolerate cooler weather. Some are hardy enough to be grown in temperate gardens. These perennials grow from rhizomes to form clumps up to 6 ft (1.8 m) high and 4 ft (1.2 m) wide, and for most of the year in warm climates (summer elsewhere) bear spikes or heads of fragrant flowers.

Cultivation
They prefer humus-rich, moist but well-drained soil in a part-shaded position. Spent stems should be cut out each season. Propagate from fresh seed or by division.

Hedychium coccineum
Red ginger lily

This species from the Himalayas forms a low clump with spreading stems and

Hedychium gardnerianum

Helenium 'Moerheim Beauty'

narrow leaves. Its spectacular erect flower spikes, which carry only a few flowers, can reach 10 in (25 cm) high. The blooms vary from pale coral to a bright red, always with the exaggerated stamen in pink. The cultivar 'Tara' has brilliant orange flowers and is more frost hardy than the species. *Zones 9–11*.

Hedychium gardnerianum
Kahili ginger
This species from the Himalayas grows to 8 ft (2.4 m) tall with long, bright green leaves clasping the tall stems. This is the most widely cultivated species; it prefers a warm climate although it will grow outside in temperate areas that have light, infrequent frosts. The fragrant red and pale yellow flowers, held in dense spikes, appear towards the end of summer. It is considered a weed in some regions such as in the north of New Zealand. *Zones 9–11*.

HELENIUM
Sneezeweed, Helen's flower
This genus found in the Americas consists of about 40 species of annual, biennial or perennial herbs. The mid-green leaves, which are alternate on erect stems, are oval to lance-shaped. Daisy-like flowerheads appear in summer and have yellow, red-brown or orange ray florets and yellow, yellow-green, red or brown disc florets.

Cultivation
Frost hardy, heleniums grow in any temperate climate as long as they get sun. The soil should be moist and well drained. Remove spent flowers regularly to prolong the flowering period. Propagate by division of old clumps in winter or from seed in spring or fall (autumn).

Helenium 'Moerheim Beauty'
This upright perennial has sprays of daisy-like, rich orange-red flowerheads with prominent, chocolate-brown central discs. They are borne in summer and early fall (autumn) above mid-green foliage. Easily grown, it gives color to borders and is useful for cut flowers. Slow growing to 3 ft (1 m) high and 24 in (60 cm) wide, it enjoys hot summers. *Zones 5–9*.

HELIANTHEMUM
Rock rose, sun rose

Helianthemum means flower of sunshine, an appropriate name for flowers that only open in bright sunlight. The genus contains over 100 species found on rocky and scrubby ground in temperate zones of the northern hemisphere. They are sturdy, short-lived, evergreen or semi-evergreen shrubs or subshrubs. The foliage ranges in color from silver through mid-green. Wild plants have flowers resembling 1 in (25 mm) wide wild roses, but garden forms can be anything from white through yellow and salmon-pink to red and orange, and some have double flowers.

Cultivation

Plant in full sun in freely draining, coarse soil with a little peat or compost added during dry periods. Propagate from seed or cuttings.

Helianthemum nummularium

A variable species from Europe and Turkey, *Helianthemum nummularium* has a neat, prostrate habit and grayish foliage. Its small but profuse flowers vary in color from yellow or cream to pink and orange. Most of the cultivars traditionally listed under this name are in fact of hybrid origin. *Zones 5–10.*

HELIANTHUS

This genus of the daisy family includes one of the world's most important oilseed plants, also used for livestock fodder, as well as the Jerusalem artichoke with edible tubers, and many ornamentals. Consisting of around 70 species of annuals and perennials, native to the Americas, they have large daisy-like, usually golden-yellow flowerheads, which are on prolonged display from summer to fall (autumn). They have hairy, often sticky leaves and tall, rough stems.

Cultivation

Frost hardy, they prefer full sun, well-drained soil and protection from wind. Fertilize in spring. Cut perennials down to the base after flowering. Propagate from seed or by division in fall or early spring.

Helianthus annuus
Common sunflower

This fast-growing, upright annual can reach a height of 10 ft (3 m) or more.

Helianthemum nummularium

Helianthus annuus

Heliconia bihai

Helianthus × multiflorus 'Triomphe de Gand'

Large daisy-like, 12 in (30 cm) wide yellow flowerheads with brown centers are borne in summer. This species produces one of the world's most important oilseeds. Newer varieties have been developed that grow to about 6 ft (1.8 m), including 'Autumn Beauty' with medium-sized flowers usually brownish red, deep red, light yellow or golden yellow; and 'Teddy Bear', a compact grower with double, dark yellow flowers. *Zones 4–11.*

Helianthus × multiflorus

Helianthus × multiflorus is a clump-forming perennial to 6 ft (1.8 m) in height and 3 ft (1 m) in spread. The domed flowers can be up to 6 in (15 cm) across and appear in late summer to mid-fall (mid-autumn). Popular cultivars include 'Capenoch Star', 'Loddon Gold', 'Soleil d'Or' and 'Triomphe de Gand'. *Zones 5–9.*

HELICONIA

Lobster claw, false bird-of-paradise

From tropical America, Southeast Asia and some Pacific Islands, these beautiful plants have spikes of colorful bracts enclosing relatively insignificant flowers. There are around 100 evergreen perennial species and hybrids in this genus. The bracts may be red, yellow or orange, or scarlet tipped with yellow and green, or lipstick red and luminous yellow. The leaves are spoon-shaped and grow to 6 ft (1.8 m) long. Heliconias make excellent cut flowers.

Cultivation

Grow only in warm, tropical gardens with a winter minimum of 64°F (18°C). Plant in humus-rich, well-drained soil in filtered sun and summer humidity. Propagate by division of rootstock in spring, ensuring there are two shoots on each division. Check for spider mites, snails and mealybugs.

Heliconia bihai

syns *Heliconia humilis*, *H. jacquinii*
Firebird, macaw flower

The large, paddle-shaped, green leaves of this species surround a flower stem of pointed, scarlet bracts tipped with green and inconspicuous white flowers. This is the most familiar species and is popular for flower arrangements. *Zones 11–12.*

Heliconia psittacorum

Heliopsis helianthoides 'Light of Loddon'

Heliconia psittacorum
Parrot flower

Ranging from eastern Brazil to the West
Indies, this smaller species is good for
mass planting. It has long-stalked, lance-
like, rich green leaves. Narrow, pinkish,
orange or pale red bracts surrounding
yellow or red flowers with green tips are
produced in summer. It is usually 3–5 ft
(1–1.5 m) tall. *Zones 11–12.*

HELIOPSIS
Orange sunflower, ox eye

The name *Heliopsis* means resembling a
sunflower, and these perennials from the
North American prairies do look like
sunflowers, though on a more manageable scale. There are about 12 species,
with stiff, branching stems and toothed,
mid- to dark green leaves. The solitary,
usually yellow flowers are up to 3 in
(8 cm) wide and make good cut flowers.

Cultivation

They thrive in fertile, moist but well-
drained soil and a sunny position. They
are all very frost hardy. Deadhead
regularly and cut back to ground level
after flowering finishes. Propagate from
seed or cuttings in spring, or by division
in spring or fall (autumn).

Heliopsis helianthoides

This species grows to 5 ft (1.5 m) tall
and 3 ft (1 m) in spread. It has coarse,
hairy leaves and golden-yellow flowers
in summer. 'Light of Loddon' has rough,
hairy leaves and strong stems that carry
dahlia-like, bright yellow, double flowers
in late summer; it grows to a height of
3 ft (1 m) and a spread of 24 in (60 cm).
Zones 4–9.

HELLEBORUS
Hellebore

Native to areas of Europe and western
Asia, these 15 perennial or evergreen
species are useful winter- and spring-
flowering plants for cooler climates.
They bear beautiful, open flowers in
white or shades of green, red and purple
and are effective planted in drifts or
massed in the shade of deciduous trees.
All are poisonous.

Cultivation

Grow in part-shade and moist, well-
drained, humus-rich soil; do not dry out
in summer. Cut off old leaves from

Helleborus orientalis

deciduous species just as the buds start
to appear. Remove flowerheads after
seeds drop. A top-dressing of compost
or manure after flowering is beneficial.
Propagate from seed or by division in
fall (autumn) or early spring. Check
for aphids.

Helleborus foetidus
Stinking hellebore
This clump-forming European perennial
has attractive, dark green, divided leaves
that remain all year. In winter or early
spring the clusters of pale green, bell-
shaped flowers, delicately edged with
red, are borne on short stems. Established plants will often self-seed readily.
Zones 6–10.

Helleborus orientalis
Lenten rose
The most widely grown of the genus,
this evergreen, clump-forming species
from Greece, Turkey and the Caucasus
grows to 24 in (60 cm) high and wide.
The large nodding flowers come in a
great variety of colors from white, green,
pink and rose to purple, sometimes with
dark spots. Very frost hardy, it flowers
in winter or early spring. The dense
foliage fades and can be trimmed back
before flowering. *Zones 6–10.*

Helleborus foetidus

HEMEROCALLIS
Daylily
These east Asian perennials have showy
flowers which come in a range of vibrant
colors. Individual blooms last only for a
day, but are borne in great numbers on
strong stems above tall, grassy foliage
and continue flowering from early
summer to fall (autumn). Flower size
varies from 3 in (8 cm) to 6 in (15 cm)
or more, single or double; plant height
ranges from about 24 in (60 cm) to
about 3 ft (1 m).

Cultivation
Position carefully when planting as the
flowers turn their heads towards the sun
and the equator. Most are fully hardy.
Propagate by division in fall or spring
and divide clumps every 3 or 4 years.
Check for slugs, snails, aphids and
spider mite.

Hemerocallis 'Apricot Queen'
Raised in the 1940s, 'Apricot Queen'
remains popular, producing a prolific

supply of buds and holding each opened flower for about 16 hours. The petals display blended shades of red and orange. It is clump-forming and grows to a height of about 3 ft (1 m). The mid-green leaves are reed-like. Being fully deciduous it is well suited to cold winter climates. A suuny position and protection from snails and slugs are recommended. *Zones 4–9.*

Hemerocallis lilioasphodelus
syn. *Hemerocallis flava*
Pale daylily, lemon daylily
This is one of the first daylilies used for breeding and is found across China. It forms large spreading clumps with leaves up to 30 in (75 cm) long. The lemon-yellow flowers are sweetly

Hemerocallis Hybrid 'Stella d'Oro'

Hemerocallis 'Apricot Queen'

scented and borne in a cluster of 3 to 9 blooms. It has a range of uses in Chinese herbal medicine: some parts may be eaten, while others may be hallucinogenic. *Zones 4–9.*

Hemerocallis Hybrids
Almost all the cultivated species of *Hemerocallis* have played their part in producing the vast range of modern daylily hybrids. A recent development is a range of miniatures, in many colors and with either broad or narrow petals: one of the most popular is 'Stella d'Oro' with clear golden-yellow flowers of almost circular outline. *Zones 5–11.*

HEPATICA
Liverleaf
Hepatica is closely related to *Anemone*, as the flower shape suggests. There are 10 species from North America, Europe and temperate Asia. They are all small, hairy, spring-flowering perennial herbs. The supposed resemblance of their leaves to a liver gave them their common and botanical names: *hepar* is Latin for liver. They have medicinal uses in liver and respiratory complaints, as well as for indigestion. There are a number of garden varieties with white, blue or purple flowers, sometimes double.

Hemerocallis lilioasphodelus

Cultivation

They occur naturally in woodlands so prefer part-shade and rich, moist but well-drained soil. Propagate from seed or by division, especially for the double varieties.

Hepatica nobilis

syns *Anemone hepatica, Hepatica triloba*
An inhabitant of mountain woods across much of Europe, this small perennial has solitary blue, pink or white ½–1¼ in (12–30 mm) flowers on long stalks. It has evergreen leaves with 3 broad, rounded lobes, usually purplish beneath. Although the plant is poisonous, it has been used as a herbal remedy for coughs and chest complaints. *Zones 5–9.*

HESPERIS

From the Mediterranean and temperate Asia, this genus consists of 60 species of biennials and herbaceous perennials allied to stocks (*Matthiola*). They have narrow, usually undivided leaves that may be toothed or toothless, and showy pink, purple or white flowers in long racemes. Some species have fragrant flowers.

Cultivation

Species are readily grown in temperate areas and will naturalize, but cultivars are sometimes more difficult. Frost hardy, they prefer full sun and moist but well-drained, neutral to alkaline, not too fertile soil. Propagate from seed or cuttings. Check regularly for mildew and watch for slugs and snails.

Hesperis matronalis
Dame's rocket, sweet rocket

Ranging from Europe to central Asia, the flowers of *Hesperis matronalis* become very fragrant on humid evenings. It has smooth, narrowly oval leaves and branching flowerheads with white to lilac flowers borne in summer. There is also a purple form. Upright in habit, it grows 12–36 in (30–90 cm) high with a spread of about 24 in (60 cm). Plants lose their vigor after a time and are best renewed every 2 to 3 years. *Zones 3–9.*

HEUCHERA
Alum root, coral bells

There are about 55 species of these evergreen and semi-evergreen perennials, native to North America and Mexico. They form neat clumps of scalloped leaves, often tinted bronze or purple, from which arise stems bearing masses of dainty, nodding, white, crimson or pink bell flowers often over a long flowering season. They are good as ground covers, in rock gardens or as edging plants.

Hepatica nobilis

Hesperis matronalis

Heuchera sanguinea

× Heucherella tiarelloides

Heuchera micrantha var. diversifolia 'Palace Purple'

Cultivation

Mostly frost hardy, they like either full
sun or semi-shade and well-drained,
coarse, moisture-retentive soil. Propagate species from seed or by division;
cultivars by division in fall or early
spring. Remove spent flower stems and
divide established clumps every 3 or 4
years.

Heuchera micrantha var. diversifolia 'Palace Purple'

This cultivar is grown for its striking,
purple, palmate leaves and panicles of
tiny white flowers in summer. It is clump
forming, with a height and spread of
about 18 in (45 cm). The leaves last well
as indoor decoration. *Zones 5–10.*

Heuchera sanguinea
Coral bells

This, the most commonly grown species,
occurs naturally from Arizona to New

Mexico. It grows to 18 in (45 cm) and
has sprays of scarlet or coral red flowers
above toothed, deeply lobed leaves.
British and American gardeners have
developed strains with a wider color
range—from pale pink to deep red—and
slightly larger flowers. Bressingham
hybrids are typical. *Zones 6–10.*

× HEUCHERELLA

This hybrid genus is the result of a cross
between *Heuchera* and *Tiarella*, both
members of the saxifrage family. Plants
are evergreen, clumping or ground-
covering perennials with tall, airy stems
of dainty pink or white flowers. These
are produced over a long season from
late spring. Leaves are rounded, lobed
and have distinct veins. When young
they are bronze-red, turning green
during summer then reddish in fall
(autumn).

Cultivation

They enjoy leafy, rich, moist but well-
drained soil. Where summers are mild,
full sun is best, but in hotter areas
dappled or part-shade suits. Propagate
by division in fall (autumn) or winter in
mild areas, spring in cooler places.

× Heucherella tiarelloides

Growing about 12 in (30 cm) tall with
flower stems rising a further 12–15 in

Hibiscus trionum

Hosta fortunei 'Albomarginata'

(30–38 cm), this fully hardy perennial spreads by creeping stolons. The leaves are lobed and toothed and form a dense, rounded mound. Small pink flowers appear on red stems. In the cultivar 'Bridget Bloom' the flowers are a soft, pastel pink and very freely produced. *Zones 5–9*.

HIBISCUS

While the genus name conjures up the innumerable cultivars of *Hibiscus rosa-sinensis*, the genus of around 220 species is quite diverse, including hot-climate evergreen shrubs and small trees, some deciduous, temperate-zone shrubs and some annuals and perennials. The leaves are mostly toothed or lobed and the flowers are of characteristic shape with a funnel of 5 overlapping petals and a central column of fused stamens.

Cultivation

The shrubby species thrive in sun and slightly acid, well-drained soil. Water regularly and feed during the flowering period. Trim after flowering to maintain shape. Propagate from seed or cuttings or by division, depending on the species. Check for aphids, mealybugs and whitefly.

Hibiscus trionum
Bladder ketmia, flower-of-an-hour

This weed of cultivation and waste places may be an annual or biennial herb or subshrub to 3 ft (1 m) high and 24 in (60 cm) wide. The hairy leaves are usually divided into deep lobes, with these further lobed or toothed. Each morning in summer and fall (autumn) it produces a sprinkling of smallish pale yellow flowers with a deep crimson, almost black center. It self seeds readily. *Zones 9–11*.

HOSTA
Plantain lily

The 40 species in this genus of frost-hardy perennials are from Japan, China and Korea. They produce wide leaves, some marbled or marked with white and others a bluish green. All-yellow foliage forms are also available. They do well in large pots, and are excellent for ground cover, or on the margins of lily ponds or bog gardens. Tall stems to about 18 in (45 cm) of nodding white, pink or shades of purple and blue, bell- or trumpet-shaped flowers appear in warmer weather.

Cultivation

They grow well in shade and rich, moist, neutral, well-drained soil. Feed regularly during the growing season. Propagate by division in early spring, and guard against snails and slugs.

Hosta fortunei

This strong-growing perennial has given rise to many hybrids. It has ovate or broad lanceolate, pleated and pointed leaves. In summer tall flower stems are produced from which hang lavender flowers. Plants grow at least 18 in (45 cm) tall but spread nearly twice as wide. 'Albomarginata' has gray-green leaves with creamy yellow to white margins; 'Albopicta' has leaves marbled or irregularly marked in 2 shades of green; and 'Aurea' is a luminous golden green. *Zones 6–10.*

Hosta 'Krossa Regal'

This hybrid has beautiful powdery gray-green leaves that are upward folded, wavy edged and distinctly pleated. *Zones 6–10.*

Hosta plantaginea

Hosta plantaginea
August lily, fragrant plantain lily

Popular for its pure white, fragrant flowers on 30 in (75 cm) stems, this Chinese species has mid-green leaves forming a mound 3 ft (1 m) across. It flowers in late summer. *Zones 3–10.*

Hosta sieboldiana

This robust, clump-forming plant from Japan grows to 3 ft (1 m) high and 5 ft (1.5 m) wide. It has puckered, heart-shaped, bluish gray leaves and bears racemes of mauve buds opening to trumpet-shaped white flowers in early summer. 'Frances Williams' has heart-shaped, puckered blue-green leaves with

Hosta fortunei 'Aurea'

Hosta 'Krossa Regal'

yellowish green margins. *Hosta
sieboldiana* var. *elegans* also has heart-
shaped, puckered leaves. *Zones 6–10.*

Hosta undulata
Wavy leafed plantain lily

Hosta undulata has creamy white, wavy
or twisted leaves that are splashed or
streaked green along their edges. Mauve
flowers on tall stems in summer complete this attractive and desirable
specimen. *Zones 6–10.*

HOUTTUYNIA

There is only one species in this genus, a
wide-spreading, creeping herbaceous
perennial from moist or wet, part- or
fully shaded parts of eastern Asia. It is a
good ground cover in moist gardens or
beside ponds and can also grow in
shallow water or boggy ground. In
summer it bears spikes of tiny yellowish
flowers with 4 pure white bracts at the
base of each spike.

Hosta sieboldiana

Hosta undulata

Houttuynia cordata

Hypericum cerastoides

Cultivation

This frost-hardy plant likes moist, leafy rich soil. In cooler climates it tolerates sun so long as the ground is moist, but in hotter places some shade is desirable. Where winters are always cold, reduce water in winter or cover the roots with a thick layer of straw. Propagate from ripe seed or from cuttings, or by division.

Houttuynia cordata

Ranging from the Himalayas to Japan, this water-loving deciduous perennial makes a good ground cover but may become invasive. It is a vigorous plant, growing to 12 in (30 cm) high with an indefinite spread. It grows from underground runners which send up bright red branched stems bearing aromatic green leaves. However, the most popular form, 'Chameleon' (syns 'Tricolor', 'Variegata') is strikingly variegated in red, cream, pink and green. *Zones 5–11.*

HYPERICUM
St John's wort

This is varied genus of 400 species of annuals, perennials, shrubs and a few small trees, some evergreen but mostly deciduous, with showy flowers in shades of yellow with a central mass of prominent golden stamens. It has a cosmopolitan distribution. Species range in size from diminutive perennials for the rockery to over 10 ft (3 m) tall.

Cultivation

Mostly cool-climate plants, they prefer full sun but will tolerate some shade. They like fertile, well-drained soil, with plentiful water in late spring and summer. Remove seed capsules after flowering and prune in winter. Propagate cultivars from cuttings in summer, and species from seed in fall (autumn) or from cuttings in summer.

Hypericum cerastoides

syn. *Hypericum rhodoppeum*
This densely mounding perennial has oval, gray-green leaves and terminal clusters of bright yellow, cup-shaped flowers in late spring and early summer. It has an upright, slightly spreading habit and grows to 12 in (30 cm) tall with an 18 in (45 cm) spread. Frost hardy, it is useful in rock gardens. *Zones 6–9.*

I, J, K

Iberis amara cultivar

Iberis sempervirens

IBERIS

This genus of around 50 species of annuals, perennials and evergreen subshrubs are mainly from southern Europe, northern Africa and western Asia. Highly regarded as decorative plants they are excellent for rock gardens, bedding and borders. Showy flowers are borne in either flattish heads in colors of white, red and purple, or in erect racemes of pure white flowers.

Cultivation

Fully to marginally frost hardy, they require a warm, sunny position and a well-drained, light soil, preferably with added lime or dolomite. Propagate from seed in spring or fall (autumn) — they may self-sow, but are unlikely to become invasive — or from cuttings in summer.

Iberis amara
Candytuft, hyacinth-flowered candytuft
Native to the UK and Europe, this is a fast-growing and erect bushy annual. Frost hardy, it has lance-shaped mid-green leaves and reaches a height of 12 in (30 cm), with a spread of 6 in (15 cm). It produces large racemes of small, fragrant, pure white flowers in early spring and summer. Various strains are available. The Hyacinth-flowered Series has large fragrant flowers in varying shades of pink. *Zones 7–11.*

Iberis sempervirens
Candytuft, evergreen candytuft
A low, spreading, evergreen subshrub, this species from southern Europe is ideal for rock gardens. It has narrow, dark green leaves and dense, rounded heads of unscented white flowers in spring and early summer. It is frost hardy, and grows 6–12 in (15–30 cm) high with a spread of about 18–24 in (45–60 cm). The cultivar 'Snowflake' has glossy, dark green leaves and semi-spherical heads of white flowers. Lightly trim after flowering. *Zones 4–11.*

IMPATIENS

This genus of around 850 species of succulent-stemmed annuals, evergreen perennials and subshrubs is widely distributed, especially in the subtropics and tropics of Asia and Africa. Many hybrid strains are perennial in mild climates, but in colder climates are usually grown as annuals. Their botanical name, *Impatiens*, refers to the impatience with which they grow and multiply.

Cultivation
Frost hardy to frost tender, they grow in sun or part-shade. They prefer a moist but freely drained soil, and need protection from strong winds. Tip prune to encourage shrubby growth and more

Impatiens, New Guinea Hybrid

Impatiens walleriana

abundant flowers. Propagate from seed
or stem cuttings in spring or summer.

Impatiens, New Guinea Hybrids

These fast-growing perennials are also
grown as annuals in cool climates. They
are frost tender and grow to a height and
spread of 12–18 in (30–45 cm). The
leaves are oval, pointed and bronze
green, or may be variegated with cream,
white or yellow. The flat, spurred
flowers are pink, orange, red or cerise,
sometimes with white markings. Cultivars include 'Concerto', with crimson-
centered deep pink flowers; 'Tango',
with deep orange flowers and bronze
leaves; and 'Red Magic', with scarlet
flowers and bronze-red leaves. They like
brightly lit positions indoors in cooler
climates or on enclosed verandahs or
patios in warmer areas. *Zones 10–12.*

Impatiens usambarensis

This tropical African species gets its
name from the Usambara Mountains on
the borders of Kenya and Tanzania,
where it was first discovered. It is
related to the better known *Impatiens
walleriana* and has been used in the
breeding of the many colorful 'busy
lizzie' hybrids in this group. *I. u* ×
walleriana displays just one of the many
possible color outcomes in such crosses.
Zones 10–12.

Impatiens usambarensis × walleriana

Impatiens walleriana
syn. *Impatiens sultanii*
Busy Lizzie

From tropical East Africa, this succulent, evergreen perennial has soft, fleshy
stems with reddish stripes and oval,
fresh green leaves. Flattish spurred
flowers ranging through crimson, ruby
red, pink, orange, lavender and white,
some variegated, are produced from late
spring to late fall (autumn). There are
many cultivars. It is marginally frost
hardy, fast growing and bushy, and
grows to a height and spread of 12–24 in
(30–60 cm); water well. *Zones 9–12.*

INCARVILLEA

This genus of the bignonia family
(Bignoniaceae) consists of 14 species
suitable for rock gardens and borders.
Some are annuals, although those in

cultivation are usually perennial. Most flower in shades of magenta and deep rose pink although one or two species come in shades of yellow or white. They are native to central and east Asia and the Himalayas.

Cultivation
Most are frost hardy, but do not tolerate overly wet or waterlogged soil in winter. They like rich, moisture-retentive, well-drained soil, in a position that receives ample sun except in the hottest part of the day. Propagate from seed.

Incarvillea delavayi
Pride of China, hardy gloxinia
This fleshy-rooted, clump-forming perennial, native to China, has handsome, fern-like foliage and erect stems bearing large, trumpet-shaped, rosy purple flowers in summer. It grows to a height of 24 in (60 cm) with a spread of 12 in (30 cm), but dies down early in fall (autumn). It is very frost hardy, but should be protected with a compost mulch during cold winters. *Zones 6–10.*

INULA
Native to Asia, Africa and Europe, this genus of about 90 species in the daisy family are mostly herbaceous perennials, although some are subshrubs, biennials or annuals. They vary in size from tiny plants suited to the rock garden up to towering perennials that exceed 10 ft (3 m) tall. Inulas have fine-petalled, invariably yellow daisies, some species of which are quite large. Several have been cultivated since ancient times; the name *Inula* was in use in Roman times.

Cultivation
Inulas are frost hardy. They grow in any well-drained, deep, fertile soil. They prefer a sunny to part-shaded aspect. Propagate from seed or by division in spring or fall (autumn).

Inula helenium
Elecampane, scabwort
This is one of the largest *Inula* species at 8 ft (2.4 m) tall with a spread of 3 ft (1 m). As it is rhizomatous, it is also one of the most invasive. It produces its large, yellow daisy-like flowers in summer and should be planted with due deference to its invasive potential. *Inula helenium* was used in medicine as a tonic, astringent, demulcent and diuretic and, because of this, is often planted in herb gardens. *Zones 5–10.*

Inula helenium

Incarvillea delavayi

IRESINE

Belonging to the amaranthus family, these tropical perennials from the Americas and Australia—some 80 species—are sometimes treated as annuals. They vary in habit from upright to ground-hugging. The flowers are insignificant, but their leaves are often brilliantly colored.

Cultivation

These frost-tender plants only make permanent garden plants in tropical to warm temperate climates. In cooler areas they can be grown in greenhouses. They prefer good loamy, well-drained soil and must be kept moist during the growth period. They need bright light, with some sun, to retain the brilliant color in their leaves. Pinch out tips in the growing season. Propagate from cuttings.

Iresine herbstii
syn. *Iresine reticulata*
Beefsteak plant, bloodleaf

Native to Brazil, this species makes an attractive tropical bedding or pot plant. Although perennial, it is often treated as an annual that is overwintered as struck cuttings in a greenhouse in cold areas. It grows to 24 in (60 cm) tall with a spread of 18 in (45 cm), but usually much less if grown as an annual. It has red stems and rounded purple-red leaves up to 4 in (10 cm) long, with notches at the tips and yellowish red veins. *Zones 10–12.*

IRIS

This wide-ranging genus of more than 200 species is named for the Greek goddess of the rainbow. Each flower has 6 petals: 3 outer petals, called 'falls', which droop away from the center and alternate with the inner petals, called 'standards'. Irises are divided into 2 main groups, rhizomatous and bulbous. Rhizomatous irises have sword-shaped leaves, are sometimes evergreen, and are subdivided into 3 groups: bearded (or flag) irises, with a tuft of hairs (the 'beard') on the 3 lower petals; beardless irises, without the tuft; crested or Evansia irises, with a raised crest in lieu of a beard.

The bulbous irises are divided into 3 groups, the Juno, Reticulata and Xiphium irises, the first 2 consisting of beautiful but mostly difficult bulbs from west and central Asia. The Xiphium irises are more easily grown; they have given rise to a group of bulbous hybrids including the so-called English, Spanish and Dutch irises; it is the latter that are commonly seen in florist shops.

Cultivation

Growing conditions vary greatly, however, as a rule rhizomatous irises, with the exception of the crested or Evansia irises, are frost hardy and prefer a sunny position. Bulbous irises are frost hardy, and prefer a sunny position with ample moisture during growth, but very little during their summer dormancy. Bulbous irises are prone to virus infection and need to be kept free of aphids, which will spread the infection. Propagate by division in late summer after flowering or from seed in fall; named cultivars by division only.

Iresine herbstii

Iresine herbstii

Iris cristata

Iris, Tall Bearded, 'Blue Shimmer'

Iris, Intermediate Bearded, 'Sunny Dawn'

Iris, Bearded Hybrids

The bearded irises have fat creeping rhizomes, sword-shaped, grayish foliage and stems bearing several large flowers. They come in an enormous range of colors—everything but true red—with many varieties featuring blended colors, contrasting standards and falls, or a broad band of color around basically white flowers (this pattern is called 'plicata').

All prefer a temperate climate, sun and mildly alkaline, well-drained soil. Do not over-water in summer. Bearded irises are subdivided into 3 groups: Dwarf Bearded, which grow about 6–15 in (15–40 cm) tall and flower earlier than the others; Intermediate Bearded, which grow to about 24 in (60 cm) tall. 'Sunny Dawn' is typical, with yellow flowers

with red beards. Tall Bearded irises are the last to bloom and grow to 3 ft (1 m) tall or higher. 'Blue Shimmer' has white flowers with liac-blue stitching. *Zones 5–10.*

Iris cristata
Crested iris

A woodland crested or Evansia iris, this creeper grows 4–9 in (10–22.5 cm) high. Native to northeast USA, in spring, it bears faintly fragrant, pale blue to lavender or purple flowers held just above the foliage; each fall has a white patch with an orange crest. It prefers moist soil in part-shade, making it suitable as a ground cover in shaded gardens; it spreads slowly by rhizomes. 'Alba' is a vigorous cultivar with white flowers. *Zones 6–9.*

Iris ensata
syn. *Iris kaempferi*
Japanese flag, higo iris

This beardless iris grows to 3 ft (1 m) tall. It has purple flowers with yellow blotches on each fall, which appear from late spring to early summer; the leaves have a prominent midrib. The many named varieties bear huge flowers, up to 10 in (25 cm) wide, in shades of white,

Iris japonica

Iris ensata

Iris, Louisiana Hybrid 'Art World'

lavender, blue and purple, often blending 2 shades and some with double flowers. They prefer part-shade in hot areas, rich, acid soil and plenty of moisture. 'Exception' has particularly large falls and deep purple flowers; 'Mystic Buddha' has purple-blue flowers with red edging. *Zones 4–10.*

Iris japonica
syn. *Iris fimbriata*
Crested iris
This is the best known of the crested or Evansia species. Native to Japan and China, it grows to 18–32 in (45–80 cm) in height, forming large clumps of almost evergreen, glossy mid-green leaves. In late winter and spring, it bears sprays of ruffled, pale blue or white flowers; each fall has a violet patch around an orange crest. It prefers an acidic soil, a lightly shaded position, and a mild climate. Keep shaded from afternoon sun. A variety with white-striped leaves, it is rather shy flowering. *Zones 8–11.*

Iris, Louisiana Hybrids
This colorful group of rhizomatous, beardless hybrid irises are evergreen with fine strap-like foliage and can build into substantial clumps; divide after 2 to 3 years. They are not fully frost hardy in very cold climates, but are becoming increasingly popular in Australia and southern USA. Although basically swamp or water irises, they will grow in the garden if kept well watered. They like a sunny position with average to damp, humus-rich soil. They rarely exceed 3 ft (1 m) high. Hybrids include 'Art World', with mauve-pink duo-toned flowers; 'Dural Dreamtime', with its fine white flower with green veins; 'Insider', a new Australian hybrid which has yellow-edged reddish brown standards and falls of reddish brown with yellow spray patterning; and 'Vermilion Treasure', with a red-violet flower with lighter spray patterning. *Zones 7–10.*

Iris pallida
Dalmatian iris

This bearded iris has fragrant, pale blue flowers with yellow beards, which are borne on 4 ft (1.2 m) high stems in late spring. It is often grown as a source of orris, a volatile substance that develops in the dried and aged rhizomes and is used in perfumes, dental preparations and breath fresheners. 'Variegata' (syn. 'Aurea Variegata') has handsome leaves striped in gray-green and cream. *Zones 5–10*.

Iris sibirica
Siberian flag

This popular beardless iris makes strongly vertical clumps of slender bright green leaves 2–4 ft (0.6–1.2 m)

Iris sibirica

Iris unguicularis

high. In late spring or early summer, flowering stems rise above the foliage with narrow-petalled, blue, purple or white flowers, often veined in a deeper color. It prefers full sun to very light shade (particularly in hot areas), a moderately moist, rich soil that may be slightly acid and water during the hottest periods. It does best in cold winter climates. Cultivars include 'Perry's Blue', with rich lilac-blue flowers with yellow markings; and 'Vi Luihn', with flowers in a rich violet shade. *Zones 4–9*.

Iris, Spuria Hybrids

Iris spuria (from northern Africa and southern France), *I. sibirica* (from eastern Europe) and allied species have been much hybridized. The more common hybrids bear numerous 4 in (10 cm) wide flowers on 4 ft (1.2 m) long stems in early summer. Colors are in the white to blue range, with some yellow and white forms. All prefer sun, rich soil and lavish watering while they are growing and flowering. *Zones 4–9*.

Iris unguicularis
syn. *Iris stylosa*
Winter iris, Algerian iris

This evergreen, beardless species is notable for its habit of bearing its

Iris pallida 'Variegata'

Knautia macedonica

Kalanchoe blossfeldiana

flowers deep down among the clumps of grassy, dark green leaves, on stems no more than 8 in (20 cm) long. Flowers are typically pale blue, but white and darker blue varieties are also available; the falls have yellow centers. It blooms from fall (autumn) to spring. It likes a warm, sheltered position, in slightly alkaline soil. *Zones 7–10*.

KALANCHOE

This genus, native to subtropical and tropical Africa and Madagascar, with some species in Asia, consists of 150 species of perennial succulents, climbers or shrubs. These vary from small, leafy succulents to tree-like shrubs. Plants grow from 6 in (15 cm) to 12 ft (3.5 m) high and bear white, yellow or orange to brown, red or purple, tubular or bell-shaped flowers in early spring, followed by seed-bearing capsules.

Cultivation

They need full sun or part-shade and well-drained soil, and only light watering in the colder months; they range from marginally frost hardy to frost tender. Propagate from stem or leaf cuttings in late spring to summer, seed at the end of spring.

Kalanchoe blossfeldiana
Flaming Katy

This small, shrubby African species reaches 12 in (30 cm) high and wide. Its multiple, upstretched branches are

covered with round to rectangular, deep green leaves with red margins and notched tips. Thick racemes of small, deep red, cylindrical flowers appear from winter to early summer; cultivated strains may be pink, yellow and also orange. Frost tender, it requires part-shade, and is a popular pot plant. *Zones 10–12*.

KNAUTIA

Consisting of 60 species of annuals and perennials, this genus is found extensively throughout temperate Eurasia. Their flowers are very like the related *Scabiosa*. These have a rosette of basal leaves through which the flower stems grow; these are branched and support some leaves.

Cultivation

These frost-hardy plants prefer sun or part-shade. They will grow happily in any well-drained loam, but require staking. Propagate from seed in fall (autumn) or by basal cuttings in spring.

Knautia macedonica

A showy species from the central Balkans to Romania, this makes an attractive subject for herbaceous borders. Its habit is similar to *Knautia arvensis*, but it grows to only 30 in (75 cm) tall, although it has larger and more attractive flowers which are usually deep purple-red, and occasionally pale pink or white. *Zones 6–10*.

KNIPHOFIA
Red-hot poker, torch lily, tritoma

There are 68 species in this southern African genus of perennials, some of which are evergreen. Upright, tufted plants with long leaves, in summer they carry showy, brightly colored, tubular flowers in dense spikes on tall bare stems. Originally the flowers were mostly flame colored, but now they can also be pink, orange or yellow. They range from head-high to miniatures growing to 24 in (60 cm) or less.

Cultivation

Frost hardy to somewhat frost tender, they like full sun, well-drained soil and plenty of water in summer. Where winter temperatures are below 5°F

Kniphofia 'Winter Cheer'

Kniphofia 'Little Maid'

(−15°C) lift and store indoors to be planted again in spring, or mulch heavily. Propagate species from seed or by division; cultivars by division.

Kniphofia ensifolia
Winter poker

This moderately frost-hardy evergreen perennial forms a dense clump, growing to 5 ft (1.5 m) tall. It has slender, sword-shaped, mid-green leaves and bears torches of prolific, lemon-yellow flowers in late fall (autumn) and winter. *Zones 8–10.*

Kniphofia 'Little Maid'

'Little Maid' is a dwarf form that reaches a height of 24 in (60 cm). It has buff-tinted soft-yellow flowers opening from pale green buds. *Zones 7–10.*

Kniphofia 'Winter Cheer'

syn. *Kniphofia* 'Zululandiae'

This evergreen, upright perennial reaches 5 ft (1.5 m) in height with a spread of 3 ft (1 m). It is fairly frost hardy and bears large torches of orange-yellow flowers in winter that gradually turn yellow. *Zones 7–10.*

Kniphofia ensifolia

Lamium album

Lamium galeobdolon 'Hermann's Pride'

LAMIUM
syns *Galeobdolon, Lamiastrum*
Deadnettle
This Eurasian genus of over 50 species of annuals and rhizomatous perennials belongs, in fact, to the mint family. Some have been used in folk medicine; some are an important source of nectar for bees. Leaves have toothed margins, arranged in opposite pairs and some-times splashed with paler gray-green or white, and short spikes or axillary whorls of white, yellow, pink or purple 2-lipped flowers, the upper lip curved over in a helmet-like shape.

Cultivation
These frost hardy plants grow in most soils. Flower color determines planting season: plant white- and purple-flowered species in spring in full sun; plant yellow-flowered species in fall (autumn) in shade. Propagate from seed or by division in early spring.

Lamium album
White deadnettle, archangel
Ranging across Europe and northern Asia, this species has foliage that superficially resembles that of the common nettle *(Urtica urens)*. An erect perennial of 12–24 in (30–60 cm) high, it produces whorls of pure white flowers from late spring to early fall (autumn). It became known as archangel because it flowers around the 8th of May, the feast day of the Archangel Michael in the old calendar. It sometimes flowers in mid-winter. *Zones 4–10.*

Lamium galeobdolon
syns *Galeobdolon luteum, G. argentatum, Lamiastrum galeobdolon*
Yellow archangel
This perennial species from Europe and western Asia spreads both by rhizomes and surface runners to form extensive, loose mats of foliage usually about 12 in (30 cm) deep, spreading over moist, shady areas beneath trees. Its leaves are variably splashed with silvery gray and in summer it bears leafy spikes of bright yellow flowers. 'Hermann's Pride' is densely mat forming and has narrow leaves streaked and spotted with silver. *Zones 6–10.*

Lamium maculatum
Spotted deadnettle
Its wild forms often regarded almost as weeds, this variable species may have erect stems to 24 in (60 cm) tall, or have a lower, more spreading habit. The strongly toothed leaves have a central blotch or stripe of pale silvery green, and leafy whorled spikes of pale pink to deep

Lathyrus odoratus

Lamium maculatum 'Roseum'

rose flowers appear in spring and summer. The cultivars mostly have a compact mat-forming habit and do not grow more than 6 in (15 cm) high. 'Roseum' has silver-striped foliage and pinkish lilac flowers. *Zones 4–10.*

LATHYRUS

This genus consists of 150 or so species of annuals and perennials, and is widespread in temperate areas, except Australasia. The uppermost pair of leaflets is usually modified into tendrils. Pea-shaped flowers come in a range of colors, from red, mauve and white to blue and yellow. *Lathyrus odoratus*, the sweet pea, has a proud place in scientific history—it was one of the plants used by Gregor Mendel (1822–84) in his hybridizing experiments which laid the foundations of genetic science.

Cultivation

These frost-hardy plants like fertile, well-drained soil in full sun. Deadhead regularly. Propagate annuals from seed; perennials from seed or by division.

Lathyrus odoratus
Sweet pea

This vigorous, climbing annual has abundant, sweetly scented flowers in white, cream, pink, blue, mauve, lavender, maroon and scarlet. They bloom several to the stem from late

Lathyrus vernus 'Cyaneus'

winter to early summer. It grows to 6 ft (1.8 m) high or more, although there are dwarf, non-climbing cultivars available. The climbers need good support, and are ideal for covering walls or fences. *Zones 4–10.*

Lathyrus vernus 'Cyaneus'
Spring vetch

This hardy herbaceous perennial is a purplish-blue-flowered form of a 20 in (50 cm) high European and west Asian species. An excellent plant for rockeries, its flowers are a distinctive shade that stands out well among other woodland plants. They are carried on racemes of up to 15 blooms, open from early spring and are held above the foliage. The leaf tips come to a simple point, not, as with climbing sweet peas, a tendril. *Zones 4–10.*

LAVATERA

Closely related to the mallows and hollyhocks, this genus of 25 species of annuals, biennials, perennials and softwooded shrubs has a scattered distribution around temperate regions of the world, mostly in Mediterranean or similar climates. A few species have colorful mallow flowers, generally produced over a long season. The plants are upright in habit with simple to palmately lobed leaves. The shrubs and perennials are not very long-lived.

Cultivation

Moderately to very frost-hardy, they prefer a sunny site and well-drained soil. Prune after flowering. Propagate annuals, biennials and perennials from seed sown *in situ* (cuttings do not strike well), and shrubs from cuttings.

Lavatera 'Barnsley'

This semi-evergreen soft shrub grows to 6 ft (1.8 m) and bears sprays of pale pink flowers with deep pink centers throughout summer. It is very frost hardy. *Zones 6–10.*

Lavatera trimestris
Annual mallow

This shrubby Mediterranean annual is grown mainly for its silken, trumpet-shaped, brilliant white or pink flowers which appear from summer to early fall (autumn). They are short lived but are borne in profusion, benefiting from regular deadheading. The annual mallow has an erect, branching habit and is moderately fast growing to a height of 24 in (60 cm) and a spread of 18 in (45 cm). 'Mont Blanc' (syn. *Lavatera* 'Mont Blanc') has pure white flowers. *Zones 8–11.*

LEONTOPODIUM
Edelweiss

Occurring wild in the mountains of Europe and temperate Asia, this genus consists of about 35 species of short-lived perennials in the daisy family. The flowerheads have a central disc of inconspicuous cream florets surrounded by a ring of overlapping, pointed bracts of unequal length, coated with sparse to dense white wool. The lance-shaped leaves are also covered with white hairs, which protect the plant from cold and intense sunlight. They suit rock gardens in cool to cold climates.

Cultivation

Plant in full sun or part-shade (in hot climates) in gritty, well-drained soil. They are frost hardy but need shelter from winter rain. Propagate from fresh seed or by division.

Lavatera trimestris 'Mont Blanc'

Lavatera 'Barnsley'

Leontopodium alpinum

Much loved by the Swiss, the European edelweiss reaches a height and spread of around 8 in (20 cm). Each silvery white flowerhead is 2–3 in (5–8 cm) across, the bracts so thickly felted they look like strips of flannel. It blooms in spring or early summer. *Zones 5–9.*

LEUCANTHEMUM

There are about 25 species of annuals or perennials in this genus from Europe and northern Asia. They are clump forming plants with variably toothed or lobed leaves that are unlike those of other chrysanthemum relatives. Long-stalked daisy-like flowerheads arise from leafy stems, with white or yellow ray florets and yellow disc florets.

Cultivation

They are largely undemanding, growing well in a border or garden bed in full sun or morning shade in moderately fertile, moist but well-drained soil. Propagate from seed or cuttings, or by division.

Leucanthemum × superbum

syns *Chrysanthemum maximum* of gardens, *C.* × *superbum*

Shasta daisy

Growing to a height and spread of 2–3 ft (60–90 cm), this robust perennial has large, daisy-like white flowerheads with pale golden centers in summer and early fall (autumn). They were once thought to be *Leucanthemum maximum*, but are now believed to be hybrids between that species and *L. lacustre*; they naturalized on Mount Shasta in Washington State, USA and attracted the attention of the famous plant breeder Luther Burbank. There are many cultivars, always white-flowered, but including doubles as well as singles, some with fringed petals. *Zones 5–10.*

LEWISIA

Bitter root

This genus honors the explorer Meriwether Lewis (1774–1838), and contains about 20 species of small perennials with deep tap roots, leathery leaves and starry flowers, native to the USA's Rocky Mountains. The roots have wonderful powers of survival: some 5 years after Lewis returned to civilization in 1806, a botanist in London, studying his dried plant specimens found one trying to grow. He planted it and the following summer it flowered.

Cultivation

They like a cool climate, full sun or part-shade in warm climates and excellent drainage, to avoid winter-wet rotting the

Leontopodium alpinum

Leucanthemum × *superbum*

Liatris spicata

Lewisia cotyledon

roots. Propagate herbaceous species from seed, and evergreen species from seed or offsets.

Lewisia cotyledon
This evergreen, which hybridizes readily, has rosettes of fleshy, toothed leaves and bears clusters of white to yellow, apricot and pink to purple flowers on upright stems. It grows to a height of 12 in (30 cm). *Lewisia cotyledon* var. *howellii* spreads to 6 in (15 cm). 'Pinkie', with pink flowers, grows 1 in (25 mm) tall and 2 in (5 cm) wide. *Zones 6–10.*

LIATRIS
Blazing star
These 40 species of perennials come from central and eastern North America. In summer they shoot up tall, cylindrical spikes of fluffy flowers from a knobby rootstock. They belong to the daisy or composite family but their spike-like inflorescences, with crowded small flowerheads opening from the top downward, are quite unlike those of other daisies.

Cultivation
They grow in most soils and conditions including damp places such as stream banks and ditches, although they prefer climates with low humidity. They thrive with minimum care, making excellent border plants. Propagate from seed or by division of old clumps in winter.

Liatris spicata
syn. *Liatris callilepis* of gardens
Gay feather, spike gay feather
This low-growing species has lilac purple flowers, although they can occur in pink and white. They are produced in crowded, fluffy spikes—like a feather duster—in late summer, opening from the top downwards, the opposite of most flowering spikes. It grows to some 24 in (60 cm) high, with thickened, corm-like rootstocks and basal tufts of grassy foliage. 'Floristan' is a seedling strain growing to 5 ft (1.5 m) tall; it is available in 2 colors: deep violet ('Floristan Violett') and white ('Floristan Weiss'). *Zones 3–10.*

LIBERTIA
These 20 species of perennials in the iris family have tufts of grass-like leaves springing from rhizomes which may be very short or long creeping. They are

found on both sides of the Pacific Ocean in New Zealand, Australia, New Guinea and the Andes of South and Central America. They grow easily in a temperate climate, producing erect, wiry stems bearing clusters of small white iris-like flowers in spring and summer.

Cultivation
Moderately frost hardy, they require a sheltered, sunny or part-shaded position and well-drained, peaty soil with plenty of moisture in spring and summer. Propagate by division or from seed.

Libertia grandiflora
New Zealand iris
This easily grown rhizomatous perennial is native to New Zealand and has decorative foliage, seed pods and flowers. It has grass-like, brown-tipped leaves over 24 in (60 cm) long. In early summer it produces tall, wiry, lightly branched flower stems with dainty white flowers, followed in fall (autumn) by golden-brown seed capsules. Loosely clump forming, it grows to a height of 3 ft (1 m) and has a spread of 24 in (60 cm). *Zones 8–11.*

Libertia peregrinans
This New Zealand species is remarkable for its long, branching rhizomes which send up sparse tufts of narrow, strongly

Libertia peregrinans

veined leaves at intervals, these turning a striking orange-brown shade in fall (autumn) and winter. It reaches 30 in (75 cm) high and grows in moist, slightly acidic, well-drained soil in full or part-shade. It has a yellowish bronze-green shorter flowering stem with white flowers with orange-brown anthers. *Zones 8–10.*

LIGULARIA
There are at least 150 species of perennials in this genus which is found mainly in temperate eastern Asia. Many are large-leafed, clump-forming plants that produce tall spires of daisy-like flowerheads, mostly in shades of yellow or orange. They are stately plants and vigorous growers, adapted to moist, sheltered sites such as stream banks and woodland glades and flowering mainly in summer and early fall (autumn).

Cultivation
Quite frost hardy, they prefer moist, well-drained soil and grow in either sun or part-shade. Propagate by division in spring or from seed in spring or fall. Watch for slugs and snails.

Libertia grandiflora

Limnanthes douglasii

Ligularia dentata

Ligularia dentata

syns *Ligularia clivorum, Senecio clivorum*
This compact species, native to China
and Japan, has showy flowerheads. It
grows to a height of 4 ft (1.2 m) and a
spread of 3 ft (1 m). It has kidney-
shaped, long-stalked, leathery, brownish
green leaves and bears clusters of large,
orange-yellow flowerheads on long
branching stems in summer. Cultivars
worth growing are 'Othello' and
'Desdemona', which has green leaves
heavily overlaid with bronze and maroon.
'Gregynog Gold' has round green leaves
and orange flowers. *Zones 4–9.*

LIMNANTHES
Meadow foam, poached egg flower

These western North American meadow
plants are annuals more often cultivated
in other countries. The genus consists of
7 species of plants with 5-petalled, cup-
shaped flowers and bright green leaves
and can be relied on to provide color
from spring to fall (autumn).

Cultivation

They prefer damp soil and full sun as
long as the roots are cool. Sow seed
directly in fall or early spring and lightly
cover. Staggered sowing ensures a
constant display best suited to the
rockery or along the pavement edge.

Limnanthes douglasii
Meadow foam

Delightful and delicate, this 6 in (15 cm)
tall plant has pale green fern-like foliage
and masses of slightly perfumed, white-
edged, golden-centered flowers. There is
also a pure gold form. It is named after
the early 19th-century collector David
Douglas, who made many important
finds in western North America.
Zones 8–10.

LIMONIUM
Statice, sea lavender

Statice is an obsolete botanical name of
this genus of around 150 species,
scattered around the world's temperate
regions mostly in saline coastal and
desert environments. They include
evergreen and deciduous subshrubs,
perennials, biennials and annuals, some
of the latter popular for their many-
colored heads of small papery flowers
which can be cut and dried for decoration. The tapering, almost stalkless
leaves appear in basal rosettes.

Cultivation

Statices like full sun and well-drained,
sandy soil. They benefit from light

Limonium sinuatum

Limonium perezii

fertilizing in spring. Propagate by division in spring, from seed in early spring or fall (autumn) or from root cuttings in late winter.

Limonium latifolium

syn. *Limonium platyphyllum*
From eastern Europe, this tall-stemmed perennial bears clusters of lavender-blue or white flowers over summer. Clump forming and large leafed, it grows 24 in (60 cm) tall and spreads 18 in (45 cm). The dried flower stems have a delicate appearance. *Zones 5–10.*

Limonium perezii

Limonium perezii comes from the Canary Islands and is a species of more or less shrubby habit with glossy leaves. The leafless flower stems bear many small flowers, whose insignificant white petals make less impact in the garden than the long-lasting, deep mauve-blue calyces. It grows about 24 in (60 cm) tall and flowers in summer. *Zones 9–11.*

Limonium sinuatum

syn. *Statice sinuata*
This bushy, upright Mediterranean perennial is usually grown as an annual. It produces dense rosettes of oblong, deeply waved leaves and masses of tiny papery flowers on winged stems. It flowers in summer and early fall (autumn) and is fairly slow growing,

Limonium latifolium

reaching a height of 18 in (45 cm) with a spread of 12 in (30 cm). The Petite Bouquet Series are dwarf plants to 12 in (30 cm) in height and with golden- or lemon-yellow, white, cream, salmon-pink, purple or blue spikelets. *Zones 9–10.*

LINARIA
Eggs and bacon, toadflax

Native mainly in the Mediterranean region and western Europe, these 100 species of adaptable annuals, biennials and perennials are related to snapdragons and have naturalized in many places. They grow to 18 in (45 cm) with masses of tiny snapdragon-like blooms in many colors. The erect stems have stalkless, usually gray-green leaves. They suit rock gardens, borders and cottage gardens.

Cultivation

They require rich, well-drained, preferably sandy soil, moderate water and full sun. Seed sown directly in fall (autumn) or very early spring will germinate in 2 weeks. Seedlings need to be thinned to a 6 in (15 cm) spacing.

Linaria purpurea
Purple toadflax

This perennial from Europe is naturalized in some areas and grows to 3 ft (1 m). It bears violet-tinged purple flowers in summer. 'Canon J. Went' is a tall example of the species with tiny pale pink flowers. *Zones 6–10.*

LINUM
Flax

This genus contains 200 species of annuals, biennials, perennials, subshrubs and shrubs, some evergreen, distributed widely in temperate regions. It includes the commercial flax, *Linum usitatissimum*, grown for fiber and oilseed. Several ornamental species have profusely blooming, 5-petaled flowers, which can be yellow, white, blue, red or pink. They suit a rock garden or border.

Cultivation

They are mostly quite frost hardy. Grow in sun in humus-rich, well-drained, peaty soil. After perennial species flower,

prune hard. Propagate annuals, biennials and perennials from seed and perennials by division. Most self-sow readily.

Linum narbonense

A perennial native of the Mediterranean region, this most handsome of all the blue flaxes has violet, funnel-shaped flowers borne on slender stems. The flowers last for many weeks in summer. It has soft, green leaves and forms clumps 18 in (45 cm) high and wide. *Zones 5–10.*

Linum perenne

syn. *Linum sibiricum*
Of wide occurrence in Europe and temperate Asia, this is a vigorous,

Linum perenne

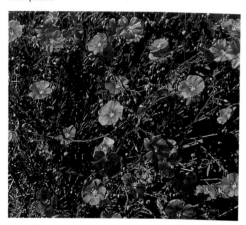

Linaria purpurea

Linum narbonense

upright perennial that forms a shapely, bushy plant 24 in (60 cm) high with a spread of 12 in (30 cm). It has slender stems with grass-like leaves and clusters of open, funnel-shaped, light blue flowers are borne throughout summer. *Zones 7–10.*

LIRIOPE

This genus contains 5 species of clump-forming, rhizomatous, evergreen perennials native to Vietnam, China, Taiwan and Japan. Some cultivars are so dark in leaf they are practically black. They do not creep, and for ground cover have to be planted 6 in (15 cm) apart. *Liriope* flowers range from white through to pale purple.

Cultivation

Grow in full sun or part-shade in well-drained soil. In early spring cut back shabby leaves, just before the new ones appear. Propagate from seed in fall (autumn) or by division in early spring.

Liriope muscari

syns *Liriope platyphylla, L. graminifolia*
This clumping, evergreen perennial is a useful ground cover. It bears erect spikes

Lobelia cardinalis

of rounded, bell-shaped, violet flowers in late summer. It grows to 12–24 in (30–60 cm) high with a spread of 18 in (45 cm). Flower spikes are held just above the foliage. 'Lilac Beauty' is a larger example of the species. *Zones 6–10.*

LOBELIA

Widespread in temperate and tropical areas, the growth habits of this genus of 370 species of annuals, perennials and shrubs vary from low bedding plants to tall herbaceous perennials or shrubs. They all have ornamental flowers and suit flower boxes, hanging baskets and rock-gardens.

Cultivation

These frost-hardy to somewhat frost-tender plants are best grown in well-drained, moist, light loam enriched with compost. Most grow in sun or part-shade but resent wet conditions in winter. Prune after flowering, and fertilize weekly with a liquid manure during the season. Propagate annuals from seed, perennial species from seed or by division and perennial cultivars by division only.

Lobelia cardinalis
Cardinal flower

This clump-forming perennial from eastern North America is useful for

Liriope muscari

Lobelia erinus

Lobelia erinus 'Cambridge Blue'

growing in wet places and beside streams and ponds. From late summer to mid-fall (mid-autumn) it produces spikes of brilliant, scarlet-red flowers on branching stems above green or deep bronze-purple foliage. It grows to a height of 3 ft (1 m) and a spread of 12 in (30 cm). *Zones 3–10*.

Lobelia erinus
Edging lobelia
This slow-growing, compact annual is native to South Africa and grows to a height of 4–8 in (10–20 cm) and spread of 4–6 in (10–15 cm). It has a tufted, often semi-trailing habit, with dense oval to lance-shaped leaves tapering at the base. It bears small, 2-lipped pinkish purple flowers continuously from spring to early fall (autumn). 'Cambridge Blue' is a popular hybrid along with 'Color Cascade', with a mass of blue to violet to pink and white flowers. *Zones 7–11*.

Lobelia × gerardii
A hybrid between the North American species *Lobelia cardinalis* and *L. siphilitica*, this robust perennial can grow as tall as 5 ft (1.5 m). It has pink, violet or purple flowers. 'Vedrariensis' is its best-known cultivar, producing racemes of violet-blue flowers in late summer; its leaves are dark green and lance-shaped. These hybrids prefer to grow in moist but well-drained soil in full sun. *Zones 7–10*.

Lobelia × gerardii

Lobularia maritima 'Violet Queen'

LOBULARIA

This genus consists of 5 species of frost-hardy, dwarf plants from the Mediterranean and the Canary Islands; they are useful for rockeries, window boxes and borders. Although there are both annual and perennial forms, the annuals are most commonly grown. They bear tiny 4-petalled, fragrant flowers in compact, terminal racemes in summer and early fall (autumn).

Cultivation

Grow in full sun in fertile, well-drained soil. Continuous flowering can be encouraged by regular deadheading. Propagate from seed in spring or, if used outdoors, from late spring to fall.

Lobularia maritima

syn. *Alyssum maritimum*
Sweet alyssum, sweet Alice

This fast-growing, spreading annual is a popular edging, rock-garden or window box plant. It produces masses of tiny, honey-scented, 4-petalled white flowers over a long season, from spring to early fall (autumn). Lilac, pink and violet shades are also available. It has a low, rounded, compact habit, and grows to a height of 3–12 in (8–30 cm) and a spread of 8–12 in (20–30 cm). 'Violet Queen' is the darkest of the garden varieties of sweet Alice. *Zones 7–10.*

LUNARIA
Honesty

The origin of the common name for this genus, allied to stocks (*Matthiola*), of 3 species of annuals, biennials and perennials is uncertain, although it could be from the way the silver lining of the seed pods is concealed in the brown husk like a silver coin, the reward of virtue that does not flaunt itself. Sprays of honesty have been popular as dried flower arrangements since the 18th century.

Cultivation

Plant in full sun or part-shade in fertile, moist but well-drained soil. Propagate perennials from seed or by division in fall (autumn) or spring, biennials from seed. They self-seed quite readily.

Lunaria annua
syn. *Lunaria biennis*
A fast-growing biennial native to southern Europe and the Mediterranean coast, this plant has attractive flowers and curious fruit. It has pointed, oval,

Lunaria rediviva

Lunaria annua

serrated, bright green leaves and bears heads of scented, 4-petalled, rosy magenta, white or violet-purple flowers in spring and early summer. These are followed by seed pods with a silvery, translucent membrane. Erect in habit, it grows to 30 in (75 cm) high with a spread of 12 in (30 cm). *Zones 8–10.*

Lunaria rediviva
Perennial honesty
This perennial grows to 3 ft (1 m) high with a spread of 12 in (30 cm). It has hairy stems, heart-shaped leaves and pale violet flowers; the fruit are silver pods. *Zones 8–10.*

LUPINUS
Lupin, lupine
This legume genus of 200 species of annuals, perennials and semi-evergreen and evergreen shrubs and subshrubs have long, erect spikes of showy pea-flowers in a range of colors including blue, purple, pink, white, yellow, orange

Lupinus, Russell Hybrids

and red. They are used as ornamentals, as animal fodder, and as a 'green manure' crop (because of their nitrogen-fixing capacity). The leaves are distinct among legumes in being palmate, with 5 or more leaflets radiating from a common stalk. They are widespread in northern temperate zones except Asia.

Cultivation

Most prefer climates with cool wet winters and long dry summers. They like full sun and well-drained, moderately fertile, slightly acidic, sandy soil. Propagate species from seed and Russell lupin cultivars from cuttings or by division.

Lupinus, Russell Hybrids

This fine strain of strong-growing lupins bear long spikes of large, strongly colored flowers in cream, pink, orange, blue or violet, some varieties bicolored, in late spring and summer. They produce a magnificent clump of deeply divided, mid-green leaves, growing to 3 ft (1 m) high. 'Noble Maiden', from the Band of Nobles series, has cream flowers; 'Polar Princess' has white flowers; and the blooms of 'Troop the Colour' are bright red. There are also dwarf strains, such as the popular 'Lulu', which grows to 24 in (60 cm) high. *Zones 3–9.*

Lupinus texensis

Lupinus texensis
Texas blue bonnet
A bushy annual to 12 in (30 cm) high, this species has bright green leaves divided into 5 small leaflets that are hairy on the undersides, and bears dark blue and white flowers in late spring. Easily grown, it thrives in poor soil and is quick to flower from seed. This is the state flower of Texas, beyond which it does not occur wild. *Zones 8–10.*

LYCHNIS
Campion, catchfly
Native to temperate regions of the northern hemisphere, these 15 to 20 species of biennials and perennials have summer flowers that range in color from white through pinks and oranges to deep red. All have flat 5-petalled flowers but in many species the petals are notched or

Lychnis × *haageana* 'Vesuvius'

deeply forked or sometimes divided into narrow teeth.

Cultivation
They are frost hardy and like cool climates, preferably in sunny sites, and any well-drained soil. Higher mountain species do best in soil that is protected from excessive solar warmth. Remove spent stems after flowering and dead-head frequently. Propagate by division or from seed in fall (autumn) or early spring.

Lychnis chalcedonica
Maltese cross
This perennial species from far eastern Europe and western Russia has been popular with gardeners since the 17th century. Its color is such a dazzling orange-red that its garden companions should be chosen with care. It flowers for a short season in early summer, grows about 4 ft (1.2 m) tall, and takes its common name from the shape of the flower. White and pink varieties and one

Lychnis coronaria

with double flowers exist, but these are fairly rare. *Zones 4–10.*

Lychnis coronaria
Rose campion, dusty miller, mullein pink

A clump-forming European perennial sometimes grown as a biennial, this striking plant grows to a height of 30 in (75 cm) and a spread of 18 in (45 cm). It forms a dense clump of silvery white downy leaves, and many-branched gray stems carry large, deep rose-pink to scarlet flowers throughout summer. 'Alba' is a white-flowered cultivar. In ancient times the flowers were used for garlands and crowns. It is drought tolerant and often self-seeds. *Zones 4–10.*

Lychnis × haageana 'Vesuvius'

syn. *Lychnis × arkwrightii* 'Vesuvius'
This hybrid is probably a cross between two Asian species, *L. fulgens* and *L. sieboldii*, though *L. chalcedonica* is also a possible parent and its exact origin is unclear. What is beyond doubt, however, is that it is a singularly striking perennial

Lychnis chalcedonica

in all respects. Often short-lived, it is nonetheless worth growing for its deep bronze foliage and its large vivid orange flowers. It reaches around 24 in (60 cm) high and blooms from midsummer. *Zones 6–10.*

Lychnis viscaria
German catchfly

This perennial is widely distributed through Europe and western Asia. Growing to 18 in (45 cm) tall and with a similar spread, it is a densely clumping plant with bronze stems and narrow dark green leaves with sticky hairs. It produces spike-like panicles of mauve to magenta flowers in early summer. 'Splendens Plena' (syn. 'Flore Pleno') has larger, bright magenta double flowers. *Zones 4–9.*

Lysimachia clethroides

LYSIMACHIA
Loosestrife

Ranging through temperate and sub-tropical regions of the northern hemisphere, this genus of mainly evergreen perennials and shrubs of the primula family consists of around 150 species. Growth habit varies from low, creeping plants to clumps with tall, spike-like racemes of crowded flowers. The 5-petalled flowers are mostly yellow or white, sometimes pink or purple. The botanical name is Latinized Greek for 'ending strife' though why they deserve this name is unclear.

Cultivation

They prefer slightly acidic soil with a good mix of organic matter and medium to moist conditions in sun or part-shade. Some grow best at the edge of a pond or stream. Propagate from seed or cuttings, or by division.

Lysimachia clethroides
Japanese loosestrife

This somewhat hairy perennial grows to 3 ft (1 m) high making a broad, leafy

Lychnis viscaria 'Splendens Plena'

Lysimachia nummularia 'Aurea'

clump of erect stems. In summer it produces tapering terminal spikes, gracefully nodding in bud but becoming erect with maturity, of crowded starry white flowers. *Zones 4–10.*

Lysimachia nummularia
Creeping Jenny, moneywort

Various medicinal properties were attributed to this vigorous creeping European perennial by herbalists. The prostrate stems take root wherever they touch damp ground, forming a dense, rapidly spreading mat usually no more than 3 in (8 cm) deep. The paired leaves are almost circular, hence *nummularia* from the Latin for coin-like, also the English 'moneywort'. The deep yellow bowl-shaped flowers are borne singly on short stalks from the leaf axils over a long summer period. 'Aurea' has pale yellow-green leaves and stems; when grown in shade it turns an interesting lime green. *Zones 4–10.*

Lysimachia punctata
Golden loosestrife, garden loosestrife

A vigorous clump-forming perennial, this species grows erect to a height of

Lysimachia punctata

3 ft (1 m) with broad mid-green leaves in whorls of 4, grading into floral bracts on the upper stems which carry in summer a massed display of brilliant yellow starry flowers. It looks best planted in large groups. It is suitable for bedding, large rock gardens, or pool and streamside plantings. *Zones 5–10.*

Lythrum salicaria

LYTHRUM
Loosestrife

This genus of annuals, perennials and
subshrubs shares the common name
'loosestrife' with *Lysimachia*, though the
2 genera are quite unrelated; however,
the long, erect flower spikes of some
species and their boggy habitats resemble some lysimachias. There are
around 35 species, scattered through all
continents except South America. They
vary from small creeping plants with
stems rooting in the mud of ditches, to
plants 6 ft (1.8 m) or more tall with
showy spikes of pink to purple flowers.

Cultivation

They grow in most soil conditions as
long as moisture is adequate, and in bogs
and other wetlands some can be invasive. Propagate from seed or by division.

Lythrum salicaria
Purple loosestrife

An Old World native, this perennial
loves wet ground, often spreading into
the shallow water at the edges of ponds.
Erect stems arise from a knotty rhizome
to a height varying from 3–6 ft (1–1.8 m)
depending on soil moisture and fertility.
It produces showy long spikes of pink to
magenta flowers from mid-summer to
fall (autumn). Purple loosestrife was
used in folk medicine; its tannins have
coagulent properties, hence staunching
the flow of blood; treatment of cholera
was one of its uses. *Zones 3–10.*

M

Macleaya cordata

Malva moschata 'Alba'

MACLEAYA
Plume poppy

This genus honors Alexander Macleay (1767–1848), who was for many years Colonial Secretary of New South Wales, Australia. The plants are sometimes offered under the name *Bocconia*, an allied genus whose members are American. The genus consists of 2 or so species of rhizomatous perennials from China and Japan that do not really resemble poppies; the deception arises because the tubular flowers shed their petals as they open. The heart-shaped leaves are gray-green to olive green.

Cultivation

These fully frost-hardy plants prefer full sun and moderately fertile, moist but well-drained soil. Protect from cold winds. Propagate from seed or cuttings or by division.

Macleaya cordata
syn. *Bocconia cordata*
This tall perennial, growing to 5–8 ft (1.5–2.4 m) high, has large, rounded, deeply veined, heart-shaped, gray-green leaves. Large, feathery, terminal flower spikes of cream tinted with pink are borne in summer. It suits the herbaceous border. It spreads from rhizomes and may become invasive. *Zones 3–10.*

MALVA
Mallow

This genus is made up of 30 species of annuals, biennials and perennials from Europe, North Africa and Asia. The flowers are similar to but smaller than the popular *Lavatera* to which they are related; they are single, 5-petalled flowers in shades of white, pink, blue or purple. They suit borders or wild gardens.

Cultivation

They flourish in sunny, well-drained aspects and tend to be more robust in not too rich soil. They are fully frost hardy. Cut plants back after the first flowers have faded. Propagate from cuttings or seed; the perennials often self-seed. Watch for rust disease in spring.

Malva sylvestris

Matthiola incana

Malva moschata
Musk mallow

Useful for naturalizing in a wild garden or odd corner, this perennial has narrow, lobed, divided leaves with a sticky, hairy texture which emit a musky, cheesy odor when crushed. It bears profuse spikes of saucer-shaped pink flowers in summer. 'Alba', a white cultivar, is very popular. It has a bushy, branching habit and can grow to a height of about 3 ft (1 m). *Zones 3–10.*

Malva sylvestris
Tall mallow, high mallow, cheeses

This erect perennial grows to 3 ft (1 m) tall, often behaving as a biennial. Its leaves are broad and heart-shaped to rounded, slightly lobed and mid- to dark green. The flowers are produced from late spring to mid-fall (mid-autumn) and in the wild form are mauve-pink with dark purple veins. Cultivars have been selected with flower colors from pure white through blues to deep purple. *Zones 5–10.*

MATTHIOLA
Stock, gillyflower

This is a genus of some 55 species of annuals, biennials and subshrubby perennials from Europe, central Asia and South Africa. The leaves are usually gray-green and the perfumed flowers can be produced from spring to fall (autumn). They make good cut flowers but stocks are prone to a few pests and diseases, including downy mildew, club-root, gray mold and cabbage root fly.

Cultivation

They prefer a sunny aspect in moist but well-drained, neutral or alkaline soil. Shelter from strong winds and stake the larger forms. Propagate from seed sown *in situ* for night-scented stock—this should be staggered to increase the flowering season.

Matthiola incana

This upright biennial or short-lived European perennial is best grown as an annual. It has a bushy habit and grows up to 24 in (60 cm) high. Fully frost hardy, it has lance-shaped, gray-green leaves and fragrant spikes of mauve flowers borne in spring. 'Mammoth Column' grows taller, and produces a single spike of scented flowers in spring in mixed or separate colors. *Zones 6–10.*

MECONOPSIS

This genus consists of about 45 species of annuals, biennials and short-lived perennials that are mostly native to the Himalayas. They bear large, exotic flowers with papery petals and a bold, central boss of stamens on tall stems. The flower stalks lengthen after flowering as the fruits develop. The hairy leaves are either simple or pinnate.

Cultivation

Mostly frost hardy, they need a moist but not over-wet, lime-free, humus-rich soil and a cool site in part- or full shade with shelter from strong winds. Propagate from seed.

Meconopsis cambrica

Meconopsis betonicifolia

syn. *Meconopsis baileyi*

Blue poppy, Tibetan poppy, Himalayan poppy

This clump-forming woodland species bears sky blue, saucer-shaped, 2–3 in (5–8 cm) wide satiny flowers with yellow stamens in late spring and early summer. Oblong, mid-green leaves occur in basal rosettes. It grows 3–5 ft (1–1.5 m) tall and 18 in (45 cm) wide. It does not bloom in the first season, and dies down completely over winter. *Zones 7–9.*

Meconopsis betonicifolia

Meconopsis cambrica
Welsh poppy

Native to western Europe and the UK, this species has slightly hairy, deeply divided, mid-green leaves that form basal rosettes. Lemon yellow or rich orange blooms are freely borne from mid-spring to fall (autumn). It grows to 12–18 in (30–45 cm) tall and 12 in (30 cm) wide. Though short lived, it self-seeds readily, given the right conditions. *Zones 6–10.*

MIMULUS
syn. *Diplacus*
Monkey flower, musk

The 180 or so species of annuals, perennials and shrubs are characterized by tubular flowers with flared mouths, often curiously spotted and mottled, which have been likened to monkey faces. The flowers come in a large range of colors, including brown, orange, yellow, red, pink and crimson. Mainly native to the cool Pacific coastal areas of Chile and the USA, most prefer bog gardens or other moist situations; some are excellent rock-garden plants.

Cultivation

Grow them in full sun or part-shade in wet or moist soil. Propagate perennials by division in spring and annuals from seed in fall (autumn) or early spring.

Mimulus × hybridus Hybrids

These popular hybrids between *Mimulus guttatus* and *M. luteus* blend parental characters in various ways. The funnel-shaped, open-mouthed flowers come in red, yellow, cream and white, or mixed variations of these colors, plus red mottling, spotting or freckling. Although reasonably hardy and perennial, they rapidly deteriorate in hot sunlight and become straggly after a few months, and so are treated as annuals. 'Ruiter's Hybrid' bears orange trumpet-shaped flowers with wavy petal margins. *Zones 6–10.*

Mimulus × hybridus 'Ruiter's Hybrid'

Mimulus luteus

Mimulus moschatus

Monarda didyma

Mimulus luteus
Yellow musk, golden monkey flower
A spreading perennial often grown as an
annual, this plant bears a profusion of
yellow flowers above mid-green foliage
throughout summer. It grows to a height
and spread of 12 in (30 cm). It is very
frost hardy. *Zones 7–10*.

Mimulus moschatus
Monkey musk
This small, creeping, water-loving
perennial grows to a height and spread
of 6–12 in (15–30 cm). It bears pale
yellow flowers, lightly dotted with
brown, in summer to fall (autumn). It
was once grown for its musk scent but,
mysteriously, it has been odorless for
many years. *Zones 7–10*.

MONARDA
Bergamot, horsemint
This is a genus of 15 species of perennials or annuals with green, sometimes
purple-tinged, veined, aromatic leaves.
They are used for flavoring teas and in
potpourris. Plants can be single stemmed
or sparsely branching, and bear 2-
lipped, tubular flowers from mid-
summer to early fall (autumn).

Cultivation
They are very frost-hardy plants
preferring full sun although some shade
is acceptable. They must be well
drained; annual species prefer sandy
soil. The perennials like moist soil and in
some climates some manure or compost.
Annuals are sown directly into their
permanent spot, and perennials are
usually grown by division of established
clumps.

Monarda didyma
Bee balm, Oswego tea
This herb was used by Native Americans and early colonists as a tea. It has
spidery white, pink or red flowers borne

in late summer. The young leaves may be used in salads, as a tea, or as a stuffing for roast meat. The species grows 3 ft (1 m) or more tall. 'Croftway Pink' grows to 30 in (75 cm) tall and has rose-pink flowers from mid-summer to early fall (autumn). *Zones 4–10*.

Monarda 'Mahogany'

This is a hybrid between *Monarda didyma* and *M. fistulosa* and is a tall variety to 3 ft (1 m) with handsome wine-red or lilac flowers from mid-summer well into fall (autumn). *Zones 4–10*.

MYOSOTIDIUM
Chatham Island forget-me-not

Though the Chatham Islands lie east of New Zealand, this forget-me-not gives a glimpse of what Antarctic flora might have been like before the continent settled at the South Pole. The scientific name of the only species, *Myosotidium hortensia*, emphasizes the plant's close relationship to the true forget-me-not, *Myosotis*.

Cultivation

Salt tolerant and marginally frost hardy, it requires semi-shade and a humus-rich, moist soil. Propagate by division or from seed. Once growing well, it should not be disturbed and will naturalize freely.

Myosotidium hortensia

This evergreen, clump-forming perennial is the giant of the forget-me-not family, growing to a height and spread of 24 in (60 cm). It has a basal mound of large, glossy, rich green, pleated leaves, and in spring and summer bears large clusters of bright purple-blue flowers, slightly paler at the edges, on tall flower stems. A white-flowered cultivar is also grown. *Zones 9–11*.

Myosotidium hortensia

Monarda 'Mahogany'

MYOSOTIS
Forget-me-not

This genus of annuals and perennials includes 34 New Zealand natives among its 50 or so species, but the most commonly cultivated are from temperate regions of Europe, Asia and the Americas. Their dainty blue (sometimes pink or white) flowers bloom in spring, and most suit rock gardens and borders. The plants fade after flowering. *Myosotis*, from the Greek for 'mouse ear', refers to the pointed leaves. They have long been associated with love and remembrance.

Cultivation

Mostly quite frost hardy, they prefer a semi-shaded setting or a sunny spot protected by larger plants, and fertile, well-drained soil. They are rarely affected by pests or diseases. Fertilize before the flowering period. Propagate from seed.

Myosotis alpestris
Alpine forget-me-not

This short-lived perennial from Europe (usually grown as an annual or biennial) forms clumps to a height and spread of 4–6 in (10–15 cm). In late spring and early summer, it bears clusters of dainty, bright blue, pink or white flowers with creamy yellow eyes. *Zones 4–10.*

Myosotis sylvatica
Garden forget-me-not

This biennial or short-lived perennial is usually grown as an annual for its bright lavender-blue, yellow-eyed flowers in spring and early summer. It forms mounds of fuzzy foliage 18 in (45 cm) tall and 12 in (30 cm) wide, with taller stems uncurling as the flower buds open. 'Blue Ball' has tiny, deep blue flowers and is good for edging. *Zones 5–10.*

Myosotis sylvatica 'Blue Ball'

Myosotis alpestris

Nelumbo nucifera

Nemesia strumosa

Nemesia caerulea

NELUMBO
Lotus

This is a genus of 2 species of deciduous, perennial water plants found in North America, Asia and northern Australia. Lotuses resemble waterlilies but differ in that they raise both leaves and flowers clear of the muddy water of the ponds in which they grow, blossoming unsullied. The leaves are waxy and almost circular, and solitary, fragrant flowers are borne on long stalks. Lotus seeds found in Japan and shown by carbon dating to be 2,000 years old have germinated and borne flowers.

Cultivation

They prefer an open, sunny position in 24 in (60 cm) of water. Propagate from seed or by division.

Nelumbo nucifera
Sacred lotus, Indian lotus

The sacred lotus has leaves that emerge 6 ft (1.8 m) or more above the water. The plant spreads to 4 ft (1.2 m) wide. Large, fragrant, pink or white, 10 in (25 cm) wide flowers are borne above large, shield-shaped, pale green leaves. This vigorous plant grows well in large ponds; Buddha is often depicted in the center of such a lotus. *Zones 8–12.*

NEMESIA

This genus of 50-odd species of annuals, perennials and subshrubs comes from South Africa. Their flowering period is short, although if they are cut back hard when flowering slows down they will flower again. The flowers are trumpet-shaped and 2-lipped, and are borne singly in the upper leaf axils or in terminal racemes. The leaves are opposite and simple.

Cultivation

They need a protected, sunny spot and fertile, well-drained soil. They do not like hot, humid climates. Pinch out growing shoots on young plants to ensure bushiness. Propagate from seed in early fall (autumn) or early spring.

Nemesia caerulea
syn. *Nemesia fruticans*
This perennial can grow up to 24 in (60 cm) high in the right conditions.

Nemophila maculata

Nemophila menziesii

Becoming slightly woody at the base, it tends to sprawl, branching into erect stems holding small mid-green leaves and terminal heads of soft pink, lavender or blue flowers. 'Elliott's Variety' is very free-flowering, with bright mauve-blue flowers with a white eye. *Zones 8–10.*

Nemesia strumosa

This colorful, fast-growing, bushy annual is a popular bedding plant. It has lance-shaped, pale green, prominently toothed leaves, and grows to a height of 8–12 in (20–30 cm) and a spread of 10 in (25 cm). Large flowers in yellow, white, red or orange are borne in spring on short terminal racemes. 'Blue Gem' is a compact cultivar with small, clear blue flowers. 'Red and White' has flowers strikingly bicolored, the upper lip bright red and the lower lip white. *Zones 9–11.*

NEMOPHILA

This is a group of 11 species of annuals with bright, open, 5-petalled flowers. Originating from western USA, they are good in borders and window boxes. They produce colorful spring–summer blooms in a range of mainly blues.

Cultivation

These quick-growing annuals grow best in full sun or part-shade in friable, moisture-retentive soil. Protect from wind and position plants away from high-traffic pathways. Regular watering helps prolong blooming. Check for aphids. Propagate from seed which can be sown *in situ* during the fall (autumn).

Nemophila maculata
Five spot

Commonly referred to as five spot because each veined, white petal has a prominent deep purple blotch at its tip, this plant grows to 12 in (30 cm) tall. It is used extensively in massed displays as plants hold their profusion of blooms above the ferny foliage over a long period during summer. *Zones 7–11.*

Nemophila menziesii
syn. *Nemophila insignis*
Baby blue-eyes

A charming little Californian wildflower, this spreading annual is a useful ground cover under shrubs such as roses, as well as in rock gardens and around edges; it is particularly effective overplanted in a bed with spring bulbs. It bears small, bowl-shaped, sapphire-blue flowers with a well-defined concentric ring of white in the center. It has dainty, serrated foliage, and grows to a height and width of 6–10 in (15–25 cm). These plants dislike heat and transplanting. *Zones 7–11.*

NEPETA

This large genus of more than 200 species of perennial, rarely annual, plants is used extensively in herbaceous borders and for edgings or as ground-cover plants. Some species are naturally compact, while others tend to be taller growing plants and may need staking.

Cultivation

Provide a well-drained soil in a sunny position. Some of the vigorous herba-ceous species make good single species ground covers. Trim lightly during the growing season and cut back each year to prevent the plants from becoming too straggly. Propagate by division, from cuttings, or from seed.

Nepeta cataria
Catnip, catmint

A native of Europe, catnip is a frost-hardy perennial with branching, upright stems growing up to 3 ft (1 m). It has aromatic, gray-green leaves and whorls

Nepeta racemosa 'Blue Wonder'

Nepeta × faassenii

of white flowers from late spring through to fall (autumn). Cats are attracted to this plant and will lie in it or play in it and sometimes dig it up. A tea made from the leaves is said to be relaxing. *Zones 3–10.*

Nepeta × faassenii
Catmint

This is a bushy, clump-forming peren-nial, which forms spreading mounds of grayish green leaves that are aromatic when crushed. The numerous flower stems carry hundreds of small, violet-blue flowers throughout summer. It grows to a height and spread of 18 in (45 cm). 'Dropmore Blue' has upright, tall flower spikes of lavender blue; 'Six Hills Giant' will bloom continuously throughout summer if spent flowers are kept clipped. *Zones 3–10.*

Nepeta racemosa

syn. *Nepeta mussinii*
Native to the Caucasus region and northern Iran, this ornamental species has generally been known as *Nepeta mussinii* in gardens, though many of the plants sold under that name are in fact the hybrid *N. × faassenii.* It is a vigorous perennial up to about 12 in (30 cm) high with gray-green, densely hairy leaves and lavender-blue summer flowers in long racemes. 'Blue Wonder' is a very free-flowering form of spreading habit with violet-blue flowers. *Zones 3–10.*

Nepeta cataria

NICOTIANA
Flowering tobacco

The 67 species of annuals, biennials, perennials and shrubs in this genus are from America and Australia and include the commercial tobacco plant. Earlier introduced species have fragrant warm-weather flowers, usually opening at night; flowers of newer strains remain open all day but have limited perfume. They are good for cutting, although the plants are sticky to handle.

Cultivation

Marginally frost hardy to frost tender, they need full sun or light shade and fertile, moist but well-drained soil. Propagate from seed in early spring. Check for snails and caterpillars.

Nicotiana alata

syn. *Nicotiana affinis*
A short-lived South American perennial often grown as an annual, this marginally frost-hardy plant bears clusters of fragrant, tubular flowers in white, red or various shades of pink which open towards evening. Rosette forming, it has oval leaves and grows to a height of about 3 ft (1 m) with a spread of 12 in (30 cm). It flowers through summer and early fall (autumn). *Zones 7–11.*

Nicotiana langsdorfii

This Brazilian annual species grows to 5 ft (1.5 m) tall and has erect and branching stems that produce masses of fine, tubular lime-green flowers during the summer months. Do not be in a hurry to deadhead the last of the blooms as they may self-seed if conditions are favorable, even though the seeds themselves are extremely small. *Zones 9–11.*

Nicotiana sylvestris

One of the few summer-flowering annuals which thrive in shade, the flowers of this species remain open even in deep shade or on overcast days. It grows to 5 ft (1.5 m) or more with tall, stately flowering stems that arise from a mass of large, bright green lush foliage. Terminal groups of long, tubular white flowers are particularly fragrant on warm summer evenings so plant it where the scent can be appreciated. *Zones 8–11.*

Nicotiana sylvestris

Nicotiana langsdorfii

Nicotiana alata

Nigella damascena

Nierembergia repens

NIEREMBERGIA
Cupflower

Comprising 23 species within the Solanaceae family, these annual and perennial herbs and subshrubs from South America make ideal plants for borders or rock garden pockets. They are slender plants with fine foliage and come in a range of colors, the most popular types bearing white or purple-blue, open, cup-shaped flowers.

Cultivation

They prefer friable, well-composted soil in full sun; water well and feed to prolong flowering. The annuals will flower from seed during their first year. In colder areas, the perennials are often grown as annuals, but in more temperate regions they can be overwintered outdoors. Propagate annuals from seed, perennials by division and the subshrubs from cuttings.

Nierembergia repens
syn. *Nierembergia rivularis*
Whitecup

This perennial species spreads by underground stems to form clumps of about 2 in (5 cm) high by 18 in (45 cm) wide. It is best grown in a contained area or rock garden as it has a tendency to become invasive. It has small, spatula-shaped bright green foliage covered, in summer, with a mass of single, open flowers, white with a golden center. *Zones 8–10.*

NIGELLA

The nigellas are a genus of about 15 species of annuals from the Mediterranean countries and western Asia. They have long been used in folk medicine. The flowers are attractive and are suitable for cutting. They have ornamental seed pods which hold their shape and are popular for flower arrangements.

Cultivation

The seedlings hate being transplanted, but if seeds are sown where the plants are to grow and some flowers are allowed to go to seed, new plants will come up for years. Plant in full sun in fertile, well-drained soil and deadhead to prolong flowering if the seed pods are not needed. Propagate from seed.

Nigella damascena
Love-in-a-mist, devil-in-a-bush

This fully frost-hardy annual bears spurred, many-petalled, pale to lilac-blue or white flowers in spring and early summer, almost hidden in the bright green, feathery foliage; these are followed by rounded, green seed pods that mature to brown. Upright and fast growing, it reaches 24 in (60 cm) in height with a spread of 8 in (20 cm). 'Miss Jekyll' is a double blue form. *Zones 6–10.*

Nolana paradoxa

Nymphaea, Hardy Hybrid 'Lucida'

NOLANA

This genus consists of 18 species of annuals, perennials and subshrubs from Chile to Peru and the Galapagos Islands. Most are clump forming to semi trailing and rarely exceed 8 in (20 cm) high. Long-tubed, bell-shaped flowers, carried singly or in small clusters, develop in the leaf axils and appear throughout the growing season. They are generally white to purple with yellow throats.

Cultivation

Plant in humus-rich, well-drained soil in sun or part-shade. Semi-trailing types suit hanging baskets. Pinch the stem tips back occasionally. They are only hardy to the lightest frosts. Propagate from seed, layers or tip cuttings.

Nolana paradoxa

This annual has a dwarf, creeping habit, and is ideal as a colorful ground cover in an open sunny position or for pots and hanging baskets. Low growing, up to 10 in (25 cm) high and 15 in (38 cm) wide, it produces masses of trumpet-shaped, purple-blue flowers, each with a pronounced white throat, over the summer. 'Blue Bird' has flowers in a rich, deep blue shade, again with the white throat. *Zones 8–11.*

NYMPHAEA
Waterlily

This worldwide genus of 50 species of deciduous and evergreen perennial aquatic plants with fleshy roots have rounded, floating leaves which are cleft at the base, and attractive large flowers which come in shades of white and cream, brilliant yellows and oranges, pinks and deep reds, blues and purple. They may be night blooming, depending on species, and sometimes fragrant.

Cultivation

Frost-hardy waterlilies grow in most climates and flower freely throughout summer. Divide the tuber-like rhizomes and replant every 3 or 4 years. Tropical waterlilies are frost tender, requiring a very warm, sunny situation. They flower from mid-summer. All need still water and annual fertilizing. Propagate from seed or by separating plantlets. Check for insects, particularly aphids; goldfish will eat most pests.

Nymphaea, Hardy Hybrids

These cold-hardy and colorful hybrids have day-blooming flowers, mostly in shades of white, yellow, pink or red, set on or just above the surface of the water. 'Atropurpurea' has reddish purple foliage complementing its dark red, wide-open flowers with golden stamens. 'Lucida' has large green leaves and attractive deep red flowers with paler outer petals, 5–6 in (12–15 cm) across. The elegant Marliacea hybrids have dark green leaves and star-shaped, semi-double, soft pink flowers with golden centers, which appear in summer. The large flowers stand slightly above the water. *Zones 5–10*.

Nymphaea, Tropical Day-blooming Hybrids
Tropical hybrids can bear day- or night-time flowers. 'Blue Beauty' is a decidu-ous or evergreen, day-blooming waterlily with large, brown-speckled, dark green leaves with purplish under-sides; the flowers are rounded, semi-double, 12 in (30 cm) across, and deep purple-blue with yellow centers and it spreads to 8 ft (2.4 m). 'St Louis Gold', with abundant daytime blooms of deep gold, is a good variety for smaller pools or tubs. *Zones 10–12*.

OENOTHERA
Evening primrose
This genus, native to the Americas, consists of more than 120 species of annuals, biennials and perennials. Their short-lived flowers, borne during summer, have 4 delicate petals, yellow or less commonly pink, red or white, and a long basal tube. Most are pollinated by nocturnal insects and only release their fragrance at night. Some do not open their petals during the day. Evening primrose oil is extracted from the plants' tiny seeds; it contains certain fatty acids believed to be beneficial to health if consumed regularly in modest quantities.

Cultivation
They are mostly frost hardy and prefer a well-drained, sandy soil in an open, sunny situation. Propagate from seed or by division, or from softwood cuttings.

Oenothera speciosa
White evening primrose, showy evening primrose
This short-lived, rhizomatous perennial bears spikes of profuse, fragrant, saucer-shaped, pink-tinted white flowers. Fresh flowerheads open daily during summer. The small leaves often turn red in hot or cold weather. Clump forming, it grows to 18–24 in (45–60 cm) in height with a spread of 18 in (45 cm) or more. 'Rosea' (syns 'Childsii', *Oenothera berlandieri*) is lower growing, with flowers edged and heavily veined rose pink, yellow in the center. *Zones 5–10*.

OMPHALODES
Navelwort
From Europe, Asia and Mexico, this genus consists of 28 species of forget-me-not–like annuals and perennials that are either evergreen or semi-evergreen. These plants make excellent ground

Nymphaea, Tropical Day-blooming Hybrid 'Blue Beauty'

Oenothera speciosa 'Rosea'

covers, and they are most suited to rock gardens.

Cultivation

They prefer shade or part-shade with moist but well-drained soil (except for *Omphalodes linifolia*, which prefers a sunny position). They are mostly frost hardy. Propagate from seed in spring or by division in fall (autumn).

Omphalodes cappadocica

This spreading perennial from Turkey has creeping underground stems. It produces numerous sprays of flat, bright purple-blue flowers in spring that arise from clumps of densely hairy, oval to heart-shaped leaves that are found at the base of the plant. It reaches a height of 6–8 in (15–20 cm) and a spread of 10 in (25 cm) and is fully frost hardy. *Zones 6–9.*

Omphalodes verna
Blue-eyed Mary, creeping forget-me-not

This semi-evergreen thrives in shady conditions. During spring, it produces long, loose sprays of flat, bright blue flowers with white eyes. This plant has heart-shaped, mid-green leaves that form clumps. It reaches a height and spread of 8 in (20 cm). *Zones 6–9.*

Omphalodes cappadocica

OPHIOPOGON
Mondo grass, snakebeard, lilyturf

This genus contains 50 or so species of evergreen perennials from eastern Asia. They have attractive, long-lived clumps of grass-like foliage springing from underground rhizomes. They are not grasses but lilies, allied to lily-of-the-valley *(Convallaria)*. The summer flowers are small and can be white or blue through to purple. The berry-like fruits each contain one seed. They are trouble-free and provide an attractive ground cover that effectively suppresses leaves.

Cultivation

They are mostly fairly frost hardy and tolerate sun or part-shade in moist, well-drained soil. Propagate by division of clumps, or from seed. To establish a quick ground cover, plant divisions at 8 in (20 cm) intervals.

Ophiopogon japonicus
syn. *Liriope japonica*
Mondo grass

This fine-leafed species is native to Japan and Korea. The dark green recurving foliage arises from deep rhizomes, spreading to form dense, soft mats up to about 8 in (20 cm) deep. Pale purple flowers are hidden among the

Omphalodes verna

Ophiopogon japonicus

Origanum vulgare 'Aureum'

Ophiopogon planiscapus 'Nigrescens'

leaves in mid-summer, followed by bright blue, pea-sized fruit. 'Kyoto Dwarf' is only 2–4 in (5–10 cm) high, with very short leaves. *Zones 8–11*.

Ophiopogon planiscapus 'Nigrescens'
syn. *Ophiopogon planiscapus* 'Ebony Night'
Black mondo grass
This cultivar is grown particularly for its distinctive purple-black rather stiff leaves about ¼ in (6 mm) wide which form slow-growing, sparse clumps. Its lilac flowers appear in clusters along the flowering stem in summer. These are followed by black fruit. It reaches a height of 10 in (25 cm) and a spread of 12 in (30 cm). It is native to Japan. *Zones 6–10*.

ORIGANUM
syn. *Majorana*
Marjoram, oregano
Native to the Mediterranean region and temperate Asia, these perennials and subshrubs in the mint family have aromatic leaves and stalked spikes or heads of small tubular flowers with crowded, overlapping bracts. Some are grown as culinary herbs; others are grown for their decorative pink flowerheads. With arching or prostrate stems arising from vigorously spreading rhizomes, they are useful for trailing over rocks, banks and walls.

Cultivation
They like full sun and a moderately fertile, well-drained soil. Trim excess growth regularly and propagate from seed in spring or by root division in fall (autumn) or spring.

Origanum vulgare
Common oregano, wild marjoram
The common oregano has a sharper, more pungent flavor than marjoram. It has a sprawling habit and grows to 24 in (60 cm) high with dark green, oval leaves and small, white or pink flowers in summer. The leaves are used, fresh or dried, in many Mediterranean-inspired dishes. In Italy, oregano is used in pizza toppings and pasta dishes. 'Aureum' has a less sprawling habit and bright greenish gold leaves. *Zones 5–9*.

ORTHROSANTHUS
The 7 species of this genus of the iris family, from tropical America and Australia, are grass-like perennials with

Orthrosanthus multiflorus

Osteospermum ecklonis 'Starshine'

Osteospermum fruticosum

short, woody rhizomes and flattened fans of sword-shaped leaves up to 18 in (45 cm) long. The flowers are blue or yellow and 6-petalled. In some species, the flowers have dark veining. They are carried in clusters of 2 to 8 blooms on wiry stems.

Cultivation

Plant in moist, well-drained soil in sun or part-shade. They grow best in a mild, frost-free climate. They are often short lived. Propagate from seed or by division of the rhizomes in late winter.

Orthrosanthus multiflorus

This native of southwestern Australia makes an erect tufted plant with narrow, grass-like leaves and spikes of starry blue to purple flowers which appear in spring. It reaches a height of 24 in (60 cm) and a spread of 12 in (30 cm). *Zones 9–10.*

OSTEOSPERMUM

This genus of 70 or so species of evergreen shrubs, semi-woody perennials and annuals is mostly indigenous to South Africa. Allied to *Dimorphotheca*, they have irregularly toothed leaves and produce a profusion of large, daisy-like flowerheads in the white, pink, violet and purple range. Most are cultivars of uncertain origin, suspected to be hybrids. Tough plants, they are useful for rock gardens, dry embankments or the front rows of shrub borders.

Cultivation

They are marginally to moderately frost hardy and prefer open, well-drained soil of medium fertility in an open, sunny spot. Propagate from cuttings or seed.

Osteospermum ecklonis
syn. *Dimorphotheca ecklonis*
Blue-and-white daisybush, sailor boy daisy
This shrub is variable in growth habit, with some erect forms of up to 5 ft (1.5 m) tall and other forms that are lower and more spreading, or even semi-prostrate. From late spring to fall (autumn), it bears profuse 3 in (8 cm) wide daisies, sparkling white with deep reddish violet centers and streaked bluish mauve on the undersides of petals. 'Starshine' has white flowers with bluish centers. *Zones 8–10.*

Osteospermum fruticosum
syn. *Dimorphotheca fruticosa*
Freeway daisy, trailing African dalsy
This is a perennial with prostrate or

trailing stems that can spread to cover large areas. Masses of palest lilac daisies are borne on stalks up to 12 in (30 cm) above the ground; the heaviest bloom is in winter. *Zones 9–11*.

Osteospermum jucundum
syns *Dimorphotheca barberae* of gardens, *Osteospermum barberae*
Trailing mauve daisy, pink veld daisy
This semi-prostrate perennial species from South Africa makes a low clump often no more than 8 in (20 cm) high and up to 3 ft (1 m) across. It bears abundant purplish pink daisies with darker central discs throughout fall (autumn), winter and spring. *Zones 8–10*.

OXALIS
Wood-sorrel
This is a genus of some 500 species of bulbous, rhizomatous and fibrous-rooted

Osteospermum jucundum

Oxalis massoniana

perennials and a few shrubs. Some have become garden weeds. The leaves are always compound, divided into 3 or more heart-shaped or more deeply 2-lobed leaflets in a palmate arrangement. The funnel-shaped flowers are usually pink, white or yellow, and are carried in an umbel-like cluster on slender stalks.

Cultivation
Most grow from bulbs or corms, which multiply readily. A position in sun or part-shade suits most, along with a mulched, well-drained soil and moderate water. Propagate by division of the bulbs or from seed in fall (autumn).

Oxalis massoniana
Its orange-toned flowers make *Oxalis massoniana* something of a novelty. From southern Africa, it was named after Francis Masson, a Scot who made notable collections in South Africa in the late 18th century. *Zones 9–10*.

Oxalis purpurea
syn. *Oxalis variabilis*
One of the showiest species in the genus, this South African native has large flowers in pink, rose, lilac or white; all have soft yellow centers. Clover-like leaves arise from bulbs to form a mound only 4 in (10 cm) high; the deep green leaflets have purple undersides and the flowers appear from late fall (autumn) until early spring. *Zones 8–10*.

Oxalis purpurea

P

Paeonia lactiflora Hybrid

Paeonia mlokosewitschii

Paeonia officinalis 'Rubra Plena'

PAEONIA
Peony

There are 33 species in this genus of deciduous perennials and shrubs from Europe, Asia, North America and China. The centers of the rose-like flowers have a mass of short stamens almost concealing the large ovaries that develop into seed pods. Flowers are mostly in shades of pink or red, but there are also white and yellow-flowered species. The majority are herbaceous, but 'tree peonies' have aboveground woody stems, and are no more than about 8 ft (2.4 m) high.

Cultivation

Most will only succeed in climates with a cold winter. They like full or filtered sunlight, and cool, moist soil. Propagate from seed, or by division for cultivars.

Paeonia lactiflora **Hybrids**

The herbaceous Chinese peonies have handsome foliage—maroon tinted when it first appears in spring—and usually scented flowers in a huge range of colors and forms. 'Beacon Flame' has deep red semi-double flowers. 'Cora Stubbs' has broad outer petals and smaller central ones in contrasting tones. 'Kelway's Glorious' has highly scented creamy white double flowers. *Zones 6–9.*

Paeonia mlokosewitschii
Caucasian peony

From late spring to mid-summer, this European peony bears big, open, pale to bright yellow flowers atop soft green leaves that have hairy undersides and are sometimes tinged purple at the edges. An erect, herbaceous perennial, it grows to 30 in (75 cm) high and wide, enjoys semi-shade and is resistant to frost. The seed pods split open to reveal black seeds on a red background. *Zones 6–9.*

Paeonia officinalis

Of European origin, this herbaceous perennial reaches a height and spread of 24 in (60 cm) and from spring to mid-summer bears single, purple or red, rose-like flowers. Although poisonous, it has been used medicinally. Of similar size, 'Rubra Plena' bears flowers that consist of clusters of many small, mid-magenta petals. *Zones 8–10.*

Papaver nudicaule

Papaver orientale

PAPAVER
Poppy

The 50 or so annual, biennial or perennial species of this genus are mainly from temperate parts of Eurasia and Africa and eastern USA. They have characteristic cupped petals and nodding buds turning skywards upon opening. Several of their close relatives take their common name, such as the tree poppy *(Romneya)*, the Californian poppy *(Eschscholzia)* or the blue poppy *(Meconopsis)*.

Cultivation
Poppies are fully frost hardy and prefer little or no shade and deep, moist, well-drained soil. Sow seed in spring or fall (autumn); many self-seed readily.

Papaver nudicaule
Iceland poppy
This tuft-forming perennial from North America and Asia Minor is almost always grown as an annual. Large scented flowers, borne in winter and spring, are white, yellow, orange or pink, and have a crinkled texture; the leaves are pale green, the stems long and hairy. It grows 12–24 in (30–60 cm) tall with a 6–8 in (15–20 cm) spread. *Zones 2–10.*

Papaver orientale
Oriental poppy
In summer this herbaceous perennial bears spectacular flowers as big as peonies in shades of pink through to red.

Papaver rhoeas (Shirley Series)

The cultivated varieties, sometimes double, come in a wide range of colors and many feature a dark basal blotch on each petal. According to variety, it grows from 18 in (45 cm) to more than 3 ft (1 m) tall. 'Cedric Morris' has shell-pink flowers with frilly petals, each with an almost black blotch at the base. *Zones 3–9.*

Papaver rhoeas
Corn poppy, field poppy, Flanders poppy
The cupped flowers on this fast-growing annual are small, delicate, scarlet and single. The cultivated varieties (Shirley Series) come in reds, pinks, whites and bicolors; they have a pale heart instead of the black cross that marks the center of the wild poppy. It grows to 24 in (60 cm) high with a 12 in (30 cm) spread. Double-flowered strains are also available. *Zones 5–9.*

PAROCHETUS
Shamrock pea, clover pea, blue pea

This genus contains a single species, a prostrate perennial with clover-like trifoliate leaves composed of leaflets slightly more than ½ in (12 mm) long. For most of the year it looks exactly like a small patch of clover. However, from late summer to winter, depending on the climate, it is studded with bright blue pea-like flowers borne singly or in pairs.

Cultivation

It is excellent for rockeries or an alpine house or as an unusual subject for a hanging basket. It prefers moist, humus-rich soil in sun or part-shade. Propagate from seed or by division.

Parochetus communis

From southwest China, Southeast Asia and the Himalayas to Sri Lanka, this deciduous species grows to a height of 4 in (10 cm) with a 12 in (30 cm) spread. The flowers are produced in succession throughout late summer and fall (autumn). *Zones 9–11.*

PELARGONIUM

The widely grown hybrid pelargoniums are popularly known as 'geraniums', but should not be confused with members of the genus *Geranium* of the same plant family. The genus *Pelargonium* consists of perhaps 280 species from South Africa, Australasia and the Middle East. Common garden and pot 'geraniums' are the Zonal pelargoniums. They have almost circular leaves with scalloped margins, often with horseshoe-shaped zones of brown, red or purple, and flower almost continuously.

Cultivation

These frost-tender plants are often treated like annuals for summer bedding in colder climates. In warmer climates they flower almost all the time, although they do not like extreme heat and humidity. They prefer light, well-drained, neutral soil. Avoid over-watering; Zonals rot at the base if soil remains wet. Propagate from softwood cuttings.

Pelargonium odoratissimum
Apple geranium

A strong, sweet smell of apples comes off the small, roughly heart-shaped, lobed, gray-green leaves of this bushy South African geranium. It reaches a height and spread of 12 in (30 cm). Flowers are small and white, sometimes with red veins in the upper petals. In warm-temperate climates, flowers may be borne almost continuously, although it dislikes hot, humid conditions. *Zones 10–11.*

Parochetus communis

Pelargonium odoratissimum

Pelargonium tricolor

This species is a sprawling, wiry-stemmed shrub about 12 in (30 cm) tall. It has narrow, hairy, gray-green leaves with a few deeply cut teeth. The distinctive flowers are pansy-like; the upper petals are red with a black base and the lower petals are white. *Zones 9–11.*

PENSTEMON

This large genus consists of 250 species of deciduous, evergreen or semi-evergreen subshrubs and perennials native to the cold temperate to subtropical northern hemisphere. The leaves appear in opposite pairs in whorls, while the flowers have 2 lobes on the upper lip and 3 on the lower. Hybrids have showy flower spikes in blues, reds, white and bicolors.

Cultivation

These marginally to very frost-hardy plants prefer fertile, well-drained soil and full sun. Propagate from seed, by division, or from cuttings of non-flowering shoots (the only method for cultivars).

Penstemon barbatus

syn. *Chelone barbata*

Coral penstemon, beard-lip penstemon

The scarlet flowers on this semi-evergreen, very frost-hardy perennial are tubular with 2 lips. They bloom on racemes from mid-summer to early fall (autumn) above narrow, lance-shaped, green leaves. The plant grows to 3 ft (1 m) high, with a spread of 12 in (30 cm). *Zones 3–10.*

Penstemon 'Evelyn'

This is a 30 in (75 cm) tall perennial hybrid with very narrow leaves and masses of slightly curved pale pink flowers. It was raised by the famous Slieve Donard nursery of Northern Ireland and is very frost hardy. *Zones 7–10.*

Penstemon barbatus

Pelargonium tricolor

Penstemon 'Evelyn'

Penstemon heterophyllus

Penstemon × gloxinioides

Pericallis × hybrida

Penstemon × gloxinioides
Border penstemon
This name applies to a group of hybrids raised in the middle of the 19th century from the species *Penstemon cobaea* and *P. hartwegii*. They have some of the largest and showiest flowers of any penstemons, mainly in rich reds and pinks and usually with a white throat. However, they are often short lived and not so cold hardy as other penstemons, and have declined in popularity. *Zones 7–9.*

Penstemon heterophyllus
Foothill penstemon, blue bedder penstemon
This very frost-hardy, summer-flowering subshrub grows to about 18 in (45 cm) tall. Its leaves are lance-shaped and slightly blue-green. The flowers vary from deep violet-pink to near blue.

Penstemon heterophyllus subsp. *purdyi* (syn. *P. h.* 'Blue Bedder') is a semi-evergreen shrub with blue tube-shaped flowers and pale green leaves. *Zones 8–10.*

PERICALLIS
Cineraria
This is a genus of some 15 species of perennials and subshrubs from Macronesia. Best known in cultivation for the florist's cineraria (*Pericallis × hybrida*), the wild species are nowhere near as fancy. The leaves, which may be in basal rosettes in the perennials, are usually oval to lance-shaped, with finely toothed edges and covered in small hairs. The flowers are usually pink, mauve or purple, and carried in open heads.

Cultivation
They like any moist, well-drained soil in part- to full shade, but few tolerate anything other than very light frosts. Propagate from seed or cuttings or by division, depending on the growth form.

Pericallis × hybrida
syns *Senecio cruentus, S. × hybrida*
This hybrid reaches 12 in (30 cm) tall and wide. It is a multi-purpose bloomer for grouping or for formal bedding in

Petunia × hybrida

Phacelia grandiflora

part-shaded spot, for window boxes or containers. The color of the daisy-like flowers ranges from pink, red, purple and crimson through to white, as well as the traditional blue. They are tolerant of heat, salt air and poor soil, but suffer in high humidity or excessive rain. *Zones 9–11.*

PETUNIA

There are around 35 species in the genus, including annuals, biennials and shrubby perennials. They have dark green, rather hairy, smooth-edged leaves and trumpet-shaped flowers in white, purple, red, blue, pink or mixed hues.

Cultivation

They are fairly fast growing, frost-tender plants, and like well-drained, fertile soil and a sunny location. They thrive where summers are hot. Sow seed under glass in early spring, or plant purchased seedlings at beginning of summer. Fertilize every month until flowering is advanced.

Petunia × hybrida

The 2 most important hybrid groups are the Grandiflora and Multiflora petunias, both with plants around 12 in (30 cm) tall at maturity. Grandifloras are very wide and shallow, while Multifloras are more compact with densely massed and somewhat narrower blooms. Nana Compacta petunias are generally less than 6 in (15 cm) high. Pendula petunias have prostrate, trailing stems. The

Grandiflora petunias are very popular, with a dazzling range of newer F1 hybrids, although they are easily rain damaged and susceptible to disfiguring botrytis rot; they include the Cascade and Supercascade Series (or Magic Series), with single flowers and somewhat trailing stems. *Zones 9–11.*

PHACELIA
Scorpion weed

This genus of around 150 species of annuals, biennials and perennials is generally shrubby, but species vary considerably, ranging from 6 in (15 cm) to over 5 ft (1.5 m) tall. Leaves are often toothed or lobed, sometimes to the point of being pinnate. They have clusters of small 5-petalled flowers at the stem tips. The flowers are usually in blue or purple shades, often with white centers. They are native to the Americas.

Cultivation

Most like any light but moist, well-drained soil in full sun. They are fully frost hardy. Propagate the annuals and biennials from seed, the perennials from seed or cuttings.

Phacelia grandiflora

This species from southern California is a 3 ft (1 m) tall annual with serrated-edged, elliptical leaves up to 8 in (20 cm) long. Its flowers are 1½ in (35 mm) wide and are mauve to white. *Zones 8–11.*

PHLOMIS

This genus consists of around 100 species of often downy-leafed perennials, subshrubs and shrubs occurring from the Mediterranran to China. Leaves are mostly large, over 4 in (10 cm) long, and densely covered with hair-like felting. The tubular flowers, borne on upright verticillasters, curl downwards and have 2 lips at the tip, the upper lip hooded over the lower. They occur in clusters of 2 to 40 blooms, depending on the species, and are usually in shades of cream, yellow, pink, mauve or purple.

Cultivation

Hardiness varies, though most tolerate moderate frosts. Plant in moist, well-drained soil in full sun or part-shade. Propagate from seed or from cuttings or by division.

Phlomis fruticosa
Jerusalem sage

This evergreen shrub, a native of southern Europe, is grown for the strikingly beautiful yellow flowers it bears in whorls from early to mid-summer, among oval, wrinkled, felty green leaves. It tolerates coastal areas quite well and grows to a height and spread of 30 in (75 cm). To keep its habit neat, prune to about half its size in fall (autumn). *Zones 7–10.*

Phlomis russeliana

Phlomis russeliana

This perennial thrives in any ordinary soil given a reasonable amount of sun. The large, heart-shaped, fresh green leaves make excellent ground cover, forming clumps around 12 in (30 cm) high and up to 24 in (60 cm) across. In summer, it bears stout stems 3 ft (1 m) high topped with several whorls of hooded, butter-yellow flowers. *Zones 7–10.*

PHLOX

This North American genus contains more than 60 species of evergreen and semi-evergreen annuals and perennials. They have profuse, fragrant flowers and symmetry of the flower clusters. The name *phlox* means 'flame', an appropriate epithet for these brightly colored, showy flowers.

Cultivation

The tall perennial phloxes like any temperate climate, though they need a lot of water while growing. The annuals grow in almost any climate. Grow in fertile soil that drains well but remains moist, in a sunny or part-shaded position. Propagate from seed or cuttings or by division.

Phlox douglasii

This evergreen perennial bears white, lavender-blue or pink flowers and grows

Phlomis fruticosa

to 8 in (20 cm) high. 'Boothman's Variety' is a dwarf form with blue-centered lavender flowers. 'Crackerjack' is a compact cultivar with crimson to magenta flowers. 'Red Admiral' is a strong-growing yet compact form with vivid crimson flowers. 'Rosea' forms a neat mat with silver-pink flowers. 'Waterloo' has deep crimson flowers. *Zones 5–10.*

Phlox drummondii
Annual phlox

This annual grows quickly to a bushy 15 in (38 cm) in height, half that in spread. In summer and fall (autumn), it bears closely clustered, small, flattish flowers with 5 petals in reds, pinks, purples and creams. It has lanceolate, light green leaves and is frost resistant. 'Sternenzauber' (syn. 'Twinkle') has

Phlox douglasii 'Rosea'

Phlox drummondii

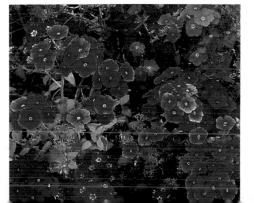

star-like flowers with pointed petals. There are dwarf strains that grow to 4 in (10 cm). *Zones 6–10.*

Phlox maculata
Meadow phlox

Phlox maculata is an herbaceous perennial that grows to 3 ft (1 m) tall and bears scented, white, pink or purple flowers in mid-summer. 'Alpha' is around 30 in (75 cm) tall with deep pink flowers. 'Miss Lingard' is up to 3 ft (1 m) tall with fragrant white flowers that some-times have a central pink ring. 'Omega' is around 30 in (75 cm) tall with fragrant white, lilac-centered flowers. *Zones 5–10.*

Phlox paniculata
Summer phlox, perennial phlox

This tall perennial can grow to more than 3 ft (1 m) high. In summer, it bears

Phlox maculata 'Omega'

Phlox paniculata

Phlox subulata

Phormium Hybrid 'Rainbow Warrior'

Phormium tenax 'Bronze Baby'

long-lasting, terminal flowerheads comprising many small, 5-lobed flowers. Colors range through violet, red, salmon and white according to variety. 'Mother of Pearl' has white to pale pink flowers suffused pink on stems up to 30 in (75 cm) tall. *Zones 4–10*.

Phlox subulata
Moss phlox
Throughout spring, this prostrate alpine perennial produces terminal masses of star-shaped flowers in blue, mauve, carmine, pink and white, the petals being notched and open. Fully frost hardy and evergreen, it is suitable for sunny rock gardens. 'McDaniel's Cushion' (syn. 'Daniel's Cushion') is best in small groups among shrubs or taller perennials. 'Marjorie' has glowing deep pink flowers. *Zones 3–10*.

PHORMIUM
New Zealand flax
Valued for the dramatic effect of their stiff, vertical leaves, these 2 species of large, clumping plants from New Zealand grow well in most conditions. The large, arching, striped leaves appear in clumps and can be dark green to green-yellow; there are many cultivars with variegated or brightly colored foliage. Height ranges from 3 ft (1 m) to 6 ft (1.8 m). The fiber of these flaxes has been used commercially, but is now largely confined to traditional Maori crafts.

Cultivation
They like almost any climate. They are fairly frost hardy, and respond well to generous watering and permanently moist conditions. Propagate from seed or by division in spring.

Phormium Hybrids
'Rainbow Warrior' is a recently released cultivar that makes a luxuriant clump of foliage. It has long arching and drooping leaves that are predominantly pinkish red and irregularly striped with bronze green. *Zones 8–11*.

Phormium tenax
The larger of the 3 New Zealand flax species, this has olive-green, strap-like leaves 6–10 ft (1.8–3 m) tall in clumps

Physalis alkekengi var. franchetii

Phygelius aequalis 'Yellow Trumpet'

about 6 ft (1.8 m) across. Foliage varies from bronze or purplish chartreuse to pink and salmon; leaves may be variegated with vertical stripes of 2 or more colors. 'Bronze Baby' has wide, fibrous, copper-toned leaves with sharply pointed ends. In summer, it bears tubular, bronze-red flowers on a strong stem from the base of the clump. *Zones 8–11.*

PHYGELIUS
Cape fuchsia
Related to *Penstemon* and *Antirrhinum* (the snapdragons) rather than *Fuchsia*, these 2 species of erect, evergreen shrubs or subshrubs—perennials in some winter conditions—are good rock-garden plants. They grow to 3 ft (1 m) high and 18 in (45 cm) wide, and bear handsome, red flowers in summer, set among dark green, oval leaves.

Cultivation
They do best in sun or part-shade and like a fertile, well-drained soil that is not too dry. Propagate from cuttings in summer.

Phygelius aequalis
This species is a suckering shrub to 3 ft (1 m) tall with dark green leaves and pale pink flowers. 'Yellow Trumpet' has leaves that are a paler green and creamy yellow flowers. *Zones 8–11.*

PHYSALIS
Ground cherry
This is a genus of around 80 species of annuals and perennials with a widespread distribution, especially in the Americas. Most form a clump of upright leafy stems 2–4 ft (0.6–1.2 m) tall. The flowers are small, usually white or yellow blotched purple, and are backed by calyces that enlarge to enclose the fruits—yellow, orange or red berries—as they develop. The fruits are often edible.

Cultivation
Hardiness varies, but most tolerate moderate frosts. They like moist, well-drained soil and a spot in sun or part-shade. Propagate from seed or by division.

Physalis alkekengi
Chinese lantern, winter cherry
This 24 in (60 cm) tall perennial found from southern Europe to Japan is notable for the vivid orange calyx that surrounds the ripening fruit. The flowers are small and white with yellow centers. The fruiting stems are often used fresh in floral arrangements or dried for winter decoration. *Physalis alkekengi* var. *franchetii* has minute, creamy white flowers. *Zones 6–10.*

PHYSOSTEGIA
Obedient plant, false dragon head

This is a genus of some 12 species of vigorous, rhizomatous perennials. They form clumps of unbranched, upright stems clothed in narrow, lance-shaped, long leaves with toothed edges. Plant size varies from 2–6 ft (0.6–1.8 m) tall. From midsummer, spikes of flowers develop at the stem tips. The flowers are tubular to bell-shaped with 2 upper lobes and 3 lower lobes. They come in shades of lavender, pink or purple and white.

Cultivation

They prefer moist, well-drained soil in sun or very light shade. Hardiness varies, though all tolerate moderate frosts. Propagate from seed or small basal cuttings or by division.

Physostegia virginiana

The showy flowers of this herbaceous perennial, which bloom in erect terminal spikes late in summer, are available in pale pink, magenta ('Vivid') or white. This native of eastern and central North America grows to 3 ft (1 m). 'Summer Spire' is around 24 in (60 cm) tall with deep pink flowers. *Zones 3–10.*

PHYTEUMA
Horned rampion

This Eurasian genus of around 40 species of small perennials is instantly

recognizable for the unusually structured flowerheads. The plants vary in size from 4–30 in (10–75 cm) tall. The flowers are borne on rounded heads and are tubular, often swelling at the base, with scarcely open tips from which the stigma protrudes; they are usually in lavender, blue or purple shades tinged with white.

Cultivation

Grow the small alpine species in light, gritty soil with added humus in a rockery or alpine house; large species will grow in a normal perennial border. Plant in sun or part-shade. Propagate from seed or by division.

Phyteuma comosum

syn. *Physoplexis comosa*

Native to the European Alps, this tufted perennial rarely exceeds 4 in (10 cm) in height. It has toothed, heart-shaped leaves and heads of violet-blue flowers. A favorite of alpine enthusiasts, it requires a gritty soil with added humus for moisture retention. *Zones 6–9.*

Physostegia virginiana 'Summer Spire'

Phyteuma comosum

Platycodon grandiflorus

Plectranthus ecklonii

PLATYCODON
Balloon flower, Chinese bellflower

The sole species in this genus is a semi-tuberous perennial with flower stems up to 30 in (75 cm) tall. Native to China, Japan, Korea and eastern Siberia, in spring it forms a clump of toothed-edged, elliptical to lance-shaped light blue-green foliage. The leafy flower stems develop quickly from midsummer and are topped with heads of inflated buds that open into broad, bell-shaped, white, pink, blue or purple flowers.

Cultivation

Very frost hardy, it likes any well-drained soil in full sun, but may take a few years to become established. Propagate from seed or by division. Because it resents disturbance, do not divide regularly.

Platycodon grandiflorus

On this species, balloon-like buds open out into 5-petalled flowers like bells, colored blue, purple, pink or white, in summer. The serrated elliptical leaves with a silvery blue cast form in a neat clump up to 24 in (60 cm) high and half that in spread. *Platycodon grandiflorus* var. *mariesii* was introduced in the late 1800s. More compact than the species, it grows to 18 in (45 cm) tall and has glossy, lance-shaped leaves. *Zones 4–10.*

PLECTRANTHUS

This genus contains more than 350 species of annuals, perennials and shrubs native to Africa, Asia and Australia. Most are rather frost tender and several species are grown as house plants, others are garden ornamentals or herbs. They generally have succulent or semi-succulent stems. The leaves are often fleshy and frequently oval to heart-shaped. The flowers are small and tubular, but are borne in sometimes showy spikes that extend above the foliage.

Cultivation

Plant in moist, well-drained soil in part-shade. Protect from frost and prolonged dry conditions. Propagate from seed or cuttings or by layering. Many will self-layer.

Plectranthus ecklonii

This shrub grows to a height of 6 ft (1.8 m) under favorable conditions, preferring a sheltered position and tolerating moderate shade. It has an erect, bushy habit with large deep green leaves that taper into their stalks and are strongly veined on the upper side. The tubular violet flowers are borne in erect terminal panicles in fall (autumn). Cutting the plant back hard in early spring induces a better show of flowers. *Zones 9–11.*

POLEMONIUM
Jacob's ladder

This genus of around 25 species of annuals and perennials is distributed over the Arctic and temperate regions of the northern hemisphere. They form clumps of soft, bright green, ferny, pinnate leaves from which emerge upright stems topped with heads of short, tubular, bell- or funnel-shaped flowers usually in white or shades of blue or pink. Dormant in winter, they develop quickly in spring and are in flower by early summer.

Cultivation

Most are very frost hardy and easily cultivated in moist, well-drained soil in sun or part-shade. Propagate annuals from seed; perennials from seed or cuttings of young shoots or by division. Some self-sow freely.

Polemonium caeruleum

Yellowy orange stamens provide a colorful contrast against the blue of this perennial's bell-shaped flowers when they open in summer. The flowers cluster among lance-shaped leaflets arranged in many pairs like the rungs of a ladder. The plant grows in a clump to a height and spread of up to 24 in (60 cm) or more. The stem is hollow and up-standing. It suits cooler climates. *Zones 2–9.*

Polemonium caeruleum

POLIANTHES

This is a sun-loving Mexican genus of about 13 clump-forming perennials, most of which are tender to both frost and dry conditions. The garden-grown species present their leaves from a basal rosette and their flowers on straight, upright stems. The genus includes the well-known tuberose, *Polianthes tuberosa*, which has been grown as a cut flower for centuries and is used extensively in the manufacture of perfumes.

Cultivation

They prefer open positions in good, well-drained garden loams and adequate moisture during the summer growing phase. The clumps should be lifted annually and the large bulbs, which once they flower will not flower again, removed. Propagate from seed.

Polianthes tuberosa
Tuberose

This species produces a mass of sweetly scented blooms in summer or early fall (autumn). A tall stem up to 3 ft (1 m) high is topped with a spike bearing

Polianthes tuberosa

clusters of tubular, star-shaped, creamy white flowers. A double variety, 'The Pearl', is more widely available than the single. The slender leaves are strap-shaped. *Zones 9–11.*

POLYGONATUM
Solomon's seal

The 30 or so species in this genus of forest-floor perennials are distributed all over the temperate zones of the northern hemisphere. King Solomon is thought to have first discovered the medicinal qualities of the plants, which are credited with healing wounds; the distilled sap of the rhizomes is still used in the cosmetics industry. They are favorites for woodland gardens.

Cultivation

They need rich, moist soil and a shady spot. Cut back to the rhizome in fall (autumn) as they are completely dormant in winter. Propagate from seed or by division of the rhizomes in spring or fall.

Polygonatum × hybridum

This hybrid species does best in cool to cold areas. In spring, the white, green-tipped, tubular flowers hang down from the drooping 3 ft (1 m) stems at the leaf axils. It is difficult to grow from seed. *Zones 6–9.*

Polygonatum × hybridum

POLYGONUM
syns *Aconogonon, Bistorta, Tovara, Persicaria affinis*
Knotweed

This is a genus of 50 to 80 species of evergreen, semi-evergreen or deciduous annuals, perennials or subshrubs. They have rounded, lance- or heart-shaped leaves 1½–10 in (3.5–25 cm) long depending on the species. The foliage often has purple-gray markings and may develop red and gold tints in fall (autumn). The flowers, usually pink or cream, are borne in sometimes showy panicles or spikes in the leaf axils and at stem tips.

Cultivation

These frost hardy plants like any well-drained soil in sun or part-shade; some may become invasive. Plant stronger growers where they can be contained. Propagate from seed or by division.

Polygonum affine
syn. *Persicaria affinis*

This evergreen Himalayan perennial has small, lance-shaped leaves that become bronze in winter. It forms a mat 12 in (30 cm) or more high with a similar spread. In late summer and fall (autumn), it bears dense spikes of small, red, funnel-shaped flowers. 'Darjeeling Red' has elongated leaves that turn bright red in fall. 'Donald Lowndes' is a compact cultivar with salmon-pink flowers that age to deep pink. *Zones 3–9.*

Polygonum affine

Portulaca grandiflora

Pontederia cordata

PONTEDERIA
Pickerel weed

The 5 or so aquatic perennials in this genus are native to river shallows in North and South America. They have distinctive, lance-shaped leaves and bell-shaped, usually blue flowers in terminal spikes. The name honors Guilio Pontedera (1688–1757), who was a professor of botany at the University of Padua.

Cultivation

Pickerel weed flourishes in almost any climate, from cold to subtropical. Plant in full sun in up to 10 in (25 cm) of water. Prune only spent flower stems, to encourage successive batches of flowers. Propagate from seed or by division in spring.

Pontederia cordata
Pickerel rush

This species grows from Nova Scotia to Florida, USA. A very frost-hardy, marginal water plant, it grows to 30 in (75 cm) with an 18 in (45 cm) spread. Its tapered, heart-shaped leaves are dark green and shiny. In summer it produces intense blue flowers in dense, terminal spikes. Zones 3–10.

PORTULACA

There are about 100 species of semi-succulent annuals or perennials in this genus, indigenous to the warm, dry regions of the world. The fleshy leaves vary in color from white to green or red. The flowers are cup-shaped, white, yellow, apricot, pink, purple or scarlet in color, and resemble roses in form.

Cultivation

They are easily grown in all climates. In cooler areas they should not be planted out until the danger of frost has passed. They need sun, well-drained soil and occasional watering. Propagate from seed or cuttings. Check for aphids.

Portulaca grandiflora
Rose moss, sun plant

This annual South American succulent is a low-growing plant which reaches 8 in (20 cm) high and spreads to 6 in (15 cm). It has small, lance-shaped, fleshy leaves and reddish stems. Its large, open flowers, usually double and borne in summer, come in bright colors including yellow, pink, red or orange. The flowers close at night and on cloudy days. It is suitable as a ground cover or in a rockery or border. Zones 10–11.

POTENTILLA
Cinquefoil

This genus consists of 500 or so perennials, some annuals and biennials, and deciduous shrubs. Many have 5-parted leaves (hence the common name cinquefoil), and range from about 1 in (25 mm) tall to about 18 in (45 cm). They bear profuse clusters of rounded, bright flowers through spring and summer. Some are used medicinally—the root bark of one species is said to stop nose bleeds and internal bleeding.

Cultivation

Plant in well-drained, fertile soil. They thrive in full sun in temperate climates. Perennials are generally frost hardy. Propagate by division or from seed; propagate shrubs from seed or from cuttings.

Potentilla nepalensis

A profusion of flowers in shades of pink or apricot with cherry red centers appears throughout summer on the slim branching stems of this Himalayan perennial. With bright green, strawberry-like leaves, this species grows to 12 in (30 cm) or more high and twice that in width. 'Miss Willmott' is an 18 in (45 cm) high cultivar with deep cerise-red flowers. *Zones 5–9.*

PRATIA

This genus, closely allied to *Lobelia*, includes 20 species of evergreen perennials native to New Zealand, Australia, Africa, Asia and South America. They have multiple branching stems and little toothed leaves. A profusion of starry flowers is followed by globular berries. Most are carpet forming and suit rockeries, but tend to overrun the garden.

Cultivation

Ranging from very frost hardy to frost hardy, they generally enjoy damp but porous soil, total sun or part-shade and protection from the elements. Water liberally during the growth period and sparingly in winter. Propagate by division or from seed.

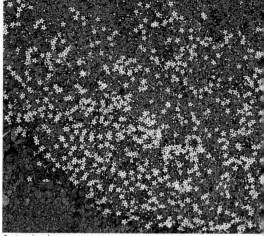

Pratia pedunculata

Potentilla nepalensis 'Miss Willmott'

Pratia pedunculata

From eastern Australia, this small-leafed, low-growing species makes a good ground cover, spreading and taking root at its nodes. In spring and early summer it bears profuse star-shaped, 5-petalled flowers, usually mid-blue to white, sometimes purple. These are followed by small berries. It is very frost hardy. *Zones 7–11.*

PRIMULA
Primrose

This popular genus of perennials consists of around 400 species. They are mainly rhizomatous, though some have poorly developed rhizomes and are short lived. The leaves are usually crowded into a basal tuft or rosette: mostly broadest toward their tips, they generally have toothed or scalloped margins. Flower shape, size and color vary so much that it is hard to generalize, though basically all have a tubular flower that opens abruptly into a funnel or flat disc, with five or more petals that are often notched at their tips.

Cultivation
Primulas like fertile, well-drained soil, part-shade and ample water. Propagate from seed or by division, or from root cuttings.

Primula auricula
This small central European perennial has yellow flowers in spring and furry leaves. Garden varieties come in a wide range of colors. In the mid-18th century a mutation resulted in flowers in shades of gray, pale green and almost black with centers covered with a white powder called 'paste'. Such flowers, called show auriculas, were once great favorites, but now have few devotees. *Zones 3–9.*

Primula japonica

Primula denticulata
Drumstick primrose
The botanical name of this very frost-hardy Himalayan perennial refers to the toothed profile of the mid-green, broadly lanceolate leaves. A vigorous grower, it reaches a height and spread of 12 in (30 cm). In early to mid-spring its open, yellow-centered flowers of pink, purple or lilac crowd in rounded terminal clusters atop thick hairy stems. *Primula denticulata* subsp. *alba* has white flowers usually on slightly shorter stems than the species. *Zones 6–9.*

Primula japonica
Japanese primrose
Forming a clump up to 24 in (60 cm) high and 18 in (45 cm) across, this fully frost-hardy perennial flowers in tiers on

Primula auricula

Primula denticulata

Primula obconica

tall, sturdy stems like a candelabra in spring and early summer. Its shiny flowers range through pink, crimson and purple to nearly pure white, usually with a distinct eye of another color. It prefers a moist situation. *Zones 5–10.*

Primula malacoides
Fairy primrose
This is a native of China. Small, open flowers bloom in spiral masses on this frost-tender perennial, sometimes grown as an annual. The single or double flowers range from white to pink to magenta. Its oval, light green leaves and erect stem have a hairy texture. It reaches a height and spread of 12 in (30 cm) or more. *Zones 8–11.*

Primula obconica
Poison primrose
Dense flower clusters grow in an umbellate arrangement on hairy, erect stems of this perennial. Native to China,

Primula malacoides

it grows to 12 in (30 cm) high and wide and flowers from winter through spring. The yellow-eyed, flattish flowers range from white to pink to purple. The light green leaves are elliptical and serrated. *Zones 8–11.*

Primula, Polyanthus Group
syn. *Primula × polyantha*
These fully frost-hardy perennials, sometimes grown as annuals, reach 12 in

Primula 'Wanda'

Primula, Polyanthus Group

Primula veris

(30 cm) in spread and height. Large, flat, scented flowers in every color but green bloom on dense umbels from winter to spring. Polyanthus are cultivars derived from *Primula vulgaris* crossed with *P. veris*, and have been grown since the 17th century. *Zones 6–10.*

Primula veris
Cowslip
A European wildflower of open woods and meadows, this species blooms a little later than the common primrose does. It is easily distinguished by the clusters of flowers carried on 6 in (15 cm) tall stalks and its sweeter scent. *Zones 5–9.*

Primula vulgaris

Primula vulgaris
English primrose, common primrose
This common European wildflower likes its cultivated conditions to resemble the cool woodland conditions of its native environment. Low growing to 8 in (20 cm) and usually frost hardy, it produces a carpet of bright flowers in spring. The flattish flowers are pale yellow with dark eyes (but garden forms come in every color), and bloom singly on hairy stems above rosettes of crinkled, lance-shaped, serrated leaves. Both the leaves and flowers are edible.

The cultivar 'Gigha White' has white flowers with yellow centers. *Zones 6–9.*

Primula 'Wanda'
This little plant disappears entirely over winter and begins to burst into flower as the new foliage develops. The leaves are deep green, heavily crinkled and about 3 in (8 cm) long. The short-stemmed flowers are deep magenta to purple with a yellow eye. It is an easily grown plant that quickly forms a small clump. It suits the front of a border; it also grows well in containers. *Zones 6–9.*

PRUNELLA
Self-heal

This is a genus of 7 species of semi-
evergreen perennials from Europe, Asia,
North Africa and North America. They
form low, spreading clumps and bear
opposite pairs of ovate to oblong,
sometimes deeply lobed leaves. Erect
flowering stems bear whorled spikes of
2-lipped tubular flowers in shades of
white, pink or purple.

Cultivation

Most spread from creeping stems that
readily take root at the nodes, making
them excellent ground covers. They are
fully frost hardy and grow in sun or
part-shade in moist, well-drained soil.
Propagate from seed or by division.

Prunella grandiflora
Large self-heal

Purple, 2-lipped flowers grow in erect
spikes above leafy stubs in spring and
summer on this species. A native of
Europe, it is good for ground cover or
rock gardens, having a spread and
height of 18 in (45 cm). 'Loveliness' has
soft mauve flowers. *Zones 5–9.*

Prunella grandiflora

PSYLLIOSTACHYS
Statice

This genus of 6 to 8 species of annuals is
found in the Middle East and central
Asia. Once included with *Statice*
(*Limonium*), they are now classified
separately. Rarely over 15 in (38 cm) tall
in flower, they form a clump of basal
leaves, sometimes hairy, that are often
deeply cut so they are almost pinnate.
The papery flowers are white, pink or
mauve, tiny and borne on upright spikes
that only rarely branch. They are often
dried or used fresh in floral arrangements.

Cultivation

Plant in moist, well-drained soil in full
sun and allow to dry off after flowering.
Propagate from seed.

Psylliostachys suworowii
syn. *Limonium suworowii*
Russian statice, rat's tail statice

Native to Iran, Afghanistan and central
Asia, this species has sticky 2–6 in (5–
15 cm) leaves and relatively large pink
flowers on wavy 6 in (15 cm) spikes.
Zones 6–10.

Psylliostachys suworowii

PTILOTUS

This is a genus of around 100 species of annuals, perennials and subshrubs from Australasia. Their stemless leaves are often rather thick and heavy. The foliage tends to be red tinted and frequently has wavy edges. The flowers are tiny, usually a shade of green, pink or purple, and are carried on shaggy spikes up to 6 in (15 cm) long.

Cultivation

These frost tender plants are easily cultivated in any well-drained soil in full sun. Propagate the annuals from seed, the perennials and shrubs from seed or cuttings.

Ptilotus manglesii

This is an Australian species that flowers from late winter to early summer when it is covered in rounded, 4 in (10 cm) spikes of pink to purple flowers. Sometimes grown as an annual, it is a short-lived spreading perennial that grows to around 12 in (30 cm) high. The leaves vary in shape: the basal leaves are oval, while the upper leaves are narrow. *Zones 9–11.*

PULMONARIA
Lungwort

Lungwort is an unappealing name for this European genus of 14 species of perennial, rhizomatous, forget-me-not-like plants—it refers to their former medicinal use. The most common species are low, spreading plants 6–10 in (15–25 cm) high with a spread of 24 in (60 cm) or more. The simple oval to lance-shaped leaves are sometimes slightly downy and often spotted silver-

Ptilotus manglesii

white. From early spring small deep blue, pink or white flowers open from pink or white buds.

Cultivation

They like cool, moist, humus-rich soil in light shade. All are very frost hardy. Propagate from seed or cuttings or by division.

Pulmonaria saccharata
Jerusalem sage, Bethlehem sage

This evergreen perennial has heavily spotted, hairy, 10 in (25 cm) leaves and has given rise to numerous cultivars with flowers in white and all shades of pink and blue. 'Highdown' is a 12 in (30 cm) cultivar with silver-frosted leaves and pendulous clusters of deep blue flowers. The Argentea Group consists of cultivars with silver leaves and red flowers that turn dark purple with age. *Zones 3–9.*

PULSATILLA
Pasque flower

These 30 species of spring-flowering, deciduous perennials are closely related to the anemones and were once included in that genus. They form mounding clumps of finely divided, almost ferny

foliaged rosettes. The leaves and flower stems are covered with downy silver-gray hairs. The flower color range includes white, pink, purple and red.

Cultivation

Most often grown in rockeries, these very frost-hardy plants also suit borders and troughs and prefer a moist, gritty, scree soil in sun or part-shade. They prefer cool to cold winters and cool summers and tend to be short lived in mild areas. Propagate from seed or by division.

Pulsatilla vulgaris

syns *Anemone pulsatilla, A. vulgaris*
Nodding, 6-petalled flowers bloom in spring on this European species. The yellow centers of the flowers are a stark color contrast to the petals, which can range through white, pink and red to purple. The finely divided leaves are pale green and very hairy. It reaches 10 in (25 cm) in height and spread. Avoid disturbing the roots. 'Alba' has pure white flowers and needs protection from sun and frost. 'Rode Klokke' (syn. 'Rote Glocke') is a free-flowering form with dark red blooms. 'Rubra' has purplish red or rusty flowers. *Zones 5–9.*

Pulmonaria saccharata

Pulsatilla vulgaris

Q, R

Ranunculus acris 'Flore Pleno'

Ramonda nathaliae

RAMONDA

This genus from Spain, the Pyrenees and the Balkans contains 3 species of ever-green perennials with rosettes of hairy, usually wrinkled leaves with toothed, wavy edges. Doing well in rock gardens or in cracks in stone walls, they have brightly colored, 4- to 5-petalled flowers, blooming in late spring and early summer.

Cultivation

Excessive water in the leaf rosettes may cause rotting, so they are best grown on an angle in part-shade and very well-drained, humus-rich soil. Propagate from seed or cuttings.

Ramonda nathaliae

This Balkan species, which reaches a height and spread of 4 in (10 cm), bears panicles of flat, 4-petalled, deep purple flowers with orange-yellow centers. The mid- to dark green leaves, hairier on the undersides than on top, grow to 2 in (5 cm) in length. *Zones 6–9*.

RANUNCULUS
Buttercup

This is a genus of some 400 species, mostly annuals and perennials from temperate regions worldwide. The flowers are bowl- or cup-shaped, 5-petalled and yellow, white, red, orange or pink. The name derives from the Latin for 'frog', due to the tendency of some to grow in bogs or shallow water. Two species are popular folk cures for arthritis, sciatica, rheumatism and the removal of warts.

Cultivation

Most thrive in well-drained soil, cool, moist conditions and sunny or shady locations. They are mostly fully frost hardy. Propagate from fresh seed or by division. Watch for powdery mildew and for attacks by slugs, snails and aphids.

Ranunculus acris
Meadow buttercup

This clump-forming perennial from Europe and western Asia has wiry stems with lobed and cut leaves. Panicles of saucer-shaped, bright yellow flowers appear in mid-summer. It grows from 8–36 in (20–90 cm) in height. 'Flore Pleno' has double, rosetted, golden-yellow flowers. *Zones 5–9*.

Ranunculus ficaria
Lesser celandine, pilewort

From southwestern Asia, Europe and northwestern Africa, this perennial has single, almost cup-shaped, bright yellow or orange flowers that appear in spring. It reaches only 2 in (5 cm) in height, and has glossy green leaves with silver or gold markings; the leaves die down after

Ranunculus ficaria

the flowers appear. 'Albus' has single, creamy white flowers with glossy petals. 'Brazen Hussy' has deep bronze-green leaves and shiny, deep golden-yellow flowers with bronze undersides. *Zones 5–10.*

RAOULIA
Vegetable sheep

This is a genus of about 20 species of evergreen perennials or subshrubs from New Zealand. They mostly form slow-growing, ground-hugging carpets of downy leaves and in summer bear small white or pale yellow, papery textured daisies. They are excellent foliage plants for rock gardens or raised beds.

Cultivation

Most require a cool-temperate climate, moist, acidic, sharply drained soil and protection from heavy winter rain. They prefer an open, sunny position or part-shade in warmer areas. Propagate from fresh seed or by division.

Raoulia australis
syn. *Raoulia lutescens*
Golden scabweed

Suitable for rock gardens, this prostrate, mat-forming perennial lays down a solid

Raoulia australis

carpet of silvery leaves ½ in (12 mm) deep over a 10 in (25 cm) spread. In summer it produces minuscule flowerheads of fluffy yellow blooms. *Zones 7–9.*

REHMANNIA

The 8 or 9 perennial species of *Rehmannia*, from China, are sometimes classed in the Scrophulariaceae family with foxgloves and snapdragons, or assigned to Gesneriaceae as cousins of the gloxinia and African violet. The uncertainty is due to the fact that the 2-lipped flowers look a bit like foxgloves, snapdragons and gloxinias. They have a delicate color, usually some shade of cool pink with pink and gold at their throats.

Cultivation

Plant in a warm-temperate climate (or a mildly warmed greenhouse in cool climates) in a sheltered spot in full sun and in rich, leafy soil. Propagate from seed or cuttings. Watch out for slugs and snails.

Rehmannia elata
syn. *Rehmannia angulata* of gardens
Chinese foxglove

This is the best known *Rehmannia* in gardens. From the mountains of China, it bears semi-pendent, tubular, bright pink flowers from summer to fall (autumn) and grows to 3 ft (1 m) high. Though perennial, it is short lived and is usually grown as a biennial. *Zones 9–10.*

RESEDA
Mignonette

This genus from Asia, Africa and Europe contains about 60 species of erect or spreading, branching annuals and perennials. They bear star-shaped, greenish white or greenish yellow flowers in spike-like racemes from spring to fall (autumn). These are attractive to bees. Mignonette used to be a favorite with perfumers and it is still cultivated in France for its essential oils.

Cultivation

Plant in full sun or part-shade in well-drained, fertile, preferably alkaline soil. Deadheading will prolong flowering. Propagate from seed in late winter.

Rehmannia elata

Reseda odorata
Common mignonette

From northern Africa, this moderately fast-growing annual is renowned for the strong fragrance of its flowers. The conical heads of tiny greenish flowers, with touches of red, and dark orange stamens are otherwise unspectacular. They appear from summer to early fall (autumn). The plants will grow to 24 in (60 cm) high and about half that in spread. *Zones 6–10.*

RHEUM

This genus contains 50 species of rhizomatous perennials, including the edible rhubarb and several ornamental plants. From eastern Europe and central Asia to the Himalayas and China, they have a striking appearance; their large basal leaves are coarsely toothed and have prominent midribs and veins. The minute, star-shaped flowers appear in summer and are followed by winged fruits.

Cultivation

These very frost-hardy plants prefer full sun or part-shade and deep, moist,

Reseda odorata

humus-rich soil. Propagate from seed or by division. Watch for slugs and crown rot.

Rheum palmatum
Chinese rhubarb

This Chinese species bears panicles of small, dark red to creamy green flowers that open early in summer. It has deep green leaves with decoratively cut edges, and reaches up to 8 ft (2.4 m) in height and 6 ft (1.8 m) in spread. 'Atrosanguineum' has dark pink flowers and crimson leaves that fade to dark green. *Zones 6–10.*

RHODANTHE
Strawflower

The 40 species of erect annuals, perennials and subshrubs in this genus all come from arid areas of Australia and recently have mostly been classified in the genus *Helipterum*. Their daisy-like, everlasting, pink, yellow or white summer flowers are used for cut flowers and in dried arrangements. They have alternate, mid-green to gray-green leaves.

Cultivation

These marginally frost-hardy plants prefer full sun and well-drained soil of poor quality. Propagate from seed.

Rhodanthe chlorocephala subsp. rosea

syns *Helipterum roseum, Acroclinium roseum*
This annual from southwestern Australia grows to a height of 24 in (60 cm) and a spread of 6 in (15 cm). The flowerheads are composed of white to pale pink bracts surrounding a yellow center, and close in cloudy weather. It is widely grown for cut flowers. *Zones 9–11.*

Rhodanthe 'Paper Star'

This cultivar, possibly a form of *Rhodanthe anthemoides*, has profuse white flowerheads. While not very long lasting as a cut flower, it is an impressive, long-flowering garden specimen of semi-prostrate habit. *Zones 7–11.*

RHODOHYPOXIS
Rose grass

There are 4 to 6 species of these small, colorful, tuberous-rooted, herbaceous perennials from South Africa in this genus, but only *Rhodohypoxis baurii* is

Rhodanthe 'Paper Star'

Rheum palmatum 'Atrosanguineum'

Rhodanthe chlorocephala subsp. rosea

Rodgersia aesculifolia

Rhodohypoxis baurii

common in gardens. Sowing seeds from named varieties will give quite a range of colors. They have grass- to strap-like hairy leaves and produce white, pink, red or purple flowers on short stalks over long periods in summer.

Cultivation
They grow well in any temperate climate where soil does not freeze to the depth of the tubers. They prefer full sun and well-drained, fertile, humus-rich soil that retains moisture in summer and is not excessively wet in winter. Propagate from seed or by division.

Rhodohypoxis baurii
This alpine plant grows 3 in (8 cm) tall, each tuber producing grassy, lightly hairy leaves and, in spring, several starry flowers 3 in (8 cm) wide. Colors range from pure white to various shades of pink and dark red. The central 3 petals close over the heart of the flower to protect it from the weather, and spring open when a pollinating insect alights. It soon forms a dense clump. *Zones 8–10*.

RODGERSIA
Native to Burma, China, Korea and Japan, this genus consists of 6 species of moisture-loving perennials. They tend to be grown more for their bold leaves than for their plumes of fluffy flowers, borne

in mid- to late summer. The stems unfurl in mid-spring and spread out to form a fan of leaves on top of stout stems.

Cultivation
They are excellent plants for marshy ground at the edge of a pond or in a bog garden in sun or part-shade. They do best in a site sheltered from strong winds, which can damage the foliage. Propagate by division or from seed.

Rodgersia aesculifolia
This Chinese species has lobed, 10 in (25 cm) wide leaves that are borne on hairy stalks, forming a clump 24 in (60 cm) high and wide. The large, cone-shaped clusters of small, starry flowers are cream or pale pink, and are borne on stout stems up to 4 ft (1.2 m) tall. *Zones 5–9*.

ROMNEYA
Tree poppy
The 2 species in this genus from North America and Mexico are summer-flowering, woody based perennials and deciduous subshrubs. They have blue-green foliage composed of alternate leaves and poppy-like, 6-petalled flowers with glossy yellow stamens.

Cultivation
They prefer a warm, sunny position and fertile, well-drained soil. They are

Roscoea cautleoides

Romneya coulteri

difficult to establish (although once established they may become invasive), and they resent transplanting. Protect the roots in very cold areas in winter. Propagate from seed or cuttings.

Romneya coulteri
California tree poppy, Matilija poppy
This shrubby Californian perennial produces large, sweetly scented, poppy-like white flowers highlighted with fluffy gold stamens. The silvery green leaves are deeply divided, their edges sparsely fringed with hairs. Fully frost hardy, it forms a bush up to 8 ft (2.4 m) high with a spread of 3 ft (1 m). *Romneya coulteri* var. *trichocalyx* has pointed, rather bristly sepals. *Zones 7–10.*

ROSCOEA
These 18 species of tuberous perennials are related to ginger (*Zingiber*), but in appearance are more reminiscent of irises. They have orchid-like flowers, which have hooded upper petals, wide-lobed lower lips and 2 narrower petals. The leaves are lance-shaped and erect. They are suitable for open borders and rock and woodland gardens.

Cultivation
They prefer part-shade and cool, fertile, humus-rich soil that should be kept moist but well drained in summer.

Provide a top-dressing of leafmold or well-rotted compost in winter. Propagate from seed or by division.

Roscoea cautleoides
Bearing its yellow or orange flowers in summer, this frost-hardy species from China grows to 10 in (25 cm) tall with a 6 in (15 cm) spread. The glossy leaves are lance-shaped and erect and wrap into a hollow stem-like structure at their base. *Zones 6–9.*

RUDBECKIA
Coneflower
This popular genus from North America has about 15 species of annuals, biennials and perennials. The plants have bright, daisy-like, composite flowers with prominent central cones (hence the common name). The single, double or semi-double flowers are usually in tones of yellow; cones, however, vary from green through rust, purple and black. Species range in height from 24 in (60 cm) to 10 ft (3 m).

Cultivation
Coneflowers prefer loamy, moisture-retentive soil in full sun or part-shade. Propagate from seed or by division in spring or fall (autumn). They are moderately to fully frost hardy. Watch for aphids.

Rudbeckia fulgida
Black-eyed Susan, orange coneflower

This rhizomatous perennial, which reaches 3 ft (1 m) high, has branched stems, mid-green, slightly hairy leaves with prominent veins, and daisy-like, orange-yellow flowers with dark brown centers. *Rudbeckia fulgida* var. *sullivantii* 'Goldsturm' (syn. *R.* 'Goldsturm') grows 24 in (60 cm) tall with crowded stems and narrow, lanceolate, green leaves. *Zones 3–10.*

Rudbeckia fulgida var. sullivantii 'Goldsturm'

Rudbeckia hirta
Black-eyed Susan

The flowerheads on this biennial or short-lived perennial are bright yellow, with central cones of purplish brown and its lanceolate leaves are mid-green and hairy. It reaches between 12–36 in (30–90 cm) tall, with a spread of 12 in (30 cm). 'Irish Eyes' is noteworthy for its olive-green center. 'Marmalade' has large flowerheads with golden-orange ray florets. Many dwarf strains of cultivars such as 'Becky Mixed' are available in a range of colors from pale lemon to orange and red; they are usually treated as annuals. *Zones 3–10.*

Rudbeckia laciniata
Cutleaf coneflower

This species is a splendid summer-flowering perennial that can reach 10 ft (3 m) tall, though 6 ft (1.8 m) is more usual. The drooping ray florets give the flowerhead an informal elegance. 'Golden Glow' is a striking, if somewhat floppy, double cultivar. 'Goldquelle' grows to around 30 in (75 cm) tall and has large, bright yellow, double flowers. *Zones 3–10.*

Rudbeckia hirta 'Irish Eyes'

Rudbeckia laciniata

S

Salpiglossis sinuata

Salvia elegans 'Scarlet Pineapple'

SALPIGLOSSIS

These natives from the southern Andes can be tricky to grow, but patient gardeners who live in mild climates with fairly cool summers will be rewarded by a short but beautiful display of flowers. They come in rich shades of crimson, scarlet, orange, blue, purple and white, all veined and laced with gold. There are 2 species of annuals and perennials providing color in borders or as greenhouse plants in cold climates.

Cultivation

Plant in full sun in rich, well-drained soil. Deadhead regularly. They are best sown directly from seed in early spring in the place they are to grow. Watch for aphids.

Salpiglossis sinuata
Painted tongue

Offering a variety of flower colors including red, orange, yellow, blue and purple, this annual blooms in summer and early fall (autumn). The 2 in (5 cm) wide, heavily veined flowers are like small flaring trumpets, while the lanceolate leaves are light green. A fast grower, it reaches a height of 18–24 in (45–60 cm) and a spread of at least 15 in

(38 cm). It is frost tender and dislikes dry conditions. *Zones 8–11.*

SALVIA
Sage

Salvia consists of some 900 species of annuals, perennials and soft-wooded shrubs with a cosmopolitan distribution. Their distinguishing feature is the tubular, 2-lipped flower with the lower lip flat but the upper lip helmet- or boat-shaped; the calyx is also 2-lipped and may be colored. Some with aromatic leaves are grown as culinary herbs. The genus name is from the Latin *salvus*, 'safe' or 'well', referring to the supposed healing properties of *Salvia officinalis*.

Cultivation

Most shrubby species tolerate only light frosts, but some perennials are more frost-hardy. Sages prefer full sun in well drained, light-textured soil with adequate summer water. Propagate from seed or cuttings, or division of rhizomatous species.

Salvia elegans
Pineapple-scented sage

This open-branched perennial or subshrub which can reach 6 ft (1.8 m) in milder areas, has a distinctive pineapple scent and flavor. Its whorls of small bright red flowers are borne in late summer and fall (autumn). The leaves are used fresh but sparingly in fruit

Salvia farinacea

Salvia involucrata 'Bethellii'

salads, summer drinks and teas. The flowers are delicious, and may be added to desserts and salads for color and flavor. 'Scarlet Pineapple' (syn. *Salvia rutilans*) is more floriferous with larger scarlet flowers which, in milder areas, will persist to mid-winter. *Zones 8–11*.

Salvia farinacea
Mealy-cup sage

This species is grown as an annual in regions that have cold winters. It is a short-lived perennial in warmer climates, although if planted in a little shade to protect it from hot afternoon sun and pruned hard in mid-fall (mid-autumn) it can live up to 5 years. Growing to some 24–36 in (60–90 cm), it bears lavender-like, deep violet-blue flowers on slender stems. It is a good cut flower. 'Victoria' has deep blue flowers. *Zones 8–11*.

Salvia greggii
Fall sage, cherry sage, autumn sage

This shrub, which can reach 3–4 ft (1–1.2 m) high has small, aromatic leaves; above the foliage rise slender stems with broad-lipped sage blossoms in red, orange, salmon, pink, pale yellow, white and blends. The flowers are produced from spring through fall (autumn) in coastal areas, and in fall and winter in the desert. Many hybrids and named selections are available. It is native to Texas and Mexico. *Zones 9–10*.

Salvia greggii

Salvia involucrata
Roseleaf sage

This tall Mexican perennial remains evergreen in mild climates but is best cut back to the ground every year to promote flowering. It has erect cane-like stems to about 5 ft (1.5 m) high and broad, long-stalked leaves that often develop red veining. The loose flower spikes terminate in groups of large mauve to magenta bracts, which are shed one by one to reveal a trio of developing flowers of the same or deeper color. It blooms over a long summer–fall (autumn) season. 'Bethellii' is a popular cultivar. *Zones 9–10*.

Salvia prunelloides

This low, tuberous-rooted perennial to 15 in (38 cm) is from Mexico. The few hairy branches bear oblong leaves to 3 in (8 cm) long. Each silky calyx carries a bright blue flower. It flowers from late summer into fall (autumn). *Zones 9–11.*

Salvia prunelloides

Salvia splendens 'Van Houttei'

Salvia uliginosa

Salvia sclarea
Biennial clary, clary sage

This native of southern Europe and Syria is a biennial and grows 3 ft (1 m) tall. Moderately fast growing and erect, it has long, loose, terminal spikes of tubular, greenish white tinged with purple flowers in summer and velvety, heart-shaped leaves. *Salvia sclarea* var. *turkestanica* has pink stems and white, pink-flecked flowers. *Zones 5–10.*

Salvia splendens
Scarlet sage

This native of Brazil, which is grown as an annual, produces dense terminal spikes of scarlet flowers in summer through early fall (autumn). It grows 3–4 ft (1–1.2 m) tall with a similar spread. In hotter climates, give some shade; it is moderately frost hardy. 'Salsa Burgundy' has deep burgundy flowers, while 'Van Houttei' has a deep dull red calyx with large lighter red flowers. *Zones 9–12.*

Salvia uliginosa
Bog sage

Long racemes of sky-blue flowers appear in summer on this upright branching perennial from South America. The leaves are toothed, elliptical to lance-shaped and up to 3 in (8 cm) long, smooth or only slightly hairy. Growing to 3–6 ft (1–1.8 m), it

Salvia sclarea

has slender curving stems. In good or moist soil it sends out underground rooting shoots and may become invasive. *Zones 8–11.*

SANGUINARIA
Bloodroot, red puccoon

The single species of the genus is a widespread woodland plant occurring from Nova Scotia through to Florida. It is a low-growing perennial herb grown for its spring display of cup-shaped flowers.

Cultivation

It prefers sandy soil but will tolerate clay soil if not too wet. It does well in sun or part-shade, and especially under deciduous trees. Propagation is by division in late summer when the leaves have died back.

Sanguinaria canadensis

This perennial has a long stout horizontal rootstock. Each bud on the stock sends up a heart-shaped leaf with scalloped edges on stalks 6 in (15 cm) long. Each leaf is up to 12 in (30 cm) across. The solitary white or pink-tinged flowers are up to 3 in (8 cm) across, single, with 8 to 12 petals and many yellow central anthers. They appear in the folds of the leaves in spring before the gray leaves fully expand, and last for about 3 weeks. *Zones 3–9.*

Sanguinaria canadensis

SAPONARIA
Soapwort

The common name of this genus consisting of 20 species of annuals and perennials comes from the old custom of using the roots for washing clothes. They contain a glucoside called saponin, which dissolves grease and dirt and which, being edible, has been used as an additive to beer to ensure that it develops a good head when poured. These are good plants for rock gardens, banks and for trailing over walls.

Cultivation

Fully frost-hardy, they need sun and well-drained soil. Propagate from seed in spring or fall (autumn) or from cuttings in early summer.

Saponaria ocymoides
Rock soapwort

This alpine perennial from Europe forms a thick carpet from which profuse terminal clusters of small, flattish flowers, colored pink to deep red, bloom in late spring and early summer. It has sprawling mats of hairy oval leaves. *Zones 4–10.*

SAXIFRAGA
Saxifrage

Both the foliage and blooms on these perennials, biennials and annuals are equally appealing. The genus comprises

Saponaria ocymoides

Saxifraga 'Ruth Draper'

Saxifraga exarata subsp. moschata

Saxifraga paniculata

some 440 species of evergreens and semi-evergreens from Eurasia and the Americas. The flowers are mostly white, sometimes spotted with pink, but other colors are also available. The genus name combines two Latin terms, 'rock' and 'to break', suggestive of either the hardiness of their rooting system or their reputed medicinal effect on bladder stones.

Cultivation
Soil, light requirements and frost hardiness vary greatly depending on the species. Propagate from seed in fall (autumn), by division or from rooted offsets in winter.

Saxifraga exarata subsp. moschata
syn. *Saxifraga moschata*
This is a delightful downy-leafed cushion-forming plant from central and southern Europe with many round-petalled flowers on 4 in (10 cm) stems. The colors range from white or creamy yellow to pink through to strong carmine pink or red. The tricky combination of full sun and moist soil with perfect drainage in winter will keep it robust and healthy. *Zones 6–9.*

Saxifraga paniculata
syn. *Saxifraga aizoon*
Livelong saxifrage
This summer-flowering evergreen perennial from Europe grows to a height and spread of 8–10 in (20–25 cm) and bears terminal clusters of 5-petalled white flowers, often with spots of reddish purple, on erect stalks. Other colors include pale pinks and yellows. The bluish green leaves form a rosette below the flower stems. Grow in full sun in well-drained, alkaline soil. 'Rosea' has bright pink flowers. 'Minima' has very small foliage and flowers. *Zones 3–9.*

Saxifraga 'Ruth Draper'
Ruth Draper was a British comedienne of the 1930s, famous for her monologue, 'You should have seen my garden last week'. Her namesake is a pretty example of a mossy saxifrage, a group that likes a moist and lightly shaded position. It bears large, cup-shaped, purple-pink flowers in early spring and grows to 2 in (5 cm) in height. *Zones 6–9.*

SCABIOSA
Scabious, pincushion flower

This genus of 80 species of annuals, biennials and perennials, from Eurasia and north Africa, bears tall-stemmed, honey-scented flowers ideal for cutting. The blooms, bearing multiple florets with protruding filaments giving a pincushion effect, range from white, yellow, red, blue and mauve to deep purple.

Cultivation

Most species will thrive in full sun in well-drained, alkaline soil. Propagate annuals from seed in spring, and perennials from cuttings in summer, seed in fall (autumn) or by division in early spring.

Scabiosa caucasica

Flat, many-petalled flowerheads in pink, red, purple or blue hues with pincushion-like centers often in a contrasting color make this summer-flowering perennial popular for borders and as cut flowers. A bushy plant with lobed mid-green leaves, it reaches a height and spread of 18–24 in (45–60 cm). 'Clive Greaves' has lilac-blue flowers; 'Staefa' is a strong grower with blue flowers; and 'Mrs Isaac House' has creamy white flowers. *Zones 4–10.*

Scabiosa caucasica

Scabiosa columbaria

This biennial or perennial grows to 24 in (60 cm) with a spread of 3 ft (1 m). Slender, erect, hairy stems produce globular heads of reddish purple to lilac-blue flowers in 1½ in (35 mm) wide heads during summer and fall (autumn). 'Butterfly Blue' is a lower growing, dense, fuzzy leafed cultivar with lavender-blue pincushion flowers over a very long period. *Zones 6–10.*

SCAEVOLA
Fan flower

This genus from Australia and the Pacific region contains 96 species of mainly temperate origin. They are mainly evergreen perennials, shrubs, subshrubs and small trees. Most have leaves that are fleshy, often hairy and occasionally succulent, borne on stout, sometimes brittle stems. Samll, fan-shaped flowers are profuse and are held on the plant for long periods. Flower color ranges from white to blue, mauve and deep purple.

Cultivation

They tolerate a wide range of soils but prefer them light and well drained; they prefer sun or part-shade. Propagate from seed or cuttings in spring or summer.

Scabiosa columbaria 'Butterfly Blue'

Scaevola 'Mauve Clusters'

This frost-hardy, spreading perennial flowers profusely in spring and summer. The small flowers present a mass of mauve against a backdrop of bright green leaves. Growing very close to the ground, it spreads as much as 6 ft (1.8 m). *Zones 9–11.*

SCHIZANTHUS
Poor man's orchid, butterfly flower

These 12 to 15 species of annuals are from the Chilean mountains. They come in shades of pink, mauve, red, purple and white, all with gold-speckled throats. They grow to about 3 ft (1 m) high and 12 in (30 cm) wide. Most of the flowers seen in gardens are hybrids, giving a colorful display over a short spring to summer season.

Scaevola 'Mauve Clusters'

Schizanthus × wisetonensis

Cultivation

They do not like extremes of heat or cold, and grow best outdoors in a mild, frost-free climate; in colder climates grow in a greenhouse. Grow in full sun in fertile, well-drained soil. Propagate from seed.

Schizanthus × wisetonensis

This erect species bears tubular to flared, 2-lipped, white, blue, pink or reddish brown flowers often flushed with yellow from spring to summer. It has lance-shaped, light green leaves and grows to 18 in (45 cm) high with a spread of 12 in (30 cm). Most garden strains are derived from this species. *Zones 7–11.*

SCHIZOSTYLIS

A single species of grassy leafed rhizomatous perennial in the iris family makes up this genus. *Schizostylis* is widely distributed in South Africa where it grows along banks of streams. The long-flowering stems terminate in clusters of bowl-shaped 6-petalled flowers in deep scarlet and pink.

Cultivation

Frost hardy, it prefers full sun and fertile, moist soil with shelter from the cold in cool-temperate climates. Divide every couple of years when it becomes crowded or propagate from seed in spring.

Schizostylis coccinea 'Mrs Hegarty'

Schizostylis coccinea
Crimson flag

This variable species can fail in prolonged dry conditions. The sword-shaped leaves are untidy unless pruned regularly and protected from thrips and slugs. It has a late summer and fall (autumn) display which in some climates, conditions and seasons can extend into winter and beyond. *Coccinea* means scarlet, and that is the usual color of this species. It is a dainty plant reaching a height of 24 in (60 cm) and spread of 12 in (30 cm). 'Mrs Hegarty' is rose pink. *Zones 6–10*.

SCUTELLARIA
Skullcap, helmet flower

The name of this cosmopolitan genus comes from the Latin *scutella*, meaning a small shield or cup, which is a rough description of the pouch of the upper calyx. There are some 300 known species consisting mainly of summer-flowering perennials, most on a rhizomatous root system; a few are annuals and rarely subshrubs.

Cultivation

They like full sun in most reasonable garden soil. They do not like parched soil in summer, but are content with ordinary watering throughout dry weather. Propagate by division in winter or from seed sown fresh in fall (autumn). Cuttings may be taken in summer.

Scutellaria incana

Scutellaria incana

This is a rounded perennial to 4 ft (1.2 m) in height with lightly serrated oval leaves and large panicles of grayish blue flowers in summer. It is widespread throughout northeastern USA. *Zones 5–9*.

SEDUM
Stonecrop

This genus, from the temperate northern hemisphere and tropical mountains, contains about 400 species of succulent annuals, biennials, perennials, subshrubs and shrubs. Quick-growing plants, they vary in habit from carpet forming to upright up to 3 ft (1 m) tall.

Cultivation

They range from frost tender to fully frost hardy, and prefer fertile, porous soil and full sun. Propagate perennials from seed, by division or from cuttings. Propagate annuals and biennials from seed sown under glass in spring.

Sedum spectabile
syn. *Hylotelephium spectabile*
Showy sedum, ice plant

Spoon-shaped, fleshy, gray-green leaves grow in clusters on the erect stems of this perennial. Flattish heads of small, pink, star-like flowers appear in late summer. It grows to a height and spread of 18 in (45 cm) and is resistant to both frost and dry conditions. *Zones 5–10*.

Sedum spectabile

Sidalcea 'Rose Queen'

Sidalcea malviflora

SIDALCEA
Prairie mallow, checker mallow

The 20 to 25 species of upright annuals or perennials with lobed, rounded leaves in this genus are found in western USA, from open grasslands to mountain forests. Pink, purple or white flowers have a silky appearance and feel, and last well as cut flowers.

Cultivation

They prefer cool summers and mild winters in good, deep, moisture-retentive soil. They tolerate some shade in hot climates. Cutting back after flowering will produce a second flush of blooms. Propagate from seed or by division.

Sidalcea malviflora
Checkerbloom

This erect perennial grows to 4 ft (1.2 m) tall with spreading fibrous roots. It has lobed leaves and loose heads of pink or white flowers resembling hollyhocks during spring and summer. Most cultivars included under this name are now believed to be hybrids with other species. *Zones 6–10.*

Sidalcea 'Rose Queen'

syn. *Sidalcea malviflora* 'Rose Queen' Large, deep pink, cupped flowers are borne in spikes in summer on this fully frost-hardy perennial. The divided leaves form a basal clump with a spread of 24 in (60 cm). The overall height is 4 ft (1.2 m) and tall plants may need staking. 'William Smith' is similar but grows only 3 ft (1 m) tall and produces flowers in 2 tones of deep pink. *Zones 6–10.*

SILENE
Campion, catchfly

This genus contains over 500 species of annuals, biennials and deciduous or evergreen perennials featuring 5-petalled summer flowers, baggy calyces and a multitude of small, elliptical, often silky leaves. They are wisespread in the northern hemisphere with a few in South America and Africa. Some exude gum from their stems; passing flies get stuck to this, hence the common name catchfly.

Cultivation

These marginally to fully frost-hardy plants like fertile, well-drained soil and full or part-sun. Propagate from seed or from cuttings.

Silene coeli-rosa

syns *Agrostemma coeli-rosa, Lychnis coeli-rosa, Viscaria elegans*
Rose of heaven

This upright annual from the Mediterranean bears pinkish purple flowers in summer. Its lance-shaped, green leaves have a grayish cast. It grows rapidly to 18 in (45 cm) with a spread of 6 in (15 cm). *Zones 6–11.*

Silene coeli-rosa

Silene laciniata

Silene laciniata

This 3 ft (1 m) tall perennial comes from California and northern Mexico. The flowers are held in small heads and are bright crimson in color. *Zones 7–11*.

Silene vulgaris

syn. *Silene uniflora*

Bladder campion, maiden's tears

This perennial has stems up to 24 in (60 cm) tall, oval leaves and white flowers with 2-lobed petals; the flowers are either solitary or in heads. It is found throughout northern Africa, temperate Asia and Europe. However, most plants sold as *Silene vulgaris* are, in fact, *S. uniflora*. *Zones 5–10*.

Silene vulgaris

SISYRINCHIUM

These natives of South and North America can self-destruct in seasons of prolific blooming, because the flower stem kills off the leaf stem from which it sprouts. The genus includes 90 marginally to fully frost-hardy species of annuals and rhizomatous perennials. It is easy to mistake the narrow leaves of the seedlings for grass.

Cultivation

Establish them in poor to moderately fertile, moist but well-drained soil. Although tolerant of part-shade, they prefer sun. They readily self-seed, otherwise propagate by division in late summer.

Sisyrinchium bellum

Sisyrinchium bellum

California blue-eyed grass

Branched stems rise up to 18 in (45 cm) on this perennial species to form a tuft with linear leaves and amethyst-purple (rarely white) flowers. It comes from California. *Zones 8–11*.

Sisyrinchium striatum
syn. *Phaiophleps nigricans*
Satin flower

Long, narrow and sword-shaped, the leaves on this fully frost-hardy, ever-green perennial are gray-green. In summer it bears slender spikes of small cream flowers, striped purple. The species, which originates in Chile and Argentina, grows 18–24 in (45–60 cm) high with a 12 in (30 cm) spread. There is also an attractive variegated form. *Zones 8–10.*

SOLENOSTEMON
Coleus, flame nettle, painted nettle

This genus comprises 60 species of low shrubby perennials, often hairy and with variegated leaves, from tropical Africa and Asia. The stems are 4-angled and the opposite leaves are often toothed.

Solenostemon scutellarioides

The flowers are small with an elongated lower lip.

Cultivation

These frost-tender plants are easily grown in milder climates with adequate summer moisture and protection from hot sun. They prefer humus-rich, moist but well-drained soil and need to be

Sisyrinchium striatum

Solidago 'Golden Wings'

pinched back to promote bushiness. Propagate from seed or cuttings.

Solenostemon scutellarioides

syns *Coleus blumei* var. *verschaffeltii, C. scutellarioides*
Native to Southeast Asia, this bushy, fast-growing perennial is grown as an annual in more temperate climates. The leaves are a bright mixture of pink, green, red or yellow and are a pointed, oval shape with serrated edges. It grows 24 in (60 cm) high and 12 in (30 cm) wide. *Zones 10–12.*

SOLIDAGO
Goldenrod

The goldenrods are a genus of about 100 species of woody based perennials, related to the asters. They flower in fall (autumn). The small, individual flowers are bright yellow. Most are too weedy to be allowed into even the wildest garden, but some are worth cultivating for their big flower clusters and there are some very attractive hybrids.

Cultivation

These fully frost-hardy plants grow well in sun or shade in any fertile, well-drained soil. Most self-seed, or they can be propagated by dividing the clumps in fall or spring.

Solidago 'Golden Wings'

This perennial grows to 5 ft (1.5 m) high with a spread of 3 ft (1 m). It has downy, lance-shaped leaves with serrated margins, and produces small, bright yellow flowers in feathery panicles early in fall (autumn). *Zones 5–10.*

Stachys byzantina

Stachys byzantina 'Primrose Heron'

STACHYS
Betony, woundwort, hedge nettle

This genus, in the mint family, contains about 300 species of annuals, perennials and evergreen shrubs. They are widespread in temperate zones and have long been used in herb gardens, many of them having supposed medicinal value, and come from a range of habitats mostly in northern temperate regions. Many are aromatic, and attract bees and butterflies. They bear tubular, 2-lipped, purple, red, pink, yellow or white flowers.

Cultivation

They like well-drained, moderately fertile soil in full sun. Propagate from seed or cuttings or by division.

Stachys byzantina

syns *Stachys lanata, S. olympica*
Lambs' ears, lambs' tails, lambs' tongues

The leaves give this perennial its common names: they are lance-shaped and have the same white, downy feel of a lamb. Unfortunately, the leaves turn to mush in very cold, humid or wet weather. It makes a good ground cover or border plant, growing to about 12–18 in (30–45 cm) high, with a 24 in (60 cm) spread. Mauve-pink flowers appear in summer. 'Primrose Heron' has yellowish green leaves. 'Big Ears' (syn. 'Countess Helen von Stein') is a large growing cultivar which bears tall spikes of purple flowers. *Zones 5–10.*

Stachys coccinea

Stokesia laevis

Stachys coccinea
Scarlet hedge nettle

This long-flowering perennial native to southwest USA and Mexico bears red flowers, although pink and white forms are available. The flowers are almost irresistible to hummingbirds. Flowering continues from spring through fall (autumn) on plants that grow 12–36 in (30–90 cm) tall and 18 in (45 cm) wide. *Zones 6–10*.

STOKESIA
Stokes' aster

This genus of a single perennial species native to the southeastern states of the USA was named after Englishman Dr Jonathan Stokes (1755–1831). An attractive late-flowering perennial, it grows about 18 in (45 cm) high and flowers from late summer to fall (autumn) if the spent flower stems are promptly removed. It is very good for cutting.

Cultivation

Plant in full sun or part-shade and fertile, well-drained soil. Water well in summer. Propagate from seed in fall or by division in spring.

Stokesia laevis

syn. *Stokesia cyanea*

This fully frost-hardy perennial has evergreen rosettes, its narrow leaves green, basal and divided. The blue-mauve or white blooms have a shaggy appearance reminiscent of cornflowers and are borne freely on erect stems. *Zones 7–10*.

STREPTOCARPUS

This genus consists of 130 species of annuals, perennials and rarely subshrubs from tropical Africa, Madagascar, Thailand, China and Indonesia. There are 3 main groups: shrubby bushy species with vigorous growth; rosetted plants; and single-leafed species producing one very large leaf up to 3 ft (1 m) long. They all bear tubular flowers with 5 lobes and hairy, veined, crinkly leaves.

Cultivation

Frost tender, they prefer part-shade and leafy, humus-rich, moist but well-drained soil. Seeding will be prevented if flowers are deadheaded and stalks are removed. Propagate from seed or cuttings or by division.

Streptocarpus Hybrids

Most *Streptocarpus* hybrids have *S. rexii* as a major parent. They generally have a rosette growth habit and large, showy, trumpet-shaped flowers in bright colors with a white throat. 'Blue Heaven' has flowers that are a strong mid-blue to pale purple. *Zones 10–11.*

SYMPHYTUM
Comfrey

This genus comprises 25 to 35 species of hairy perennials from damp and shaded places in Europe, North Africa and western Asia. They grow rapidly and may become invasive. The leaves are alternate and rather crowded at the base of the plant. The flowers are held in shortly branched heads of pink, blue, white or cream. Each flower consists of a tube terminating in 5 triangular lobes.

Cultivation

They are easily grown in sun or part-shade in moist, well-dug soil with added manure. Propagate from seed or cuttings, or by division.

Symphytum 'Goldsmith'

syn. *Symphytum* 'Jubilee'
'Goldsmith' grows to 12 in (30 cm) and has leaves edged and blotched with cream and gold; the flowers are blue, pink or white. *Zones 5–10.*

Streptocarpus Hybrid 'Blue Heaven'

Symphytum 'Goldsmith'

T

Tagetes lemmonii

Tagetes patula

TAGETES
Marigold

These familiar summer plants have single or double flowers in shades of orange, yellow, mahogany, brown and red, which contrast brightly with the deep green leaves. Some of the 50 or so species have aromatic foliage, hence *Tagetes minuta*'s common name of stinking Roger. It is said that the roots exude substances fatal to soil-borne pests, leading to their extensive use as companion plants.

Cultivation

These fast-growing plants thrive in warm, frost-free climates. Grow in full sun in fertile, well-drained soil. Dead-head regularly. Propagate from seed in spring after frost has passed. Watch for slugs, snails and botrytis.

Tagetes lemmonii
Mountain marigold

Native to Arizona and adjacent regions of Mexico, this species is unusual in being a shrub of 3–5 ft (1–1.5 m) high, of somewhat sprawling habit. The leaves are light green and pinnately divided into narrow segments; they are very aromatic, giving off a smell like ripe passionfruit when brushed against. In fall (autumn) and winter it bears small golden-yellow flowerheads, sometimes continuing through most of the year (encouraged by cutting back in early summer). *Zones 9–11.*

Tagetes patula
French marigold

This fast-growing, bushy annual reaches 12 in (30 cm) in height and spread. It was introduced to European gardens from its native Mexico via the south of France, hence its common name. The double flowerheads, produced in summer and early fall (autumn), re-semble carnations. They bloom in red, yellow and orange. The leaves are deep green and aromatic. 'Dainty Marietta' is an all-yellow cultivar with single flowerheads. *Zones 9–11.*

TANACETUM
syn. *Pyrethrum*

In Greek mythology, immortality came to Ganymede as a result of drinking tansy, a species of this genus of rhizoma-tous perennial daisies. Even in recent times, it has been used (despite being potentially quite poisonous) for promot-ing menstruation and treating hysteria, skin conditions, sprains, bruises and rheumatism. The 70 or so species of this

Tanacetum parthenium 'Golden Moss'

genus from northern temperate zones have daisy-like flowers.

Cultivation

Moderately to very frost hardy, they prefer full sun in well-drained, dryish soil. Do not overwater. They spread readily and need to be kept under control. Propagate by division in spring or from seed in late winter or early spring.

Tanacetum coccineum

syns *Chrysanthemum coccineum, Pyrethrum roseum*

Painted daisy, pyrethrum

This frost-hardy, erect perennial has dark green, feathery, scented leaves that are finely dissected. Its single, or sometimes double, long-stalked flowerheads may be pink, red, purple or white, appearing from late spring to early summer. The species grows 2–3 ft (60–90 cm) tall with a spread of 18 in (45 cm) or more. 'Brenda' has striking magenta single flowers. 'Eileen May Robinson' is one of the best single pinks. 'James Kelway' has deep crimson-pink flowers. *Zones 5–9.*

Tanacetum parthenium

syn. *Chrysanthemum parthenium*

Feverfew

Feverfew is an aromatic plant which was once used to dispel fevers and agues,

Tanacetum coccineum

and as an antidote for over-indulgence in opium. It bears clusters of single or double white-petalled, daisy-like flowers over a long summer period. This short-lived perennial is frost hardy, and reaches 24 in (60 cm) high. 'Golden Moss' is a dwarf cultivar with a height and spread of 6 in (15 cm); it has golden, moss-like foliage and is often grown as an edging or bedding plant. *Zones 6–10.*

THALICTRUM

Meadow rue

Over 300 species make up this genus of perennials known for their fluffy, showy flowers. The branches of their slender, upstanding stems often intertwine. The leaves are finely divided. Blooming in spring and summer, the flowers have no petals, but instead have 4 or 5 sepals and conspicuous stamen tufts. They serve well in borders and in the margins of bush gardens.

Cultivation

Grow these frost-hardy plants in sun or part-shade in any well-drained soil; some species need cool conditions. Propagate from fresh seed in fall (autumn) or by division in spring.

Thalictrum aquilegiifolium
Greater meadow rue

This clump-forming Eurasian perennial grows to 3 ft (1 m) tall and has a spread of 18 in (45 cm). Pink, lilac or greenish white flowers in fluffy clusters on strong stems are produced in summer. Each gray-green leaf comprises 3 to 7 small, elliptical, toothed leaflets in a feather-like arrangement, resembling the leaves of some *Aquilegia* species. *Zones 6–10.*

Thalictrum delavayi

syn. *Thalictrum dipterocarpum* of gardens
Lavender shower

Rather than fluffy heads, this graceful, clump-forming perennial from western China bears a multitude of nodding, lilac flowers in loose panicles, with prominent yellow stamens. The flowers are borne from the middle to end of summer. The finely divided leaves give the mid-green foliage a dainty appearance. Reaching 4 ft (1.2 m) high, this species has a spread of 24 in (60 cm). 'Hewitt's

Thalictrum delavayi

Double' has rounded, pompon-like, mauve flowers. *Zones 7–10.*

THUNBERGIA

This genus of 90 to 100 species of mainly twining climbers and evergreen, clump-forming shrubs, was named after the 18th-century Swedish botanist Dr Carl Peter Thunberg. Native to Africa, Asia and Madagascar, their leaves are entire or lobed, and the mostly trumpet-shaped blooms are borne individually from the leaf axils or in trusses.

Thalictrum aquilegiifolium

Cultivation

They range from marginally frost hardy to frost tender, and prefer temperatures above 50°F (10°C). They grow in any reasonably rich soil with adequate drainage. Full sun is preferred, except during the summer months, when part-shade and liberal water should be provided. Propagate from seed or cuttings.

Thunbergia alata
Black-eyed Susan

Native to tropical Africa, this vigorous annual or perennial (in frost-free areas) climber grows quickly to 10 ft (3 m). It is marginally frost hardy. Its deep green, cordate leaves are up to 3 in (8 cm) long. It bears masses of 2 in (5 cm) wide orange flowers with black throats from early summer to fall (autumn). *Zones 9–12.*

THYMUS
Thyme

This Eurasian genus consists of over 300 evergreen species of herbaceous perennials and subshrubs, ranging from prostrate to 8 in (20 cm) high. Chosen for their aromatic leaves, they are frequently featured in rockeries, be-

tween stepping stones or for a display on banks. Some are used in cooking. The flowers are often tubular and vary from white through pink to mauve. Thyme has been associated with courage, strength, happiness and wellbeing.

Cultivation

They are mostly frost hardy. Plant out from early fall (autumn) through to early spring in a sunny site with moist, well-drained soil. Propagate from cuttings in summer or by division.

Thymus × *citriodorus*
syn. *Thymus serpyllum* var. *citriodorus*
Lemon-scented thyme

This delightful rounded, frost-hardy shrub grows 12 in (30 cm) high and has tiny oval lemon-scented leaves and pale lilac flowers. The leaves are used fresh or dry in poultry stuffings or to add lemon flavor to fish, meat and vegetables. 'Anderson's Gold' is a yellow-foliaged spreader that is inclined to revert to green. *Zones 7–10.*

Thunbergia alata

Thymus × *citriodorus* 'Anderson's Gold'

Tiarella cordifolia

Thymus serpyllum 'Pink Ripple'

Thymus serpyllum
Wild thyme, creeping thyme, mother of thyme

This European native grows to a height of 10 in (25 cm) and spread of 18 in (45 cm), forming a useful ground cover. Its creeping stem is woody and branching, and the scented, bright green leaves are elliptical to lanceolate. The bluish purple flowers are small and tubular with 2 lips, and are borne in spring and summer. It is frost hardy and will take moderate foot traffic, but needs replanting every few years to maintain a dense cover. 'Pink Ripple' has bronze-pink flowers. *Zones 3–9.*

TIARELLA
Foamflower

The foamflowers are a genus of 5 species of forest-floor perennials native to North America. They resemble their relatives, the heucheras, and can be hybridized with them. They grow from thick rootstocks, with their decorative leaves growing close to the ground. The airy sprays of small white flowers are borne on bare stems about 12 in (30 cm) tall; pale pink forms occur rarely.

Cultivation

Very frost hardy, they like cool-temperate climates, and make good ground covers for a woodland-style garden. Plant in part- to deep shade in moist, well-drained soil. Propagate from seed or by division in early spring.

Tiarella cordifolia
Foamflower, coolwort

This vigorous spreading evergreen blooms profusely in early to late spring producing terminal spikes of tiny, creamy white flowers with 5 petals. Its leaves are mostly pale green, lobed and toothed, with dark red marbling and spots; the basal leaves take on an orange-red hue in winter. When in flower, it has a height and spread of 12 in (30 cm) or more. *Zones 3–9.*

TITHONIA
Mexican sunflower

This genus of 10 species consists mainly of annuals, biennials and perennials. Originating in Central America and the West Indies, they are related to sunflowers and bear large, vivid yellow, orange or scarlet daisy-like flowerheads in summer and fall (autumn). The leaves are often hairy on the undersides and sharply lobed.

Cultivation

Marginally frost hardy, they thrive in

hot, dry conditions, but need plenty of water. They prefer well-drained soil and full sun. Deadhead regularly and prune hard after flowering to encourage new growth. Propagate from seed sown under glass in late winter or early spring.

Tithonia rotundifolia

This bulky annual needs plenty of room in the garden as it can easily grow to 5 ft (1.5 m) tall with a spread of 3 ft (1 m). Its leaves are heart-shaped. It is a great plant for hot color schemes, both in the garden and as a cut flower, with its 4 in (10 cm) wide, zinnia-like flowers of orange or scarlet. 'Torch' bears bright orange or red flowerheads and grows to 3 ft (1 m). *Zones 8–11.*

TORENIA
Wishbone flower

This genus of 40 to 50 species of erect to spreading, bushy annuals and perennials comes from tropical African and Asian woodlands. They have oval to lance-shaped, entire or toothed, opposite leaves. In summer, they bear racemes of trumpet-shaped, 2-lipped flowers with 2-lobed upper lips and 3-lobed lower lips.

Torenia fournieri

Cultivation

Torenias prefer a warm, frost-free climate. In cooler climates, they should not be planted out until after the last frost. Grow in fertile, well-drained soil in part-shade in a sheltered position. Pinch out the growing shoots of young plants to encourage a bushy habit. Propagate from seed in spring.

Torenia fournieri
Bluewings

This branching annual has light to dark green ovate or elliptical leaves with toothed edges. Frost tender, it grows fairly rapidly to a height of 12 in (30 cm) and a spread of 8 in (20 cm). Its flowers, borne in summer and early fall (autumn), are pansy-like and a deep purplish blue, turning abruptly paler nearer the center, and with a touch of yellow. Red, pink and white varieties are also available. *Zones 9–12.*

Tithonia rotundifolia

TRADESCANTIA

syns *Rhoeo, Setcreasea, Zebrina*

Spiderwort

This genus consists of 50 or more species of perennials, some evergreen, from the Americas. Some are rather weedy, but the creeping species (wandering jew) make useful ground covers. Some upright species have pure blue flowers, a hard color to find for the late-summer garden. Most trailing types are frost tender and are usually grown as greenhouse pot plants, except in mild-winter climates where they make good ground cover.

Cultivation

Grow in full sun or part-shade in fertile, moist to dry soil. Cut back ruthlessly when they become straggly. Propagate by division or from tip cuttings in spring, summer or fall (autumn).

Tradescantia, Andersoniana Group

This group of hybrids covers a range of plants formerly listed under *Tradescantia* × *andersoniana* or *T. virginiana*. They are mainly low-growing perennials with fleshy, strap-like leaves and heads of 3-petalled flowers. Although the foliage clump seldom exceeds 18 in (45 cm)

Tradescantia, Andersoniana Group hybrid

high, the flower stems can reach 24 in (60 cm). There are many hybrids in a range of white, mauve, pink and purple flower shades. 'Alba' has white flowers. *Zones 7–10.*

Tradescantia virginia

This is the most widely grown species and grows to about 3 ft (1 m) tall. It bears its flowers in long succession from summer until well into fall (autumn). Garden varieties have been selected with larger flowers and a wide color range, from white through to deep blue and purple. They like a shaded spot and a rich moist soil. Cut them down ruthlessly at the end of autumn. *Zones 4–9.*

TRICYRTIS

Toad lilies

The common name of this genus of about 20 species seems to have biased gardeners against the toad lilies, but these clumping rhizomatous summer-flowering perennials from the woodlands of Asia are quite attractive in their quiet colorings and markings. The flowers, which are star-, bell- or funnel-shaped, with opened-out tips, are held in the

Tradescantia, Andersoniana Group 'Alba'

axils of the leaves. The leaves are pointed and appear on erect or arching, hairy stems.

Cultivation

Grow these very frost-hardy plants in part-shade in humus-rich, moist soil; in areas with cool summers, they need a warm spot. Propagate from seed in fall (autumn) or by division in spring.

Tricyrtis hirta

This upright Japanese species bears 2 in (5 cm) wide, star-shaped white flowers spotted with purple from late summer to fall (autumn). The branching stems are 3 ft (1 m) long. *Zones 5–9*.

TRILLIUM
Wake robin, wood lily

Among North America's most beautiful wildflowers, this genus in the lily family contains 30 species of rhizomatous, deciduous perennials; they also occur naturally in northeastern Asia. Upright or nodding, solitary, funnel-shaped flowers with 3 simple petals are held just above a whorl of 3 leaves. They flower in spring and make good ornamentals in wild gardens and shady borders.

Trillium grandiflorum

Cultivation

Very frost hardy, they prefer a cool, moist soil with ample water and shade from the hot afternoon sun. Slow to propagate from seed in fall or by division in summer, they are long lived once established.

Trillium grandiflorum
Snow trillium, wake robin

This showy, clump-forming trillium is the easiest to grow, reaching 12–18 in (30–45 cm) in height. The pure white flowers, borne in spring, fade to pink as they age. The double-flowered white form, 'Flore Pleno', is beautiful but rare, and has arching stems and oval, dark green leaves. *Zones 3–9*.

TROLLIUS
Globe flower

The perennial globe flowers resemble their cousins the buttercups in their bright yellow flowers and their liking for wet ground, but they have a more sedate habit. The flowers are also often bigger, and their larger number of petals gives them the appearance of being double. Spring is the main flowering season, but they often flower in fall (autumn) too. They are native to northern temperate regions.

Tricyrtis hirta

Trollius chinensis

Tropaeolum majus

from Chile to Mexico. In warm areas, nasturtiums can survive for several years, self-sowing freely and flowering all year. The flowers can be single or double, about 2 in (5 cm) across, and come in red, orange, russet, yellow, cream and even blue. In the 19th century a white cultivar was bred, only to be lost.

Cultivation
Frost hardy to frost tender, most prefer moist, well-drained soil in full sun or part-shade. Propagate from seed, basal stem cuttings or tubers in spring. Watch out for aphids and cabbage moth caterpillars.

Tropaeolum majus
Garden nasturtium, Indian cress
The stem is trailing and climbing on this fast-growing, bushy South American annual. Its leaves are rounded and marked with radial veins. It blooms in summer and fall (autumn); its 5-petalled flowers spurred, open and trumpet-shaped, come in many shades from deep red to pale yellow. It grows to a spread of 3 ft (1 m) and a height of up to 18 in (45 cm). The hot-tasting leaves and flowers of this species are sometimes added to salads. The Alaska Hybrids have single flowers in a range of colors and prettily variegated leaves. *Zones 8–11.*

Cultivation
Very frost hardy, they grow in moist soil provided they are watered generously, but the boggy edge of a pond or stream suits them better. They like some shade. Propagate from seed in spring or fall or by division.

Trollius chinensis
syn. *Trollius ledebourii*
Chinese globe flower
This is one of the lesser known but still very desirable species. It grows 2–3 ft (60–90 cm) tall and bears its shining flowers in spring above handsomely slashed foliage. The flower color varies from light to deep yellow. It is a fast grower, but is not invasive. *Zones 5–9.*

TROPAEOLUM
Nasturtium
The 87 species of annuals, perennials and twining climbers in this genus are

U, V

Valeriana officinalis

Vancouveria planipetala

VALERIANA
Valerian
This genus consists of more than 150 species of herbaceous perennials, herbs and subshrubs, few of which have any ornamental value. Those that do, are suitable for borders and rock gardens. The name is from the Latin *valere* (keep well) in recognition of the medicinal properties of some species. Before modern tranquilizers were introduced, the root from *Valeriana officinalis* was used to treat nervous conditions.

Cultivation
Very frost hardy, they thrive in almost any soil, in sun or part-shade. Propagate from seed or by division of established plants in fall (autumn).

Valeriana officinalis
Cat's valerian, common valerian, garden heliotrophe
This clump-forming, fleshy perennial, which is attractive to cats, grows to 4 ft (1.2 m) tall with a spread of 3 ft (1 m). It occurs naturally throughout Europe and eastwards to Russia and western Asia. It bears rounded flowerheads of white to dark pink flowers in summer on erect hairy stems. The leaves are opposite with serrated margins. *Zones 3–9.*

VANCOUVERIA
There are 3 species in this genus of graceful, creeping, woodland plants with slender rhizomes. These perennial herbs and shrubs are native to western North America and are related to *Epimedium*. The leaves are rounded and often 3 lobed; the flowering stem, 8–16 in (20–40 cm) long, is normally leafless. The small pendulous flowers are white or yellow, and borne in spring or summer.

Cultivation
Useful as a ground cover in cool shaded areas, these frost-hardy plants prefer a cool position in peaty soil. Propagate by division, or from fresh ripe seed in spring.

Vancouveria planipetala
Redwood ivy, inside-out flower
This plant grows to 18 in (45 cm) in height with a 3 ft (1 m) spread. The stems are creeping, prostrate and branching. The evergreen leaves are thick and leathery with a wavy margin. The flower stem is leafless, up to 18 in (45 cm) tall, and the flowers are white, tinged with lavender and borne in spring. *Zones 7–9.*

Verbascum bombyciferum

Verbascum chaixii 'Album'

Verbascum 'Letitia'

VERBASCUM
Mullein

This genus consists of semi-evergreen to evergreen perennials, biennials and shrubs from Europe and the more temperate zones of Asia. Foliage ranges from glossy to velvety. Many of the 250 or so species are considered weeds. However, several are desirable in the garden for their stately habit and long summer-flowering season — the flowers do not open from the bottom up, but a few at a time along the spike.

Cultivation

They are fully to moderately frost hardy but will not tolerate winter-wet conditions. Plant in well-drained soil in an open, sunny location. Propagate from seed in spring or late summer or by division in winter. Some self-seed readily.

Verbascum bombyciferum

This biennial from Asia Minor has silvery gray, furry, large leaves and grows 6 ft (1.8 m) tall. It bears golden-yellow, cup-shaped flowers in summer, sometimes in terminal spikes. *Zones 6–10.*

Verbascum chaixii

This species from southern Europe can be relied on to live long enough to form clumps. The flowers, borne on 3 ft (1 m) tall stems in summer, are normally yellow. The white form 'Album' is usually finer. *Zones 5–10.*

Verbascum 'Letitia'

This small-growing hybrid between *Verbascum dumulosum* and *V. spinosum* has slender, felted, silver-gray foliage. From mid-spring onwards, it produces masses of delicate lemon-yellow flowers on short, branched stems. It is ideal for a rock garden or as a container plant in a sunny position. The flowers are sterile, so propagation is by division. *Zones 8–10.*

VERBENA

Originating in Europe, South America and North America, this genus of 250 or more species of biennials and perennials is characterized by small, dark, irregularly shaped and toothed leaves. They bloom in late spring, summer and fall (autumn). An agreeably spicy aroma is associated with most verbenas.

Cultivation

Marginally frost hardy to frost tender, they do best where winters are not severe. Establish in medium, well-drained soil in full sun or part-shade. Propagate from seed in fall or spring, stem cuttings in summer or fall, or by division in late winter.

Verbena bonariensis

This tall South American perennial is often grown as an annual, primarily for its deep purple flowers which top the sparsely foliaged 4–5 ft (1.2–1.5 m) stems from summer to fall (autumn). The deeply toothed leaves cluster in a mounded rosette, which easily fits in the front or middle of a border; the floral stems give a vertical line without much

Verbena bonariensis

mass. Frost hardy, it self-seeds readily and survives with minimal water, even in dry areas. *Zones 7–10.*

Verbena × hybrida
Garden verbena

This trailing perennial blooms in summer to fall (autumn). Its fragrant flowers appear in dense clusters, many showing off white centers among the hues of red, mauve, violet, white and pink. It suits summer beds and containers. 'Homestead Purple' is a sturdy cultivar with rich red-purple flowers. 'La France' has bright pink flowerheads. 'Silver Ann' has heads of light pink flowers with darker blooms at the center. 'Sissinghurst' has mid-green leaves and bears stems of brilliant pink flowerheads in summer. *Zones 9–10.*

Verbena × hybrida

Verbena rigida

Verbena rigida

syn. *Verbena venosa*

A South American native, this tuberous-rooted perennial is an excellent species for seaside cultivation. It reaches a height of 18–24 in (45–60 cm) with a spread of 12 in (30 cm). The dense spikes of pale violet to magenta flowers are borne from mid-summer. 'Silver Jubilee' bears a mass of red flowers right through the growing season. *Zones 8–10.*

VERONICA
Speedwell

The genus was named after Saint Veronica who, pious legend relates, wiped the face of Christ with her veil and was rewarded with having his image imprinted on it. The 200 or so species are herbaceous perennials, ranging from prostrate, creeping plants 6 ft (1.8 m) high giants. The small flowers are gathered in clusters of various sizes and are borne in abundance in summer, mainly in blue, although white and pink are also common.

Veronica austriaca

Cultivation

Fully to moderately frost hardy, they like any temperate climate, and are not fussy about soil or position. Propagate from seed in fall (autumn) or spring, from cuttings in summer or by division in early spring or early fall (autumn).

Veronica austriaca

syn. *Veronica teucrium*

This clump-forming European perennial grows to 10–18 in (25–45 cm) tall with long, slender stems bearing bright blue, saucer-shaped flowers in late spring. The leaves vary in shape from broadly oval to narrow and are either entire or deeply cut. Propagate by division in fall (autumn) or from softwood cuttings in summer. *Zones 6–10.*

Veronica gentianoides
Gentian speedwell

This mat-forming perennial found from the Caucasus to southwest Asia has wide, dark green leaves from which rise spikes of pale blue or white flowers in spring. It reaches 18 in (45 cm) in height. *Zones 4–9.*

Veronica gentianoides

Viola hederacea

Veronica spicata

Veronica spicata
Digger's speedwell, spike speedwell
This very frost-hardy European perennial reaches a height of 24 in (60 cm)
and a spread of up to 3 ft (1 m). Its
stems are erect, hairy and branching.
Spikes of small, star-shaped, blue
flowers with purple stamens bloom in
summer. *Veronica spicata* subsp. *incana* has
spreading clumps of silvery, felty leaves
and deep violet-blue flowers. 'Rosea' is a
pink-flowered form. *Zones 3–9.*

VIOLA
Violet, heartsease, pansy
This genus of annuals, perennials and
subshrubs has up to 500 species occurring in temperate zones. Most are
creeping plants, either deciduous or
evergreen, with slender to thick rhizomes.
Flowers of wild species have 3 spreading
lower petals and 2 erect upper petals,
with a short nectar spur projecting to the
rear of the flower. Many species produce
cleistogamous flowers, with smaller petals
that do not open properly, and able to
set seed without cross-pollination.
Hybridization has produced garden
pansies, violas and violettas, with showy
flowers in very bright or deep colors.

Cultivation
Most cultivated species tolerate light
frosts; many are fully frost hardy.
Pansies and violas are grown as annuals
or pot plants in full sun, but appreciate
shelter from wind; sow seed in late
winter or early spring, planting in late
spring in well-drained soil. Propagate
perennials by division or from cuttings.

Viola hederacea
syns *Erpetion reniforme, Viola reniformis*
Australian native violet
The small, scentless flowers borne on short stems on this creeping evergreen perennial are mostly white with a lilac blotch in the throat; they appear from spring to fall (autumn). Its stems are prostrate, suckering and mat forming, spreading widely and growing 2–4 in (5–10 cm) high. Its leaves are kidney-shaped with irregular edges. *Zones 8–10.*

Viola odorata
Sweet violet
A sweet perfume wafts from the flowers of these well-known florists' violets, sold in small bunches. It is a spreading, rhizomatous perennial from Europe, which grows 3 in (8 cm) tall and may spread indefinitely on cool, moist ground. Its dark green leaves are a pointed kidney shape with shallowly toothed edges. Spurred, flat-faced

Viola odorata

flowers in violet, white or rose appear from late winter through early spring. It boasts many cultivars. *Zones 6–10.*

Viola, Perennial Cultivars
Primarily of *Viola lutea, V. amoena* and *V. cornuta* parentage, these hardy perennial plants are long flowering, year round in mild climates. 'Jackanapes' has brown upper petals and yellow lower petals. *Zones 6–10.*

Viola, Perennial Cultivar 'Jackanapes'

Viola septentrionalis
Northern blue violet

This spring-flowering perennial from North America bears large flowers with a spur, in hues usually of bluish purple but sometimes white. The hairy green leaves are pointed and oval to heart-shaped and have toothed edges. The plant has creeping and suckering stems and grows 6–8 in (15–20 cm) high and wide. *Zones 7–10.*

Viola tricolor
Wild pansy, Johnny jump up, love-in-idleness

This annual, biennial or short-lived perennial produces neat flowers with appealing faces, in shades of yellow, blue, violet and white, in fall (autumn) and winter in mild climates if cut back in late summer. It has soft, angular, branching stems and lobed oval to lance-shaped leaves. It grows to a height and spread of 6 in (15 cm) and self-seeds readily. *Viola tricolor* 'Bowles' Black' is a

striking cultivar with black velvety petals and a yellow center. *Zones 4–10.*

Viola × wittrockiana
Viola

This hybrid group of compactly branched perennials are almost always grown as biennials or annuals. Offering flowers of a great many hues, the numerous cultivars bloom in late winter

Viola × wittrockiana

Viola septentrionalis

Left: *Viola tricolor*

through spring and possibly into summer in cooler climates. The flowers are up to 4 in (10 cm) across and have 5 petals in a somewhat flat-faced arrangement. They grow slowly, reaching about 8 in (20 cm) in height and spread. This is a complex hybrid group, including both pansies and violas, the latter traditionally distinguished by the flowers lacking dark blotches, but there are now intermediate types with pale-colored markings. Hybrids in the Imperial Series are large-flowered pansies. The Joker Series are of an intermediate type, with a range of very bright contrasting colors such as orange and purple. The Accord Series of pansies covers most colors and has a very dark central blotch. Other seedling strains include the Universal and Sky Series. 'Universal Orange' has bronze-orange flowers; 'Universal True Blue' has rich purple-blue flowers with a yellow center. *Zones 5–10*.

Viola × *wittrockiana* 'Universal True Blue'

Viola × *wittrockiana* 'Universal Orange'

W, X, Y, Z

Xeranthemum annuum

Wahlenbergia gloriosa

WAHLENBERGIA
Bluebells
This is a genus of about 200 species of
annual or perennial herbs with a wide
distribution, mostly in the southern
hemisphere. They have variable foliage
and flowers range from wide open stars
to tubular bells, all with 5 prominent
lobes, in shades of blue, purple or white.
They are usually small in stature and are
suitable for the rock garden or border.

Cultivation
Grow in a well-drained, humus-rich soil
in full sun or light shade. Propagate
from seed or by division in spring.

Wahlenbergia gloriosa
Royal bluebell, Australian bluebell
This perennial herb with spreading
rhizomes and erect stems to about 8 in
(20 cm) high is a native of Australian
alpine regions and is the floral emblem
of the Australian Capital Territory. It
has dark green lance-shaped leaves to
1½ in (35 mm) long with wavy, toothed
margins and bears a profusion of royal-
blue or purple bell-shaped flowers on
separate fine stems in summer. It is fully
frost hardy. *Zones 8–10.*

XERANTHEMUM
Immortelle
The 5 or 6 annuals in this genus are
natives of the Mediterranean region,

extending to Iran. They are called
immortelles or everlasting flowers
because the dried flowerheads retain
their color and form for many years. The
erect, branching stems have narrow,
hoary leaves. Flowerheads are solitary
on long stems and the small fertile
flowers are surrounded by papery bracts
which may be white, purple or pink.

Cultivation
Moderately frost hardy, they grow best
in a sunny position in fertile, well-
drained soil. Propagate from seed which
should be sown in spring where the
plants are to grow.

Xeranthemum annuum
Immortelle
A good source of dried flowers, this
annual blooms in summer, producing
heads of purple daisy-like flowers;
whites, pinks and mauves, some with a
'double' appearance are also available.
The leaves are silvery and lance-shaped
and the plants grow to around 24 in
(60 cm) high and 18 in (45 cm) wide.
Mixed Hybrids include singles and
doubles in shades of pink, purple,
mauve, red or white. *Zones 7–10.*

ZANTEDESCHIA
Arum lily, calla lily, pig lily
Indigenous to southern and eastern
Africa and Lesotho, this well-known

Zantedeschia aethiopica

Zantedeschia elliottiana

genus of the arum family consists of 6
species of tuberous perennials. The
inflorescence consists of a showy white,
yellow or pink spathe shaped like a
funnel, with a central finger-like, yellow
spadix. The leaves are glossy green and
usually arrowhead-shaped.

Cultivation

Consisting of both evergreen and
deciduous species, this genus includes
frost-tender to moderately frost-hardy
plants; most are intolerant of dry
conditions. Most prefer well-drained soil
in full sun or part-shade, although
Zantedeschia authiopica will grow as a
semi-aquatic plant in boggy ground that
is often inundated. Propagate from
offsets in winter.

Zantedeschia aethiopica
White arum lily, lily-of-the-Nile

Although normally deciduous, in
summer and early fall (autumn) this
species can stay evergreen if given
enough moisture. It can also be grown in
water up to 6–12 in (15–30 cm) deep.
This species reaches 24–36 in (60–90 cm)
in height and spread, with large clumps
of broad, dark green leaves. The large
flowers, produced in spring, summer
and fall (autumn), are pure white with a
yellow spadix. 'Green Goddess' has
interesting green markings on the
spathes. *Zones 8–11.*

Zantedeschia, New Zealand Mixed Hybrid 'Mango'

Zantedeschia elliottiana
Golden arum lily

This summer-flowering hybrid species
has a yellow spathe surrounding a
yellow spadix, sometimes followed by a
spike of bright yellow berries. It grows
24–36 in (60–90 cm) tall with a spread
of 24 in (60 cm). The heart-shaped,
semi-erect leaves have numerous white
spots or streaks. *Zones 8–11.*

Zantedeschia, New Zealand Mixed Hybrids

These hybrids of *Zantedeschia rehmannii*
and *Z. elliottiana* have flowers in a range
of colors from red, pink and bronze to
orange. Some have spotted leaves. Most
reach a height of 24 in (60 cm). Not as
easy to grow as their parents, they need
warmth and very rich soil. The orange
red tones of 'Mango' vary with cultivation, a slightly alkaline soil giving richer
color than an acid one. *Zones 8–11.*

ZINGIBER
Ginger

This genus consists of about 100 species of evergreen perennials with thick, branching, aromatic rhizomes and leafy, reed-like stems. They bear flowers in axils of colorful, waxy bracts in short spikes or globular heads on stalks arising from the rhizomes. One species produces the culinary root and stem ginger.

Cultivation

These frost-tender plants need a hot position with high humidity and plentiful water in summer, less in winter. Give them plenty of space to spread. Propagate from rhizome divisions in spring.

Zingiber zerumbet
Wild ginger

This clump-forming, upright species is native to India and Southeast Asia. It has narrow, 12 in (30 cm) long leaves. On separate, tall stems are overlapping green bracts ageing to red, surrounding white or gold flowers. The rhizomes are bitter to eat, but can be used in potpourri. *Zones 10–12.*

Zinnia elegans

ZINNIA
Zinnia

This genus of 20 species of erect to spreading annuals, perennials and sub-shrubs has daisy-like, terminal flower-heads in many colors including white, yellow, orange, red, purple and lilac. Found throughout Mexico and Central and South America, some are grown for cut flowers and in mixed borders.

Cultivation

These plants are marginally frost hardy and should be grown in a sunny position in fertile soil that drains well. They need frequent deadheading. Propagate from seed sown under glass early in spring.

Zinnia elegans
Youth-and-old-age

This sturdy Mexican annual is the best known of the zinnias. The wild form has purple flowerheads, and blooms from summer to fall (autumn). It grows fairly rapidly to 24–30 in (60–75 cm), with a smaller spread. Garden varieties offer hues of white, red, pink, yellow, violet, orange or crimson in flowers up to 6 in (15 cm) across. The Dreamland series is compact and heavy flowering — typical of F1 Hybrid bedding zinnias. 'F1 Dreamland Ivy' has pale greenish yellow flowers. The Thumbelina series has 2 in (5 cm) wide flowerheads on plants only 6 in (15 cm) high. *Zones 8–11.*

Zingiber zerumbet

REFERENCE TABLE

Name	Type*	Zone	Color	Planting time	Flowering season
Abelmoschus moschatus	A	8-12	pale yellow	spring	summer
Acaena 'Blue Haze'	P	7-10	blue-gray	spring	late spring-early summer
Acanthus mollis	P	7-10	white, purple, gray	autumn	summer
Acanthus spinosus	P	7-10	white, purple-red	autumn	summer
Achillea 'Coronation Gold'	P	4-10	golden yellow	winter	summer
Achillea 'Moonshine'	P	3-10	yellow	winter	summer
Achillea tomentosa	P	4-10	yellow	winter	summer
Aconitum napellus	P	5-9	blue, purple	autumn	summer-autumn
Actinotus helianthi	P	9-10	creamy white	spring, summer	summer
Adonis vernalis	P	3-9	yellow	autumn	spring-early summer
Agapanthus 'Loch Hope'	P	9-11	violet blue	spring, autumn	summer
Agapanthus praecox	P	9-11	lavender-blue	spring, autumn	summer
Agastache foeniculum	P	8-10	purple	spring	summer
Ageratum houstonianum	A	9-12	blue	spring	summer-autumn
Agrostemma githago	A	8-10	pink	spring, autumn	summer
Ajuga reptans	P	3-10	deep blue	spring, autumn	spring
Alcea rosea	A	4-10	pink, purple, cream, yellow	late summer-spring	spring-summer
Alchemilla mollis	P	4-9	greenish yellow	late winter-early spring	summer
Alonsoa warscewiczii	P	9-11	orange-red	spring-autumn	late winter-autumn
Alpinia zerumbet	P	10-12	white & yellow	spring-early autumn	spring
Alstroemeria aurea	P	7-9	orange	spring	summer
Alstroemeria Ligtu hybrids	P	7-9	cream, orange, red, yellow	spring	summer
Alstroemeria psitticina	P	8-10	crimson, green	spring	summer
Amaranthus caudatus	A	8-11	dark red	spring	summer
Amaranthus tricolor	A	8-11	red	spring	summer
Ammi majus	P	6-10	white	spring	summer-autumn
Amsonia tabernaemontana	P	3-9	pale blue	spring	summer
Anagallis arvensis	A	7-10	orange	spring, autumn	spring-autumn
Anagallis monelli	A	7-10	blue, scarlet	spring, autumn	summer
Anaphalis margaritacea	P	4-9	yellow	spring	summer
Anchusa azurea	P	3-9	blue	autumn, spring	spring-summer
Anchusa capensis	P	8-10	blue	autumn, spring	early summer
Androsace lanuginosa	P	6-9	pink	spring	summer-autumn
Anemone blanda	P	6-9	white, pink, blue	summer	spring
Anemone coronaria	P	8-10	pink, scarlet, purple, blue	summer	spring
Anemone hupehensis	P	6-10	white, mauve	summer	autumn

Name	Type*	Zone	Color	Planting time	Flowering season
Anemone x hybrida	P	6-10	white to deep rose	summer	spring
Angelica archangelica	P	4-9	green	spring	summer
Anigozanthos Bush Gems series	P	9-11	yellow, gold, green, orange, red, burgundy	spring	spring
Anigozanthos manglesii	P	9-10	deep green, red	spring	spring
Anigozanthos 'Regal Claw'	P	9-11	orange	spring	spring
Anthemis retica	P	5-9	white	spring, autumn	spring-summer
Anthemis tinctoria	P	4-10	bright golden	spring, autumn	spring-summer
Antirrhinum hispanicum	P	7-10	mauve-pink	spring, autumn	summer
Aquilegia canadensis	P	3-9	red, yellow	spring, autumn	spring-summer
Aquilegia 'Crimson Star'	P	3-10	crimson	spring, autumn	spring-summer
Aquilegia, McKana hybrids	P	3-10	pink, blue, yellow, white, red, purple	spring, autumn	spring-summer
Aquilegia vulgaris	P	3-10	pink, crimson, white, purple	spring, autumn	spring-summer
Arabis blepharophylla	P	7-10	pink-purple	summer	spring
Arabis caucasica	P	4-10	white	summer	spring
Arctotis fastuosa	P	9-11	orange	spring, autumn	summer
Arctotis hybrids	P	9-11	yellow, orange	spring, autumn	summer-autumn
Arenaria montana	P	4-9	white	late winter, spring	summer
Argemone mexicana	A	8-11	yellow	spring	summer
Argranthemum frutescens	P	8-11	white	spring, autumn	winter-spring
Armeria maritima	P	4-9	white-pink	spring, autumn	spring-summer
Artemisia ludoviciana	P	4-10	brownish-green	spring	summer
Arthropodium cirratum	P	8-10	white	spring, autumn	early summer
Aruncus dioicus	P	3-9	greenish, creamy white	late winter, spring	summer
Asperula arcadiensis	P	5-9	pink-pale purple	spring	summer
Asphodeline lutea	P	6-10	yellow	winter-spring	summer
Asphodelus albus	P	5-10	white	winter-spring	spring
Astelia chathamica	P	9-10	buff yellow	autumn-spring	summer
Aster alpinus	P	3-9	mauve-blue, pink, white	spring, autumn	summer
Aster amellus	P	4-9	pink, purple-blue	spring, autumn	summer
Aster ericoides	P	4-10	white	spring, autumn	summer-autumn
Aster novae-angliae	P	4-9	pink, cerise	spring, autumn	summer-autumn
Astilbe 'Straussenfeder'	P	6-10	rose pink	winter	summer
Astrantia major	P	6-9	pink, white	spring	summer
Aubrieta deltoidea	P	4-9	mauve-pink	late winter-spring	spring
Aurinia saxatilis	P	4-9	yellow	late winter-spring	spring-summer
Baptisia australis	P	3-10	purple-blue	autumn	summer
Begonia fuchsioides	P	10-12	coral-red to pale pink	spring	summer-autumn

Name	Type*	Zone	Color	Planting time	Flowering season
Begonia scharfii	P	10-12	pinkish-white	spring	summer-autumn
B. Semperflorens- cultorum group	P	9-11	pink, white, red	spring	summer-autumn
Belamcanda chinensis	P	8-11	cream, yellow, apricot, orange-red	late winter-spring	summer
Bellis perennis	P	3-10	white	autumn-spring	winter-summer
Bergenia cordifolia	P	3-9	purple-pink	spring	winter-spring
Bergenia x schmidtii	P	5-10	rose-pink	spring	winter-spring
Blandfordia grandiflora	P	9-11	brick-red, yellow	late winter-spring	early summer
Boltonia astoroides	P	4-9	white, pale pink, mauve	late winter-spring	spring-summer
Borago officinalis	A/B	5-10	sky-blue	late winter-spring	spring-summer
Brachycome iberidifolia	A/P	9-11	mauve-blue, white, pink, purple	spring, autumn	summer-autumn
Brachycome multifida	P	9-11	mauve-pink	spring, autumn	spring-summer
Brachycome 'Sunburst'	P	9-11	yellow fading to cream	spring, autumn	spring
Bracteantha bracteata	A/P	8-11	golden-yellow	spring	summer-autumn
Browallia speciosa	P	9-11	purple-blue	spring	summer-autumn
Brunnera macrophylla	P	3-9	violet	spring	spring-summer
Bulbinella floribunda	P	8-10	orange-yellow	summer-autumn	winter-spring
Bulbinella hookeri	P	8-10	golden-yellow	summer-autumn	winter-spring
Calceolaria Herbeohybrida group	A	9-11	yellow, deep red, orange	summer	summer
Calendula officinalis	A	6-10	orange, yellow, cream	spring-autumn	spring-autumn
Callistephus chinensis	A	6-10	purple, blue, pink, white	spring	summer-autumn
Caltha palustris	P	3-8	golden-yellow	autumn-early spring	spring
Campanula 'Burghaltii'	P	4-9	gray-mauve	late winter-spring	summer
Campanula glomerata	P	3-9	purple-blue	late winter-spring	summer
Campanula lactiflora	P	5-9	lilac-blue	late winter-spring	summer
Campanula medium	B	6-10	violet-blue, pink, white	winter-spring	spring-early summer
Campanula portenschlagiana	P	5-10	violet-blue	late winter-spring	late spring-summer
Campanula rotundifolia	P	3-9	lilac-blue, white	late winter-spring	summer
Campanula vidalii	P	9-11	pale pink to white	spring	spring-summer
Canna x generalis	P	9-12	orange-red, yellow, apricot, cream	spring-early summer	summer-autumn
Canna indica	P	9-12	dark red	spring-early summer	summer-early winter
Catananche caerula	P	7-10	lavender-blue	late winter-spring	summer
Celmisia semicordata	P	7-9	white	late winter-spring	spring
Celosia argentea	A	10-12	silvery-white	spring	summer
Centaurea cyanus	A	5-10	blue, pink, white	late winter-spring	spring-summer
Centaurea macrocephala	P	4-9	yellow	spring-early summer	summer
Centranthus ruber	P	5-10	red, pink, white	late winter-spring	spring-autumn
Cerastium tomentosum	P	3-10	white	late winter-spring	late-spring-summer

Name	Type*	Zone	Color	Planting time	Flowering season
Chelone obliqua	P	6-9	rosy-purple	late winter-spring	summer-autumn
Chrysanthemum carinatum	A	8-10	multicolored	late winter-spring	spring-summer
Cimicifuga simplex	P	3-9	white	spring-early summer	late autumn
Clarkia unguiculata	A	7-11	orange, pink, purple	autumn, spring	summer
Clematis integrifolia	P	3-9	purple-blue	summer	spring
Cleome hassleriana	A	9-11	rose-pink to white	spring	summer-autumn
Clintonia umbellata	P	4-9	white	late winter-spring	late spring-summer
Clivia miniata	P	10-11	orange-scarlet	spring-summer	winter-spring
Codonopsis convolvulacea	P	5-9	violet to white	late winter-spring	spring
Consolida ambigua	A	7-11	pink, white, purple	spring, autumn	summer
Convallaria majalis	P	3-9	white	autumn	spring
Convolvulus sabatius	P	8-11	lilac-blue	spring, autumn	spring-autumn
Coreopsis grandiflora	P	6-10	golden-yellow	spring, autumn	spring-summer
Coreopsis lanceolata	P	3-11	golden-yellow	spring, autumn	summer
Coreopsis verticillata	P	6-10	yellow	spring, autumn	spring-autumn
Corydalis flexuosa	P	5-9	blue	late winter-spring	spring-summer
Corydalis lutea	P	6-10	yellow	late winter-spring	spring-autumn
Cosmos atrosanguineus	P	8-10	dark maroon	spring	summer-autumn
Cosmos bipinnatus	A	8-11	pink, red, purple, white	spring-early summer	summer-autumn
Crambe cordifolia	P	6-9	white	spring	summer
Cynara cardunculus	P	6-10	mauve	spring	summer
Cynoglossum amabile	A	5-9	blue, white, pink	late winter-spring	spring-summer
Dahlia x hortensis	A	8-10	scarlet	late winter-spring	autumn
Dahlia, Waterlily	A	8-10	white, pink	late winter-spring	summer-autumn
Dahlia, Semi-cactus	A	8-10	bronze, orange, yellow, purple-pink	late winter-spring	summer-autumn
Delphinium, Belladonna group	P	3-9	blue, white	spring	summer
Delphinium cardinale	P	8-9	red	spring	spring-summer
Delphinium grandiflorum	P	3-9	blue	spring	summer
Delphinium, Pacific hybrids	P	7-9	blue, purple, white	late winter-early summer	summer
Dendranthema x grandiflorum	P	4-10	white, yellow, bronze, pink, purple, red	spring-autumn	autumn
Dianella tasmanica	P	8-10	blue, purple-blue	spring, autumn	spring-summer
Dianthus barbatus	P	4-10	white, pink, carmine, crimson-purple	summer	spring-summer
Dianthus chinensis	A	7-10	pink, red, lavender, white	autumn, spring	spring-summer
Dianthus, Modern Pinks	P	5-10	white, pink, crimson	summer	spring-autumn
Dianthus, Old-fashioned Pinks	P	5-9	white, pale pink, magenta, red	summer	spring-summer
Dianthus superbus	P	4-10	purple-pink	summer	summer
Diascia rigescens	P	8-10	pink	autumn	summer

Name	Type*	Zone	Color	Planting time	Flowering season
Diascia 'Rose Queen'	P	8-10	pink	spring, autumn	late spring-summer
Dicentra formosa	P	3-9	pink, red	autumn	spring-summer
Dicentra spectabilis	P	2-9	pink, white	autumn	spring-summer
Dictamnus albus	P	3-9	white, pink, lilac	summer	summer
Dietes bicolor	P	9-11	pale yellow	spring, autumn	spring-summer
Dietes iridioides	P	8-11	white	spring, autumn	spring-summer
Digitalis x mertonensis	P	4-9	pink, salmon	autumn	summer
Digitalis purpurea	P	5-10	purple, pink, magenta, white, yellow	autumn	summer
Dimorphotheca pluvialis	A	8-10	white & purple	spring	winter-spring
Dodecatheon meadia	P	3-9	white, pink	autumn	spring
Doronicum columnae	P	5-9	yellow	autumn-early summer	spring
Doronicum pardalianches	P	5-9	yellow	autumn-early summer	spring-summer
Dorotheanthus bellidiformis	A	9-11	yellow, white, red, pink	spring-early summer	summer
Doryanthes excelsa	P	9-11	red	spring, autumn	spring-summer
Doryanthes palmeri	P	9-11	scarlet	spring, autumn	spring
Dryas octopetala	P	2-9	white	spring	late spring-summer
Echinacea purpurea	P	3-10	rosy purple	winter-spring	summer
Echinops ritro	P	3-10	purple-blue	late winter-spring	summer
Echium plantagineum	A	9-10	blue-purple, red	spring, summer	spring-summer
Echium vulgare	B	7-10	violet	spring, summer	spring-summer
Epilobium angustifolium	P	2-9	rose-pink	spring, autumn	summer
Epilobium canum subsp. *canum*	P	8-10	bright red	spring, autumn	summer-autumn
Epimedium x versicolor	P	5-9	pink, yellow	autumn	spring
Eranthis hyemalis	P	5-9	yellow	spring	winter-spring
Eremurus x isabellinus	P	5-9	white, pink, salmon, yellow, apricot, copper	autumn	summer
Erigeron 'Charity'	P	5-9	lilac-pink	spring	spring-summer
Erigeron foliosus	P	5-9	blue, yellow center	spring	spring-summer
Erigeron karvinskianthus	P	7-11	white, pink, red	spring	spring-summer
Erodium pelargoniiflorum	P	6-9	white with purple veins	summer	spring-autumn
Eryngium bourgatii	P	5-9	blue, gray-green	late winter-spring	summer-autumn
Eryngium giganteum	P	6-9	blue, pale green	late winter-spring	summer
Erysimum x allionii	P	3-10	yellow, orange	spring	spring
Erysimum 'Golden Bedder'	P	8-10	cream, yellow, orange, red	spring	winter-spring
Erysimum bicolor	P	9-11	pale yellow	spring	spring
Eschscholzia caespitosa	A	7-10	yellow	spring	summer-autumn
Eschscholzia californica	P	6-11	orange, bronze, yellow, scarlet, cream, mauve, rose	spring	summer-autumn
Etlingera elatior	P	11-12	scarlet	spring	spring

Name	Type*	Zone	Color	Planting time	Flowering season
Eucomis bicolor	P	8-10	green, greenish white	spring	summer
Eupatorium megalophyllum	P	10-11	lilac	spring	spring
Euphorbia characias	P	8-10	bracts yellow-green	spring-summer	summer
Euphorbia griffithii	P	6-9	yellow, bracts orange	spring-summer	summer
Euphorbia marginata	A	4-10	bracts white	spring-summer	summer
Euphorbia myrsinites	P	5-10	chartreuse	spring-summer	spring
Euphorbia polychroma	P	6-9	chrome-yellow	spring-summer	spring-summer
Eustoma grandiflorum	B	9-11	purple, pink, blue, white	spring	spring & autumn
Exacum affine	B	10-12	purple-blue	spring	summer
Felicia amelloides	P	9-11	blue	spring	spring-autumn
Filipendula vulgaris	P	3-9	white	spring, autumn	summer
Fragaria 'Pink Panda'	P	4-10	pink	late winter-spring	spring-autumn
Francoa sonchifolia	P	7-10	pale pink	spring	summer-autumn
Gaillardia aristata	P	6-10	yellow, red center	spring	summer-autumn
Gaillardia x grandiflora	P	5-10	red, orange, yellow, burgundy	spring	summer
Gaura lindheimeri	P	5-10	white, pink	autumn	spring-autumn
Gazania rigens	P	9-11	orange	winter-spring	spring-summer
Gazania, Sunshine hybrids	P	9-11	yellow, orange, cream, chocolate striped	winter-spring	spring-summer
Gentiana septemfida	P	3-9	blue	autumn	summer-autumn
Gentiana sino-ornata	P	6-9	deep blue	autumn	autumn
Geranium 'Johnson's Blue'	P	5-9	lavender-blue	spring	summer
Geranium macrorrhizum	P	4-9	pink, purple, white	spring	spring-summer
Geranium maderense	P	9-10	pinkish magenta	spring	winter-summer
Geranium phaeum	P	5-10	brownish purple	spring	spring-summer
Geranium renardii	P	6-9	white	spring	summer
Geranium sanguineum	P	5-9	magenta	spring	summer
Geranium sylvaticum	P	4-9	purple-blue	spring	spring-summer
Gerbera jamesonii	P	8-11	white, pink, yellow, orange, red	autumn & spring	spring-summer
Geum chiloense	P	5-9	scarlet	autumn	summer
Gilia capitata	A	7-9	lavender blue	spring	summer-autumn
Glaucium flavum	P	7-10	golden-yellow, orange	spring & autumn	summer
Goodenia macmillanii	P	9-11	pink, purple streaks	spring-autumn	spring-summer
Gunnera manicata	P	7-9	greenish red	autumn & spring	summer
Gypsophila paniculata	P	4-10	white	spring & autumn	summer
Gypsophila repens	P	4-9	white, lilac, purple	spring & autumn	summer
Hacquetia epipactis	P	6-9	bright yellow	autumn-early spring	spring
Hedychium coccineum	P	9-11	pale coral, bright red	most of year	summer

Name	Type*	Zone	Color	Planting time	Flowering season
Hedychium gardnerianum	P	9-11	red, pale yellow	most of year	summer-autumn
Helenium 'Moerheim Beauty'	P	5-9	orange-red	late winter-spring	summer-autumn
Helianthemum nummularium	P	5-10	yellow, cream, pink, orange	late winter-spring	spring-summer
Helianthus annuus	A	4-11	yellow	autumn, spring	summer
Helianthus x multiflorus	P	5-9	yellow, gold, lemon, bronze	autumn, spring	summer-autumn
Heliconia bihai	P	11-12	white, bracts scarlet	spring	summer
Heliconia psittacorum	P	11-12	yellow, red, green; bracts pink, orange, red, green	spring	most of year
Heliopsis helianthoides	P	4-9	golden-yellow	spring	summer
Helleborus foetidus	P	6-10	pale green	autumn, spring	winter-spring
Helleborus orientalis	P	6-10	white, green, pink, rose, purple	autumn, spring	winter-spring
Hemerocallis 'Apricot Queen'	P	4-9	apricot	autumn, spring	summer-autumn
Hemerocallis liliosphodelus	P	4-9	lemon-yellow	autumn, spring	summer-autumn
Hemerocallis hybrids	P	5-11	orange, brick red, yellow, pink, cream	autumn, spring	summer-autumn
Hepatica nobilis	P	5-9	blue, pink, white	spring	summer
Hesperis matronalis	P	3-9	white to lilac	spring, autumn	summer
Heuchera micrantha var. diversifolia	P	5-10	white	autumn, spring	summer
Heuchera sanguinea	P	6-10	scarlet, coral red	autumn, spring	summer
x Heucherella tiarelloides	P	5-9	pink	autumn	summer
Hibiscus trionum	A	9-11	pale yellow	spring	summer-autumn
Hosta fortunei	P	6-10	lavender	spring	summer
Hosta 'Krossa Regal'	P	6-10	white to pale mauve or violet	spring	summer-autumn
Hosta plantaginea	P	3-10	white	spring	summer-autumn
Hosta sieboldiana	P	6-10	mauve-white	spring	summer
Hosta undulata	P	6-10	mauve	spring	summer
Houttuynia cordata	P	5-11	yellow	winter-spring	summer
Hypericum cerastoides	P	6-9	bright yellow	autumn	spring-summer
Iberis amara	A	7-11	white	spring, autumn	spring-summer
Iberis sempervirens	P	4-11	white	spring, autumn	spring-summer
Impatiens, New Guinea hybrids	P	10-12	pink, orange, red, cerise	spring	most of year
Impatiens usambarensis	P	10-12	red, pink, white	spring	most of year
Impatiens walleriana	P	9-12	crimson, red, pink, orange, lavender, white	spring	most of year
Incarvillea delavayi	P	6-10	rosy purple	late winter-spring	summer
Inula helenium	P	5-10	yellow	spring, autumn	summer
Iresine herbstii	P	10-12	deep red & pink foliage	spring	summer
Iris, Bearded Hybrids	P	5-10	all colors except true red	autumn	spring-summer
Iris cristata	P	6-9	pale blue, lavender, purple	autumn	spring-summer
Iris ensata	P	4-10	white, lavender, blue, purple	autumn	spring-summer

Name	Type*	Zone	Color	Planting time	Flowering season
Iris japonica	p	8-11	pale blue, white	autumn	winter-spring
Iris, Louisiana Hybrids	P	7-10	blue, mauve, white, purple, chocolate	autumn	summer
Iris pallida	P	5-10	pale blue	autumn	spring
Iris sibirica	P	4-9	purple, blue, white	autumn	summer
Iris, Spuria Hybrids	P	4-9	white to blue, yellow	autumn	early summer
Iris unguicularis	P	7-10	pale blue, white, dark blue	autumn	autumn-spring
Kalanchoe blossfeldiana	P	10-12	red	spring	spring
Knautia macedonia	P	6-10	purple-red, pink, white	autumn	summer
Kniphofia ensifolia	P	8-10	lemon-yellow	spring	autumn-winnter
Kniphofia 'Little Maid'	P	7-10	yellow	spring	winter-summer
Kniphofia 'Winter Cheer'	P	7-10	orange-yellow	spring	winter-summer
Lamium album	P	4-10	white	spring	spring-autumn
Lamium galeobdolon	P	6-10	bright yellow	autumn	summer
Lamium maculatum	P	4-10	pale pink to deep rose	spring	spring-summer
Lathyrus odoratus	P	4-10	white, cream, pink, blue, mauve, lavender, maroon, scarlet	autumn-early spring	winter-summer
Lathyrus vernus 'Cyaneus'	P	4-10	purple-blue	autumn-early spring	spring
Lavatera 'Barnsley'	P	6-10	pale pink	spring, autumn	summer
Lavatera trimestris	A	8-11	white, pink	spring	summer-autumn
Leontopodium alpinum	P	5-9	white	late winter-spring	spring-summer
Leucanthemum x superbum	P	5-10	white	winter-spring	summer-autumn
Lewisia cotyledon	P	6-10	white, yellow, apricot, pink, purple	late winter-spring	summer
Liatris spicata	P	3-10	lilac-purple, pink, white	winter	summer
Libertia grandiflora	P	8-11	white	autumn-spring	spring-summer
Libertia peregrinans	P	8-10	white	autumn-spring	spring-summer
Ligularia dentata	P	4-9	orange-yellow	spring, autumn	summer
Limnanthes douglasii	A	8-10	white edge, gold-centered	autumn, spring	spring-autumn
Limonium latifolium	P	5-10	lavender-blue, white	spring, autumn	summer
Limonium perezii	P	9-11	white, calyces mauve-blue	spring, autumn	summer
Limonium sinuatum	P	9-10	yellow, white, cream, salmon-pink, purple, blue	spring, autumn	summer-autumn
Linaria purpurea	P	6-10	purple	autumn, spring	summer
Linum narbonense	P	5-10	violet	autumn	summer
Linum perenne	P	7-10	light blue	autumn	summer
Liriope muscari	P	6-10	violet	autumn	summer
Lobelia cardinalis	P	3-10	scarlet-red	winter-spring	summer-autumn
Lobelia erinus	A	7-11	pinkish purple	late winter-early spring	spring-autumn
Lobelia x gerardii	P	7-10	pink, violet, purple	late winter-spring	summer
Lobularia maritima	A	7-10	white	spring	spring-autumn

Name	Type*	Zone	Color	Planting time	Flowering season
Lunaria annua	B	8-10	magenta, white, violet-purple	autumn, spring	spring-summer
Lunaria rediviva	P	8-10	pale violet	autumn, spring	spring-summer
Lupinus, Russell Hybrids	P	3-9	cream, pink, orange, blue, violet	late winter-spring, autumn	spring-summer
Lupinus texensis	A	8-10	dark blue & white	autumn, spring	late spring
Lychnis x haageana 'Vesuvius'	P	6-10	orange	autumn, spring	summer
Lychnis chalcedonica	P	4-10	orange-red	autumn, spring	summer
Lychnis coronaria	P	4-10	rose-pink, scarlet	autumn, spring	summer
Lychnis viscaria	P	4-9	mauve to magenta	autumn, spring	early summer
Lysimachia clethroides	P	4-10	white	winter-spring	summer
Lysimachia nummularia	P	4-10	yellow	winter-spring	summer
Lysimachia punctata	P	5-10	yellow	winter-spring	summer
Lythrum salicaria	P	3-10	pink to magenta	late winter-spring	summer-autumn
Macleaya cordata	P	3-10	cream	spring	summer
Malva moschata	P	3-10	pink	spring	spring
Malva sylvestris	P	5-10	mauve-pink	spring	spring-autumn
Matthiola incana	B	6-10	mauve	spring	spring
Meconopsis betonicifolia	P	7-9	sky-blue	summer	spring-summer
Meconopsis cambrica	P	6-10	lemon-yellow, orange	summer	spring-autumn
Mimulus x hybridus Hybrids	P	6-10	red, yellow, cream, white	spring	summer
Mimulus luteus	P	7-10	yellow	spring	summer
Mimulus moschatus	P	7-10	pale yellow	spring	summer-autumn
Monarda didyma	P	4-10	white, pink, red	spring	summer-autumn
Monarda 'Mahogany'	P	4-10	wine-red, lilac	spring	summer-autumn
Myosotidium hortensia	P	9-11	purple-blue	summer or autumn	spring-summer
Myosotis alpestris	P	4-10	blue, pink, white	autumn	spring-summer
Myosotis sylvatica	P	5-10	lavender-blue	autumn	spring-summer
Nelumbo nucifera	P	8-12	pink, white	spring	summer
Nemesia caerulea	P	8-10	pink, lavender, blue	autumn or spring	summer
Nemesia strumosa	A	9-11	yellow, white, red, orange	autumn or spring	spring
Nemophila maculata	A	7-11	white & purple	autumn	summer
Nemophila menziesii	A	7-11	blue	autumn	spring-summer
Nepeta cataria	P	3-10	white	spring-summer	spring-autumn
Nepeta x faassenii	P	3-10	violet-blue	spring-summer	summer
Nepeta racemosa	P	3-10	lavender-blue	spring-summer	summer
Nicotiana alata	P	7-11	white, red, pink	early spring	summer-autumn
Nicotiana langsdorfii	A	9-11	lime-green	early spring	summer
Nicotiana sylvestris	A	8-11	white	early spring	summer

Name	Type*	Zone	Color	Planting time	Flowering season
Nierenbergia repens	P	8-10	white	spring	summer
Nigella damascena	A	6-10	lilac-blue, white	autumn or spring	spring-summer
Nolana paradoxa	A	8-11	purple-blue	spring	summer
Nymphaea, Hardy Hybrids	P	5-10	white, yellow, pink, red	spring	summer-autumn
Nymphaea, Tropical day-blooming	P	10-12	blue, purple, red, pink, yellow, white	spring	summer-autumn
Oenothera speciosa	P	5-10	white, pink tips	spring or autumn	summer
Omphalodes cappodocica	P	6-9	purple-blue	spring	spring
Omphalodes verna	P	6-9	blue	spring	spring
Ophiopogon japonicus	P	8-11	pale purple	autumn	summer
Ophiopogon planiscapus 'Nigrescens'	P	6-10	lilac	autumn	summer
Origanum vulgare	P	5-9	pink	spring	summer
Orthrosanthus multiflorus	P	9-10	blue, purple	winter	spring
Osteospermum ecklonis	P	8-10	white, reddish centers	summer	spring-autumn
Osteospermum fruticosum	P	9-11	pale lilac	summer	summer-autumn
Osteospermum jucundum	P	8-10	purplish pink	summer	autumn-spring
Oxalis purpurea	P	8-10	pink, rose, lilac, white	autumn	autumn-spring
Oxalis massoniana	P	9-10	orange	autumn	spring-summer
Paeonia lactiflora Hybrids	P	6-9	red, white, yellow, pink, apricot	winter-early spring	spring
Paeonia mlokosewitschii	P	8-10	yellow	winter-early spring	spring-summer
Paeonia officinalis	P	8-10	purple, red	winter-early spring	spring-summer
Papaver nudicaule	P	2-10	white, yellow, orange, pink	spring or autumn	winter-spring
Papaver orientale	P	3-9	scarlet, orange, dusky pink, blackish centers	spring or autumn	spring-summer
Papaver rhoeas	A	5-9	scarlet	apring or autumn	spring-summer
Parochetus communis	P	9-11	blue	late summer-winter	summer-autumn
Pelargonium odoratissimum	P	10-11	white	spring-autumn	summer
Pelargonium tricolor	P	9-11	red & white	spring-autumn	summer
Penstemon barbatus	P	3-10	scarlet	spring or autumn	summer-autumn
Penstemon 'Evelyn'	P	7-10	pale pink	spring or autumn	summer-autumn
Penstemon x gloxinioides	P	7-9	red, pink	spring or autumn	summer
Penstemon heterophyllus	P	8-10	violet-pink, blue	spring or autumn	summer
Pericallis x hybrida	P	9-11	pink, red, purple, crimson, white, blue	spring-late summer	summer
Petunia x hybrida	A	9-11	pink, purple, red, blue, white	spring	spring-autumn
Phacelia grandiflora	A	8-11	mauve to white	late winter-spring	spring-summer
Phlomis fruticosa	P	7-10	yellow	late winter-spring	summer
Phlomis russeliana	P	7-10	butter-yellow	late winter-spring	summer
Phlox douglasii	P	5-10	white, lavender-blue, pink	late winter-spring	spring-summer
Phlox drummondii	A	6-10	red, pink, purple, cream	spring	summer-autumn

Name	Type*	Zone	Color	Planting time	Flowering season
Phlox maculata	P	5-10	white, pink, purple	late winter-spring	mid-summer
Phlox paniculata	P	4-10	violet, red, salmon, white	winter-spring	summer
Phlox subulata	P	3-10	blue, mauve, carmine, pink, white	late winter-spring	spring
Phormium Hybrids	P	8-11	foliage pinkish red	spring	summer
Phormium tenax	P	8-11	bronze-red	spring	summer
Phygelius aequalis	P	8-11	pale pink	summer	summer
Physalis alkekengi	P	6-10	white, yellow centers	late winter-spring	summer
Physostegia virginiana	P	3-10	pale pink, magenta	winter-spring	summer
Phyteuma comosum	P	6-9	violet-blue	late winter-spring	late spring-early summer
Platycodon grandiflorus	P	4-10	blue, purple, pink, white	winter-spring	summer
Plectranthus ecklonii	P	9-11	violet	spring	autumn
Polomonium caeruleum	P	2-9	blue	spring	early summer
Polianthes tuberosa	P	9-11	creamy white	spring	summer-autumn
Polygonatum x hybridum	P	6-9	white, green tips	spring or autumn	spring
Polygonum affine	P	3-9	red	spring	summer-autumn
Pontederia cordata	P	3-10	blue	spring	summer
Portulaca grandiflora	A	10-11	yellow, pink, red, orange	summer	summer
Potentilla nepalensis	P	5-9	pink, apricot, red centers	autumn	summer
Pratia pedunculata	P	7-11	mid-blue to white, purple	autumn	spring-summer
Primula auricula	P	3-9	gray, pale green, almost black	late winter-spring	spring
Primula denticulata	P	6-9	pink, purple, lilac	late winter-spring	mid-spring
Primula japonica	P	5-10	pink, crimson, purple, white	late winter-spring	spring-summer
Primula malacoides	P	8-11	white, pink, magenta	late summer-spring	spring-summer
Primula obconica	P	8-11	white, pink, purple	late summer-spring	winter-spring
Primula, Polyanthus group	P	6-10	all colors	late summer-spring	winter-spring
Primula veris	P	5-9	orange-yellow	late summer-spring	spring-summer
Primula vulgaris	P	6-9	pale yellow, white, pink	autumn-early spring	late winter-summer
Primula 'Wanda'	P	6-9	deep magenta to purple	autumn-early spring	spring
Prunella grandiflora	P	5-9	white, pink, purple	spring or autumn	spring-summer
Psylliostachys suworowii	A	6-10	pink	spring	summer
Ptilotus manglesii	P	9-11	pink to purple	spring	winter-summer
Pulmonaria saccharata	P	3-9	white, pink, blue	winter-early spring	early spring
Pulsatilla vulgaris	P	5-9	white, pink red, purple	late winter-early spring	spring
Ramonda myconi	P	6-9	white, pink, blue, lavender, purple	spring	spring-summer
Ranunculus acris	P	5-9	bright yellow	spring or autumn	midsummer
Ranunculus ficaria	P	5-10	bright yellow	spring, autumn	spring
Raoulia australia	P	7-9	yellow	spring	summer

Name	Type*	Zone	Color	Planting time	Flowering season
Rehmannia elata	P	9-10	bright pink	winter	summer-autumn
Reseda odorata	A	6-10	greenish	late winter	summer-autumn
Rheum palmatum	P	6-10	dark red to creamy green	winter-early spring	summer
Rhodanthe chlorocephala subsp. *rosea*	A	9-11	pink, yellow, white	spring	summer
Rhodanthe 'Paper Star'	P	7-11	white	spring-early summer, autumn	most of year
Rhodohypoxis baurii	P	8-10	white, pink, dark red	spring	spring-early summer
Rodgersia aesculifolia	P	5-9	cream, pale pink	autumn	mid-spring
Romneya coulteri	P	7-10	white, orange center	late winter-spring	late summer
Roscoea cautleoides	P	6-9	yellow, orange	late winter-spring	summer
Rudbeckia fulgida	P	3-10	orange-yellow	spring or autumn	summer-autumn
Rudbeckia hirta	P	3-10	orange-yellow, orange-red	spring or autumn	summer-autumn
Rudbeckia laciniata	P	3-10	golden yellow	spring or autumn	summer
Salpiglossis sinuata	A	8-11	red, orange, yellow, blue, purple	spring	summer-autumn
Salvia elegans	P	8-11	bright red	spring	summer-autumn
Salvia farinacea	A	8-11	violet-blue	spring	summer
Salvia greggii	P	9-10	red, orange, salmon, pink, pale yellow, white	spring	spring-autumn
Salvia involucrata	P	9-10	mauve, magenta	spring	summer-autumn
Salvia prunelloides	P	9-11	blue	spring	summer-autumn
Salvia sclarea	B	5-10	greenish white, tinged purple	spring	summer
Salvia splendens	A	9-12	scarlet	spring	summer
Salvia uliginosa	P	8-11	sky-blue	spring	summer
Sanguinaria canadensis	P	3-9	white	late summer	spring
Saponaria ocymoides	P	4-10	pink, deep red	spring or autumn	spring-summer
Saxifraga exarata subsp. *moschata*	P	6-9	white, creamy yellow, pink, red	autumn	spring
Saxifraga paniculata	P	3-9	white	autumn	spring
Saxifraga 'Ruth Draper'	P	6-9	purple-pink	autumn	early spring
Scabiosa caucasica	P	4-10	pink, red, purple, blue	autumn	summer-autumn
Scabiosa columbaria	P	6-10	reddish-purple, lilac blue	autumn	summer-autumn
Scaevola 'Mauve Clusters'	P	9-11	mauve	spring or summer	spring-summer
Schizanthus x wisetonensis	A	7-11	white, blue, pink, reddish brown	summer, autumn	spring-summer
Schizostylis coccinea	P	6-10	scarlet	spring	summer-autumn
Scutellaria incana	P	5-9	grayish blue	autumn	summer
Sedum spectabile	P	5-10	pink	spring	late summer
Sidalcea malviflora	P	6-10	pink, white	late winter-spring	spring-summer
Sidalcea 'Rose Queen'	P	6-10	deep pink	late winter-spring	summer
Silene coeli-rosa	A	6-11	pinkish purple	spring or autumn	summer
Silene laciniata	P	7-11	bright crimson	spring or autumn	summer-autumn

Name	Type*	Zone	Color	Planting time	Flowering season
Sisryinchium bellum	P	8-11	amethyst-purple	summer	late spring
Sisryinchium striatum	P	8-10	cream, striped purple	summer	summer
Solenostemon scutellarioides	P	10-12	leaves pink, green red, yellow	spring-summer	summer (winter house plant)
Solidago 'Golden Wings'	P	5-10	yellow	spring or autumn	autumn
Stachys byzantina	P	5-10	mauve-pink	spring, early autumn	summer
Stachys coccinea	P	6-10	red	spring, autumn	spring-autumn
Stokesia laevis	P	7-10	blue-mauve, white	autumn	summer-autumn
Streptocarpus Hybrids	P	10-11	lilac, purple, blue, pink, crimson	spring, autumn	winter-early summer
Symphytum 'Goldsmith'	P	5-10	blue, pink, white	spring, autumn	spring
Tagetes lemmonii	A	9-11	golden yellow	spring	autumn-winter
Tagetes patula	A	9-11	red, yellow, orange	spring	summer-autumn
Tanacetum coccineum	P	5-9	pink, red, purple, white	late winter-early spring	spring-summer
Tanacetum parthenium	P	6-10	white	late winter-early spring	summer
Thalictrum aquilegiifolium	P	6-10	pink, lilac, greenish white	autumn	summer
Thalictrum delavayi	P	7-10	lilac	autumn	summer
Thunbergia alata	A	9-12	orange	spring	summer-autumn
Thymus x citriodorus	P	7-10	pale lilac	summer	spring- summer
Thymus serpyllum	P	3-9	bluish-purple	summer	spring-summer
Tiarella cordifolia	P	3-9	creamy white	spring	summer
Tithonia rotundifolia	A	8-11	orange, scarlet	late winter-early spring	summer-autumn
Torenia fournieri	A	9-12	purplish-blue	spring	summer-autumn
Tradescantia, Andersoniana Group	P	7-10	white, mauve, pink, purple	spring, summer or autumn	late summer
Tradescantia virginia	P	4-9	white to deep blue, purple	spring, summer or autumn	late summer
Tricyrtis hirta	P	5-9	white	autumn	summer
Trillium grandiflorum	P	3-9	white	autumn	spring
Trollius chinensis	P	5-9	light to deep yellow	spring	spring
Tropaeolum majus	A	8-11	red, orange, yellow, cream	spring	summer-autumn
Valeriana officinalis	P	3-9	white to dark pink	autumn	summer
Vancouveria plantipetala	P	7-9	white	spring	spring
Verbascum bombyciferum	B	6-10	golden-yellow	spring	summer
Verbascum chaixii	P	5-10	yellow	spring	summer
Verbascum 'Letitia'	P	8-10	lemon-yellow	spring	spring-summer
Verbena bonariensis	P	7-10	deep purple	autumn, spring	summer-autumn
Verbena x hybrida	P	9-10	red, mauve, violet, white, pink	autumn, spring	summer-autumn
Verbena rigida	P	8-10	pale violet to magenta	autumn, spring	summer
Veronica austriaca	P	6-10	bright blue	autumn, spring	late spring
Veronica gentianoides	P	4-9	pale blue, white	autumn, spring	late spring

Name	Type*	Zone	Color	Planting time	Flowering season
Veronica spicata	P	3-9	blue	autumn, spring	summer
Viola hederacea	P	8-10	white	spring	summer
Viola odorata	P	6-10	violet, white, rose	spring	winter-spring
Viola, Perennial cultivars	P	6-10	all colors except true blue	spring	most of year
Viola septentrionalis	P	7-10	blue-purple, white	spring	spring
Viola tricolor	P	4-10	yellow, blue, violet, white	spring	autumn-winter
Viola x wittrockiana	A	5-10	all colors	spring	winter-spring
Wahlenbergia gloriosa	P	8-10	blue, purple	spring	summer
Xeranthemum annuum	A	7-10	white, pink, mauve	spring	summer
Zantedeschia aethiopica	P	8-11	white	winter	spring-autumn
Zantedeschia elliottiana	P	8-11	yellow	winter	spring-autumn
Zantedeschia, NZ Mixed	P	8-11	red, pink, bronze, orange	winter	spring-autumn
Zingiber zerumbet	P	10-12	greenish yellow	spring	summer
Zinnia elegans	A	8-11	white, red, pink, yellow, violet, orange, crimson	spring	summer-autumn

* A = annual   B = biennial   P = perennial

INDEX